Getting the Most from
AutoCAD LT

W Ditch BSc, Cert Ed

Lecturer, Wearside College, Sunderland

ARNOLD

A member of the Hodder Headline Group
LONDON • SYDNEY • AUCKLAND

This book is dedicated to the memory of my parents,
Thelma Emily and Walter

First published in Great Britain in 1996 by
Arnold, a member of the Hodder Headline Group,
338 Euston Road, London NW1 3BH

British Library Cataloguing in Publication Data
A catalogue record for this book is available from the British Library

ISBN 0 340 61421 8

Printed and bound in Great Britain by The Bath Press, Somerset

Contents

Preface

AutoCAD LT is fast becoming the standard choice for those computer users who require a relatively cheap, yet powerful CAD system. Based on the industry standard – AutoCAD – it has a long and distinguished pedigree. Full drawing compatibility with AutoCAD is also provided, ensuring that your CAD investment is preserved, should you later wish to upgrade.

Despite the much lower price, surprisingly little has been omitted from AutoCAD LT. Existing users of AutoCAD will immediately recognize the pull-down menus, dialogue boxes and the wide range of commands. The fact that AutoCAD LT uses the same drawing database as AutoCAD Release 12 means that existing Release 12 drawings can be loaded into AutoCAD LT without any problems. A file conversion utility allows Release 13 drawings to be converted into AutoCAD LT compatible format.

This book is intended for both new *and* experienced users of AutoCAD. Readers who are relatively new to CAD (and possibly lacking computing experience in general) will find that the initial chapters progressively introduce the basic principles of using a CAD package. As each feature or command is introduced, a clear explanation is given of its method of use, with typical examples demonstrating the purpose and likely context. A series of *tutorials* are used to demonstrate important concepts in a step by step manner, while *drawing exercises* allow the reader to apply their newly found knowledge in typical situations. An alphabetically arranged reference section provides a summary of each AutoCAD LT command in a compact form. This section allows you to find the command you need quickly, and shows the many ways in which each command can be invoked. This latter information encourages you to develop your own fast and effective drawing style.

Experienced CAD users will appreciate the information on customizing AutoCAD LT, including the creation of linetypes, hatch patterns, script files, parts lists and special purpose menu systems. The supplied diskette illustrates many of these concepts and demonstrates the use of customization to enhance productivity. In particular, the special purpose menu system, with its range of pre-defined blocks, shows that a single general purpose CAD package may be extended for use in a wide variety of specialist applications. A range of options are provided, allowing the creation of complex 3-dimensional structures from basic building blocks.

Acknowledgements

Thanks are due to AutoDesk, Inc. who kindly provided the author with an evaluation copy of the AutoCAD LT Release 1 software.

1   Introduction

Typographical Conventions

Given that many readers will flip regularly between this book and the
AutoCAD LT manual, this process has been simplified as far as possible by
the use of similar typographical styles. The conventions used in this book
are:-

Spacebar

Any key on the keyboard. This is normally used to indicate that the user
should press a particular key. A commonly used example is the Enter or
Return key, which is shown as ⏎.

Ctrl + C

Where two keys must be pressed simultaneously, this is shown using a
'plus' sign. For example Ctrl + C means "while holding down the Control
key, briefly press C".

or

Use the mouse to move the pointer to the required position and then click
the indicated button on the mouse (left or right). When using the *object snap*
feature it is necessary to hold down the Shift key and then click the right
mouse button. This is written as Shift + .

Sans serif

A 'sans serif' font is used for 'command dialogues', with boldface reserved
for text which must be entered by the user. For example

Command: **LINE**⏎

File

Options which must be selected by the user from the pull-down menu
system, or from a displayed dialogue box are shown in bold, with any
available keyboard short-cut underlined.

UPPERCASE

The names of AutoCAD commands, settings (system variables), named
objects (names of layers, linetypes, hatch patterns, system variables etc.)
and the names of DOS commands.

Initial Caps	The names of AutoCAD objects or entities, such as Lines, Arcs, Circles, Polylines, Doughnuts and Polygons are written with the first letter capitalized.
Courier	Text in ASCII files, which may be created or altered using a text editor program (used in Chapter 8 only).

Installing the Supplied Utility Diskette

The utility diskette is intended to support Chapter 8 by providing examples of AutoCAD LT customization.

The main application is a custom menu system which provides an enhanced 3-dimensional drawing facility. With this menu system loaded, a **3D construction** area becomes available from the **D**raw pull-down menu, as shown below.

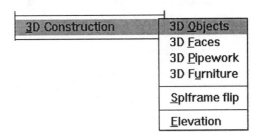

When one of the '3D' options is selected, an icon menu is displayed which allows the user to insert 3-dimensional Block definitions into the current drawing. A typical icon menu is shown below.

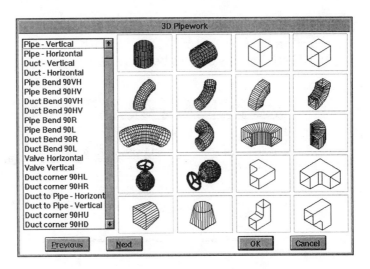

For your convenience, a batch file has been provided which will copy all required files from the supplied diskette to your hard disk. (This file assumes that you have installed AutoCAD LT into the directory C:\ACLTWIN.) To run this batch file from DOS type:

A:\> **INSTALL** ↵

Users of AutoCAD LT Release 2 should then use the PREFERENCES command and set the **Menu File** edit box to 3D\3D, as shown below.

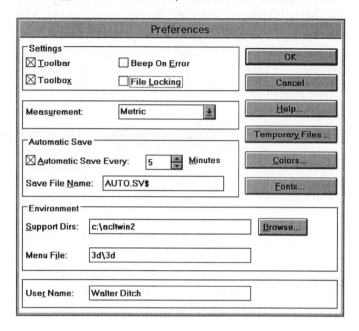

Users of Release 1 will need to use the Windows Program Manager to create a new program item for AutoCAD LT, with the working directory set to C:\ACLTWIN\3D, as shown below.

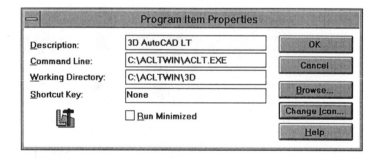

2   A First Session with AutoCAD LT

Assumed Knowledge

When writing a book which focuses on a particular software package (such as AutoCAD LT) the author must make certain assumptions about the knowledge and abilities of a typical reader. For the purposes of keeping the book to a reasonable size (and price), I have assumed that you:

❑   have assembled the various components of your computer and that you know how to switch the computer on and off (without loss of data);

❑   have a basic appreciation of computer architecture, including disk drives and their use (including formatting), keyboards and use of the mouse;

❑   are familiar with the Windows operating environment. Important concepts here include entering and exiting Windows, using the mouse (clicking left, right, double-clicking and dragging), executing programs (working with programs and folders), using pull-down menus and dialogue boxes (pressing buttons, selecting items from lists and using edit boxes) and working with data files (creating, opening, saving and deleting documents).

Although the above list may seem daunting to readers who are relatively inexperienced in the use of computers, it is necessary to make these assumptions to avoid duplicating material which is freely available in most computer manuals. It should also be said that the majority of users find Windows to be quite 'intuitive' in use and are soon able to master the concepts involved.

If you experience any problems then refer in the first instance to the documentation which accompanies your system. On-line help information is also available both for DOS, and for Windows. When using DOS, help can be obtained simply by typing **HELP** at the command prompt. With Windows, pressing function key F1 will normally cause relevant (or *context sensitive*) help information to be displayed. In addition, most Windows programs provide either a help button, or a pull-down menu area which is dedicated to this purpose.

Installing the AutoCAD LT Software

At the time of writing, the AutoCAD LT software is supplied on six 3½ inch diskettes. Although the chances of anything going wrong during the installation process are quite small, it is a good idea to make backup copies of each diskette, prior to commencing the installation process. This may save you the inconvenience (and embarrassment) of having to order replacement diskettes.

There are several possible methods for the creation of backup diskettes. One approach is to create a temporary directory on your hard disk for each diskette, and then copy all files from each diskette in turn. In the event of a problem, the content of each directory may be copied back onto a series of blank (formatted) diskettes. Another technique is to use the DISKCOPY command from DOS.

To begin the installation, insert the first diskette into a disk drive (drive A: with most computers, but possibly B:) and then from the Windows Program Manager, use the **File** pull-down menu and choose the **Run** option.

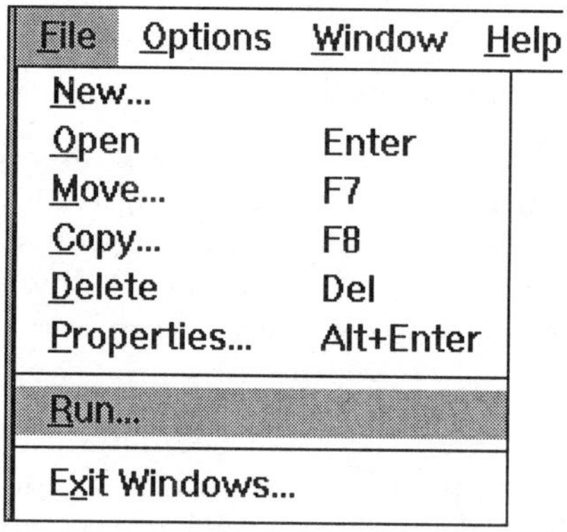

File	Options	Window	Help
New...			
Open	Enter		
Move...	F7		
Copy...	F8		
Delete	Del		
Properties...	Alt+Enter		
Run...			
Exit Windows...			

Figure 2–1. Using the Program Manager to run the installation software.

At the displayed dialogue box, type **A:\SETUP** (or **B:\SETUP** if you are using drive B:) in the **Command Line:** edit box and click the **OK** button.

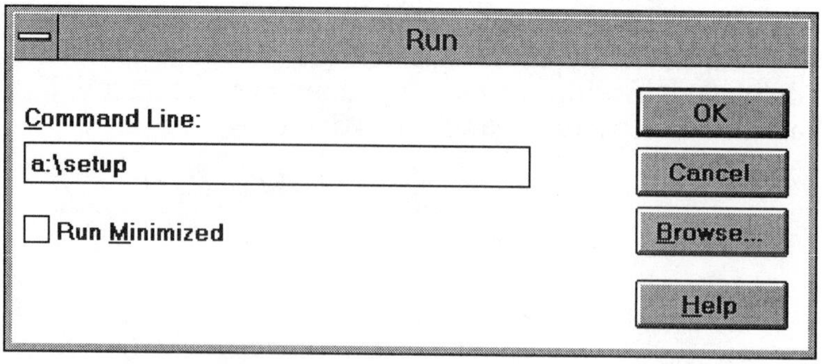

Run

Command Line:

a:\setup

☐ Run Minimized

OK

Cancel

Browse...

Help

Figure 2–2. The Run (program) dialogue box.

When the installation process begins, you will be asked to give details about yourself and your organisation (if any), which are then used to 'personalize' the AutoCAD LT software. In addition, several options are presented which relate to the software installation process itself. At this stage you can decide which files to install, and where they should be placed (i.e. the drive and sub-directory names). Unless you have a good reason for doing otherwise, I would suggest that you perform a full installation, accepting the 'default' options at each stage (as typified by Figure 2–3 below).

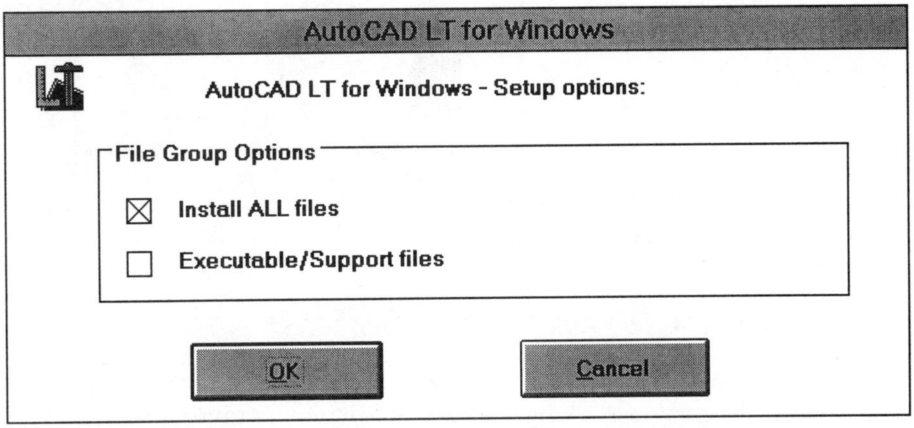

Figure 2–3. The default installation process.

The installation process for Releases 1 and 2 of AutoCAD LT are almost identical, except for a slight increase in the hard disk storage requirements with Release 2. (This is 10 MB for Release 1 and 16 MB for Release 2, assuming a full installation.)

One significant difference is that Release 1 offers the option of installing several sub-directories of Windows *Metafiles*, which are arranged as a symbol library. This option has been removed in the latest version of the software, although a simpler 'clipart' sub-directory is provided as standard with Release 2.

Once the installation process has been completed, you will find that an AutoCAD LT folder has been created in Windows, containing the program icon, together with a tutorial program and a text file viewer. This file viewer (which uses the Windows Write word processor program) displays the contents of the file README.DOC, and contains last minute information not available in the manual.

Introducing AutoCAD LT

To run AutoCAD LT, first double-click on the folder's icon to cause it to 'open' (if it is not open already). The appearance of the opened folder should be similar to that shown in Figure 2–4 below.

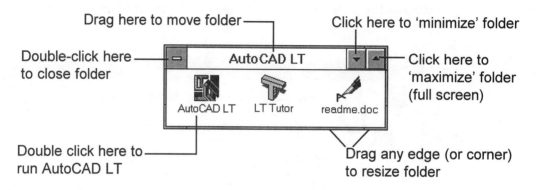

Figure 2–4. The AutoCAD LT folder.

Once the correct folder has been opened, double-click the AutoCAD LT icon to run the program. A typical screen display is given by Figure 2–5.

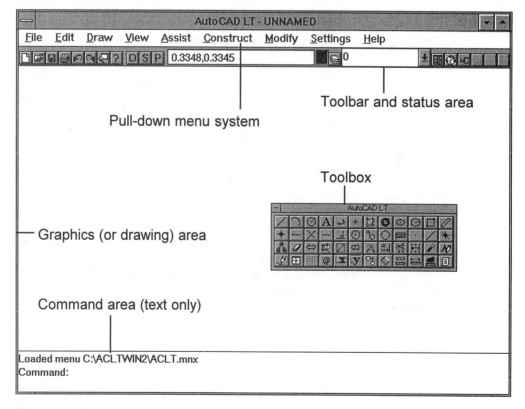

Figure 2–5. The AutoCAD LT screen.

The AutoCAD LT Screen

The exact appearance of the AutoCAD LT screen depends on a number of factors, including the screen resolution, whether the active window has been expanded to fill the entire display and the selected character size (large or small). Commonly used screen resolutions are:

❑   640 × 480 pixels;

❑   800 × 600 pixels;

❑   1024 × 768 pixels;

❑   1280 × 1024 pixels.

On most systems, the screen resolution may be altered by running the Display Driver Setup utility (after which it is normally necessary to 'restart' Windows). Generally speaking, you should select the highest screen resolution which will give satisfactory performance. Factors to consider include the size and quality of the monitor, the speed with which the graphics display is updated, and the number of colours which are available at the selected screen resolution. If you are going to use your computer for hours at a time, a few minutes experimenting with the graphics setup may increase your productivity, and prevent eye strain!

Now consider each section of the AutoCAD LT screen of Figure 2–5 in turn.

The AutoCAD LT Window

The window used by AutoCAD LT is similar in many respects to the program folder of Figure 2–4. Notice that the *Title bar* contains the name of the program, followed by the drawing filename (if any). To the left of the Title bar is the *Control menu* button. Clicking this button once calls up a short menu, while double-clicking causes the application to finish running. To the right of the Title bar are the *Minimise* and *Maximise* buttons. Clicking the Minimise button temporarily suspends the program, allowing you to run another program. The 'minimised' program appears as an *icon* at the bottom of the screen. Double-clicking this icon causes the suspended program to resume its operation. Clicking the Maximise button causes the application window to expand to fill the entire screen (which is preferred by most users). Once the program window has been maximised, the maximize button is replaced by a double-headed arrow called the *Restore* button. Clicking Restore once causes the window to return to its previous size.

Assuming that the window has not been maximized, it is possible to have more than one window open on the desktop area, although only one window can be 'active' at any time. Windows can be placed side by side, or may overlap. With overlapping windows, it is the active window which appears 'on top'. Clicking once on a window causes it to become active. The active window can be resized at any time by using the mouse to drag either an edge or a corner of the window. To move the window to a different area of the screen, move the cursor to the title bar and then drag the window to its new location. (These features may also be selected by clicking the active window's Control menu button.)

The Pull-down Menu Area

The pull-down menu system is generally considered to be the easiest way of accessing AutoCAD LT commands – particularly by inexperienced users. Although its operation seems pretty obvious, there are a number of subtle features which should be understood. Consider Figure 2–6, which illustrates one section of the menu system.

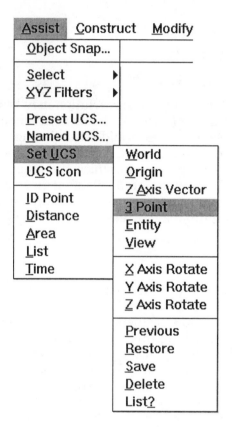

Figure 2–6. An active pull-down menu system.

The menu system may be controlled either using the mouse, or with the keyboard. Clicking anywhere on the menu bar with the mouse causes the indicated menu section to be displayed. A command which is currently visible may then be activated simply by pointing and clicking with the mouse. Notice that once a menu area is displayed, the keyboard cursor keys (↑, ↓, ← and →) may be used to move the highlighted menu bar up, down, left or right, after which the highlighted command may be activated by pressing ↵. Pressing Esc at any time has the effect of closing the open menu (which may need to be repeated several times in some cases).

Examining the menu bar more carefully reveals that each title has a single underlined character, and that each underlined letter is unique. Once a particular menu section is active, pressing the required *keyboard shortcut* key causes that command (or menu area) to become active.

Assuming that the menu system is not currently active, pressing the Alt key once will cause an item on the menu bar to become highlighted (pressing Alt again has the reverse effect). Thus, commands may be activated by pressing the correct sequence of keys. For example, pressing Alt, followed by D and then C has the effect of selecting the **Circle** option from the **Draw** pull-down menu.

Looking back at Figure 2–6 once again, we can see that some menu options have an arrow at the right-hand side, while others are terminated by a series of dots. An arrow means that selecting that item will cause a *cascading* (or 'child') menu to appear. (Arranging the menu system in this way allows groups of related items to be placed in a subsidiary menu area and causes the main menu system to appear less cluttered.) If an item terminated by three dots is selected, a *dialogue box*, such as that shown in Figure 2–7 will appear. Where an item has neither an arrow nor a series of dots, then selecting that option will cause the named AutoCAD LT command to be executed immediately.

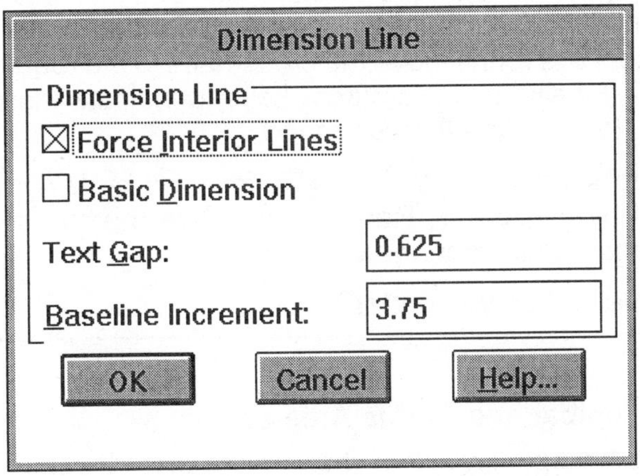

Figure 2–7. A typical AutoCAD LT dialogue box.

Before moving on to consider the next section of the AutoCAD LT screen, there are a couple of points about menus, which are worth making at this stage.

Firstly, AutoCAD LT Release 1 has <u>two</u> different menu systems. The *Full menu* is intended for advanced users, while a *Short menu* is provided for newcomers to CAD. Users of Release 1 can 'toggle' between these two menu systems by choosing the required option from the 'Settings' pull-down menu area. In Release 2, the name of the current menu system is defined by the PREFERENCES command. This allows customs menu systems to be loaded, as we will see later.

Secondly, as an aid to productivity, several frequently required options have been placed onto a special menu area which always appears at the current cursor position. If you hold down the Shift key and simultaneously click the right mouse button (Shift + ⌐⊕), a *Cursor menu* will appear, from where commonly required options may be selected. This ergonomic feature speeds up the drawing process by eliminating the need to move the cursor up to the menu bar, select an item and then move back to the drawing area for frequently used items such as *object snap*.

Tutorial 1   Accessing Commands using the Menu Bar

This tutorial demonstrates three different ways to access the CIRCLE command by using the Menu bar.

1. Mouse only. Move the mouse over the Menu bar and click on **Draw**. Now select the **Circle** option from the displayed menu, which will cause a cascading menu to appear. Using the mouse, pick the **Center, Radius** option. By pointing and clicking in the graphics area, indicate the required coordinates for the centre of the Circle, followed by a point somewhere on the circumference, which will define the radius.

2. Cursor keys. Press the [Alt] key once to cause an option on the menu bar to become highlighted. Now use the left and right cursor keys ([←] and [→]) to highlight the **Draw** title and then press [↓] (or [↵]) to cause the menu to drop down. Use the cursor keys to highlight the **Circle** option and then press [→] (or [↵]) to display the Circle child menu. Highlight the **Center, Radius** option and then press [↵]. With the cursor keys (only) move the cross-hairs to the required centre coordinate and press [↵]. Finally, use the cursor keys to indicate the required radius and then press [↵] to complete the command.

3. Keyboard shortcut keys. Type [Alt], followed by **D** (**Draw**) and then **C** (**Circle**), followed by **R** (**Center, Radius**). Now use the mouse to indicate the required centre and radius coordinates.

    Which method do you prefer?

The Toolbar and Status Area

The exact appearance of the Toolbar area depends on the graphics resolution, with higher resolutions allowing more buttons to be displayed at the right-hand side. A typical Toolbar is shown in Figure 2–8.

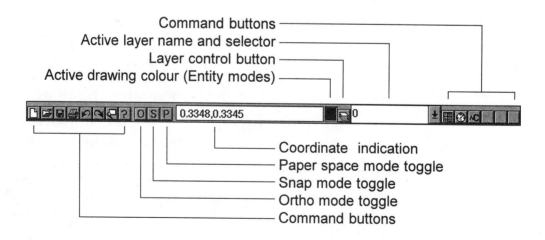

Figure 2–8. The Toolbar area.

We will be looking at some of the more basic aspects of the Toolbar area shortly, while features such as Layer control will be left to a later chapter. For the moment notice that the coordinate display constantly changes as you move the cross-hairs around the screen. Also, try turning the Snap button on and off and see the effect that this has on the movement of the cursor and on the coordinate display.

The Toolbox

The Toolbox area contains a series of buttons, each of which selects either an AutoCAD LT command, or an operating mode such as an object snap setting. By clicking the Toolbox button in the Toolbar area (see margin), the Toolbox may be toggled through its four operating modes. These are:

❑ vertical ribbon at the left of the screen;

❑ off;

❑ vertical ribbon at the right of the screen;

❑ mobile window.

Which mode to use is a matter of personal preference. Notice in any case that holding the mouse over a button for a second or more, causes the name of the command or option to appear as a 'ToolTip'. This feature, combined with the actual appearance of each icon, helps you to quickly find the required facility, as shown in Figure 2–9.

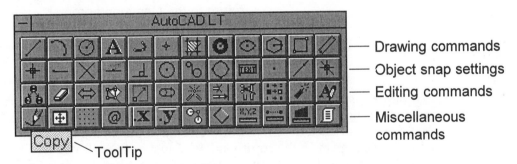

Figure 2–9. The Toolbox displayed as a mobile window.

Another useful feature is the logical arrangement of the commands in the mobile Toolbox window. Notice that the top row consists entirely of *drawing* commands which are used to create objects such as Lines, Circles etc. The second row deals with *object snap* settings, which allow indicated points to refer to existing drawing features such as endpoints of Lines or centres of Circles. The third row contains *editing* commands which are used to modify existing objects or construct new objects from existing drawing features. Finally, the bottom row contains miscellaneous commands. (Also notice that the Toolbox window may be dragged using its title bar, and can be closed by double-clicking its control menu button.)

As an exercise, move the cursor slowly over the various icons and try to match the appearance of each icon with the command name. (You will need to learn to recognize these icons to become proficient at using the Toolbox!) If you are feeling adventurous, try using some of the drawing commands to create a simple drawing (and use the ERASE command to correct your mistakes).

The Command Area

If you refer back to Figure 2–5, you will see that the lower three lines of the AutoCAD LT screen are called the *Command area*, which is a text-only window. The software indicates its readiness to accept commands by displaying a 'Command:' prompt in this area. During command entry, the Command area displays the 'dialogue' between the program and the user.

As an example, the following short sequence shows the instructions issued by the user (shown in bold) when drawing a single Line, and the computer's response at each stage.

Example

Command: **LINE** ⏎   - Start the LINE command. (Either ⏎ or Spacebar may be used as a 'command separator' here.)

From point: **100,100**   - Give a <u>start</u> point for the Line. (Use the mouse to indicate a point in the graphics area.)

To point: **200,100**   - Give an <u>end</u> point for the Line. (Use the mouse once again.)

To point: ⏎   - Press ⏎ to finish the LINE command, and return to the Command prompt.

Command: - Press ⏎ to repeat the <u>last</u> command, or type a new command name.

Although this example seems to refer only to the entry of commands using *typed input*, this is <u>not</u> the case. Even if you pick the LINE command from the **Draw** pull-down menu, or click the LINE button in the Toolbox, the LINE command name will always appear in the command area, just as though you had typed it! (The only difference is that with typed input you must press ⏎ or Spacebar to separate one keyboard entry from the next.)

It is a good idea to develop the habit of checking this area of the screen on a regular basis, because what you <u>think</u> AutoCAD LT is doing and what it is <u>actually</u> doing are not always the same thing! If for example the Command area is displaying a prompt such as 'Select objects:', this obviously means that an AutoCAD LT command is in progress (the ERASE command perhaps). Typing **LINE** at this prompt will simply generate an error message. Users who fail to take notice of these warning messages may be suprised when a large section of their drawing mysteriously disappears!

This kind of problem can easily be overcome. To cause the Command prompt to be displayed, just hold down the Ctrl key and then briefly press C (normally written as Ctrl + C). In some rare cases (the DIM command for example), you may need to repeat this process <u>twice</u> to fully exit a command which is in progress.

We have just seen that pressing [Ctrl] + [C] has the effect of cancelling an AutoCAD LT command which is in progress. The use of this particular key combination stems from the DOS-based ancestry of the full version of the AutoCAD software. The relatively recent conversion to the Windows environment leads to some minor peculiarities when it becomes necessary to cancel a partly completed operation. This is because Windows itself uses the [Esc] key for this <u>same</u> purpose. (Many Windows-based applications use the [Ctrl] + [C] combination to copy a highlighted item to the *Clipboard* – the Notepad program in the Accessories folder is a typical example.) To summarize:

❑   to cancel an AutoCAD LT command, press [Ctrl] + [C];

❑   to close an open dialogue box, press [Esc] or click the 'cancel' button;

❑   to close an open pull-down menu, press [Esc].

Returning to an examination of the Command area, one obvious problem is that previous dialogue scrolls out of view very quickly, as the command area is only three lines high! If for some reason you need to look 'further back' – to recall the last entered coordinate perhaps – then pressing function key [F2] will cause a scrollable text window to appear containing previous command dialogue. (Pressing [F2] again allows a return to the graphics screen.)

Using typed input to enter commands seems rather cumbersome, when compared with the pull-down menu system or the Toolbar and Toolbox features. However, some commands are <u>only</u> available by using typed input. In addition, many AutoCAD LT commands may be entered in abbreviated form. For example, the LINE command may be shortened to **L**, while CIRCLE may be entered as **C**. Thus to draw a Line using typed input, simply press L, followed by a suitable command separator ([↵], [Spacebar] or ⌐ᐡ). A complete list of these abbreviations is given in the Appendix, while a few of the more commonly used are given in Table 2–1 below.

Table 2–1. Commonly used command abbreviations.

A	ARC	F	FILLET	R	REDRAW
B	BLOCK	H	HATCH	S	STRETCH
C	CIRCLE	I	DDINSERT	T	DTEXT
D	DIM	L	LINE	Z	ZOOM
E	ERASE	M	MOVE		
G	GRID	P	PAN		

Note: The provision of a scrollable text window is a considerable improvement over the single text page provided by DOS-based versions of AutoCAD. DOS versions of AutoCAD use function key [F1] to swap between the text and graphics screens. Because Windows uses this same key to access the <u>on-line</u> help facility, Windows-based versions of AutoCAD and AutoCAD LT must use function key [F2] to swap between the text and graphics screens.

Learning to interpret the information presented in the Command area can be particularly useful when some of the more complex commands are used. Consider the ARC command, which offers a variety of Arc definition techniques, as shown in Figure 2–10.

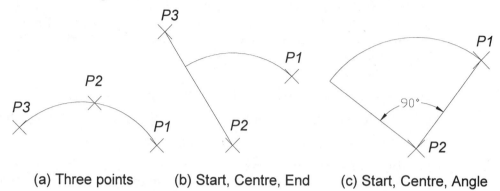

(a) Three points   (b) Start, Centre, End   (c) Start, Centre, Angle

Figure 2–10. Some methods used to define Arcs.

AutoCAD LT allows you to define an Arc using any of the above methods, and there is some flexibility concerning the <u>order</u> in which defining points are entered. (You can also give the Start and End coordinates, followed by the included angle.) By reading the information presented in the Command area carefully, you can see the range of options which are available at any time and the default entry method. Now examine the following command dialogue, which produces a three point Arc.

Command: **ARC** ↵	- Start the ARC command.
Center/<Start point>:	- Enter the start point (*P1*).
Center/End/<Second point>:	- Enter the second point (*P2*).
End point:	- Enter the third point (*P3*).

Notice that at any time, each option is separated from the next by a 'forward slash' (/) character and that the default entry method is shown inside angular brackets. So, if you enter a <u>coordinate</u> at the 'Center/<Start point>:' prompt, this will be interpreted as the <u>start</u> <u>point</u> of the Arc (*P1*).

For each of the options which is available, one or more letters is <u>capitalized</u>. To select an option, rather than the default, simply type the letter(s) which are shown in upper case. Thus to specify the <u>centre</u> of the Arc, at the 'Center/<Start point>:' prompt, type **C** followed by either ↵ or [Spacebar]. The prompt will then change to 'Center:', allowing you to give the specified information. To illustrate this technique, the following dialogue demonstrates the entry of an Arc by defining the centre, start and end (hence angle) coordinates.

Command: **ARC** ⏎	- Start the ARC command.
Center/<Start point>: **C**	- Choose the 'Center' option.
Center:	- Enter the centre coordinate (**P2**).
Start point:	- Enter the start point (**P1**).
Angle/<End point>:	- Enter the end point (**P3**), or type **A**, followed by ⏎ and then type an angle (i.e. **90** ⏎).

It is an interesting exercise to compare the range of options which is available from the pull-down menu system for a particular command, with that displayed in the command area. In most cases, the pull-down menu simply provides an easier way to access the same range of command options.

Tutorial 2   Using the Toolbox and Typed Input

This tutorial compares the entry of the LINE command using the Toolbox, and with typed input.

1. Toolbox. Select the LINE icon in the Toolbox to activate the LINE command. (What happens if another command was in progress when the LINE icon is selected?) By pointing and clicking in the graphics area, draw several joined lines. Notice that entering a command separator at the 'To point:' prompt, has the effect of leaving the LINE command. Entering the same command separator again restarts the LINE command, allowing a Line to be entered which is not joined to the previous Line. (If you actually want the Line to be joined to the last Line, then enter a command separator at the 'From point:' prompt. The start point will then be inherited from the endpoint of the last drawn Line.) Notice also while drawing Lines that entering **U** ⏎ at the 'To point:' prompt causes the last Line segment to be erased (**U** is short for UNDO), and that pressing **C** ⏎ has the effect of joining the first and last points (**C** is short for CLOSE).

2. Typed input in full. Type **LINE** ⏎ to start the LINE command and then follow the above procedure. (You may have to press Ctrl + C at least once to cancel an AutoCAD LT command which is in progress, prior to entering the LINE command.)

3. Typed input using command abbreviations. Type **L** ⏎ to start the LINE command and then follow the above procedure. (You may have to press Ctrl + C at least once to cancel an AutoCAD LT command which is in progress, prior to entering the LINE command.)

Compare your findings with those of Tutorial 1 and decide for yourself which method of command entry you prefer.

Producing Your First Drawing

Before you actually create a drawing, it is a good idea to 'configure' or 'fine-tune' AutoCAD LT, so that its operation is suited to your own personal style of working. The most basic configuration options are provided by the PREFERENCES command, which is considered below. Other drawing-specific settings, most of which are available from the **Settings** pull-down menu, are also available, and will be considered shortly.

Personal Preferences

If you type **PREFERENCES** at the Command prompt, or choose the **Preferences...** option from the **File** pull-down menu, the dialogue box of Figure 2–11 will be displayed.

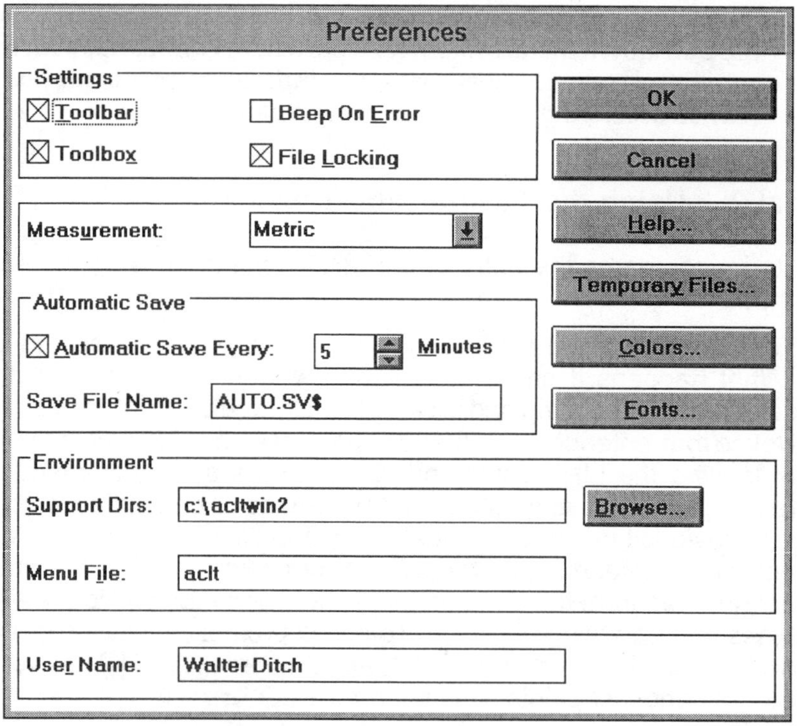

Figure 2–11. The Preferences dialogue box.

Examining this dialogue box carefully shows that it consists of five sections, with a further series of dialogue boxes available from buttons along the right edge of the window. (Notice that the button titles all end with '...'.)

The settings which are controlled by this dialogue box are stored in the text file ACLT.INI (which by default is found in the directory C:\ACLTWIN). This file is opened each time AutoCAD LT is started, so any changes made here will also affect future drawing sessions. (If you are curious about AutoCAD LT's internal operation, you may like to print this text file and try to understand its content!)

The Settings area of the dialogue box controls whether:

❑   the Toolbar and Toolbox areas are displayed;

❑   errors cause an audible beep;

❑   *file locking* is activated.

The file locking feature is really intended for <u>networked</u> computer environments, where several computers are linked together and are able to share files and hardware resources such as printers and plotters. A potential problem with this kind of arrangement is that two or more users (on different computers) may simultaneously try to open the <u>same</u> drawing and then carry out <u>different</u> drawing operations. File locking is intended to prevent this situation from arising.

What actually happens is that when the <u>first user</u> opens the drawing file, a temporary lock file is created (so for example, when a drawing called TEST.DWG is opened, a lock file called TEST.DWK would be created in the same directory). When the <u>second user</u> tries to open this same file across the network, AutoCAD LT notices the existence of the lock file and prevents duplicate access to the drawing file. Once user 1 has finished, the lock file is erased. At this point user 2 will be able to open the file without any problem (user 1 is then barred, using the same mechanism).

Note: In fact there are <u>several</u> types of lock file, each having its own unique file extension and principle of operation (refer to the *AutoCAD LT for Windows User Guide* for more details).

The use of file locking is a good idea on networked systems, but it can cause problems in some circumstances. If for example there is a power cut while you are working on a drawing, then the lock file will <u>not</u> be deleted at the end of the drawing session. (This can also happen if you fail to exit AutoCAD LT and Windows before turning off the computer, or if you suffer a software 'crash'.) When you next attempt to access the drawing, you will be refused access!

To unlock files which have been accidentally locked, type **FILES** (or **UNLOCK**) at the Command prompt, or choose **U**nlock **File...** from the **F**ile pull-down menu. The Unlock Files dialogue box will then be displayed. (Note that the last letter of the file extension is 'K' with most types of lock file, so settting the file extension to '*.??K' in the **File N**ame: edit box is generally effective.)

The second area of the PREFERENCES dialogue box controls the 'measurement' system, and selects between 'Metric' and 'English' settings. This can be rather misleading and should not be confused with the DDUNITS command, which will be considered shortly. The **Measurement:** option actually selects whether English or international (ISO) hatch patterns, linetype definitions and prototype drawings are used, when these AutoCAD LT features are accessed.

Note: The default prototype drawing is either ACLT.DWG or ACLTISO.DWG depending on the above setting. Similarly, linetype definitions are loaded from either ACLT.LIN or ACLTISO.LIN. Lastly, hatch pattern definitions are available in two files – ACLT.PAT or ACLTISO.PAT.

The *automatic save* feature is well worth using as it protects you from losing your work due to unforseen circumstances such as a power cut, or from doing something really silly with your drawing. When this feature is enabled (a 'cross' appears in the *check box*), a copy of your drawing is regularly and automatically saved to the specified filename. This file must have a file extension of '.SV$', which distinguishes it from a normal AutoCAD drawing (which would have an extension of '.DWG').

An obvious question to ask is 'If a disaster happens, how do I get my drawing back?' Well, the first thing to say is that you probably won't be able to recover <u>all</u> of your drawing, but you should be able to retrieve your work up to the point at which the last automatic save occurred. There are two basic methods which you can follow, depending on which release of AutoCAD LT you are using.

❑ Release 1. From the **File** menu, select the **Open...** option, which will display a dialogue box. Now change the entry in the **File Name:** edit box to '*.SV$' and press ⏎ (or click the **OK** button). The name of the backup file should now appear in the files section, allowing it to be selected and opened in the normal way.

❑ Release 2. Rename the file so that it has a '.DWG' extension. At the DOS prompt for example, assuming that the backup file is called BACKUP1.SV$ and that the required filename is BACKUP1.DWG, type:

C:\ACLTWIN> **REN BACKUP1.SV$ BACKUP1.DWG** ⏎

Although this feature does provide some protection against accidental loss of data, bear in mind that this is not a substitute for keeping regular backup copies of all important information. In the event, for example, of a hard disk 'crash', <u>all</u> information on the hard disk may be lost (including the backup file)!

The Environment section of the PREFERENCES dialogue box determines where AutoCAD LT will look for support files. Unless you are an expert, this option should be left at the default setting.

When you work with AutoCAD LT, information is initially stored in RAM as this provides rapid access. When this area becomes full, temporary files are created on your hard disk (which obviously results in slower program execution). In certain circumstances (normally disastrous) these temporary files may not be deleted at the end of the current drawing session. The task of periodically performing 'garbage removal' on your hard disk may be simplified if all temporary files are stored in a single directory (perhaps of the same name – as controlled by clicking on the **Temporary Files...** button). For example, you can create a directory called C:\TEMP from DOS by typing:

C:\ACLTWIN> **MD \TEMP** ⏎

Lastly, the **Colors...** and **Fonts...** buttons on the PREFERENCES dialogue box permit you to fine tune the appearance of the AutoCAD LT system. The first button allows you to change the foreground and background colour of any item in the desktop area, while the second controls the size and appearance of textual information in the graphics and text windows. (If you get into a mess when changing screen colours then clicking the **System Colors** button will return you to the original or default settings.)

Drawing Setup

Whenever you create a new drawing, it is worth spending a few moments thinking about what you are going to do and planning, before launching into action. Perhaps it may be worth producing a pencil sketch of the intended drawing so that you can finalize the drawing layout and any related sizes. Once the important points have been decided, you can create a new drawing by selecting the **New...** option from the **File** pull-down menu, or by pressing the appropriate button in the Toolbar (see margin).

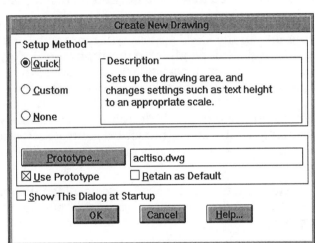

Figure 2–12. The Create New Drawing dialogue box.

This is one area which has changed significantly in Release 2 of AutoCAD LT, when compared with Release 1. You are now offered 3 different methods of creating a new drawing – the **Quick**, **Custom** and **None** options, as shown in Figure 2–12 above. These differ in the degree of detail which is offered during the drawing setup process. The **Quick** option allows the selection of basic units of measurement, the size of the drawing area and drawing aids such as the grid and snap features. **Custom** drawing setup defines these features in greater detail, and also allows a pre-drawn *Title Block* or border to be selected. (This advanced option also makes use of paper space and model space which will be introduced in a later chapter.) Finally, the **None** option proceeds directly to the creation of the drawing, using AutoCAD LT's own internal settings.

An important point to note in the dialogue box of Figure 2–12 is the *prototype* drawing. A prototype is simply an existing drawing which will be used as the basis for the new drawing. In other words, if you select a prototype, the new drawing will be an identical copy of the prototype drawing.

The efficient use of prototype drawings can save you a lot of time, as they can eliminate a great deal of duplication of effort. Prototype drawings also encourage standardization because default features such as *system variables* (settings) and styles will be inherited from the prototype. As you gain experience you may wish to create a library of prototype drawings, each of which is suited to a particular application.

If you have chosen either the **Quick** or **Custom** drawing setup options, then a drawing setup dialogue box will appear when you click the **OK** button. The next two decisions concern the required size of the drawing area (in drawing units) and which system of units (metric or imperial for example) you are going to use. These closely related items will depend on the application.

By convention, drawings are entered onto the CAD system 'actual size', so 1 drawing unit in the CAD system will represent 1 unit on the design (1 mm, 1 metre, 1 inch etc. – depending on the application). Any scaling of the drawing – to fit the drawing onto a particular size of paper when your design is printed for example – will be performed later. The accurate entry of design information is a basic principle of most CAD systems, particularly if design calculations are to be performed on the data, or if design information may be exported to another application at a later stage (numerical control software for example). There are also advantages to adopting this principle, even when a paper-based drawing is the only intention.

❑ The elimination of the need to scale all lengths prior to their entry, speeds up the drawing process considerably and removes a potential source of error.

❑ Drawing *inquiry* commands may be used at any time to check the accuracy of your design.

❑ Dimensions may be added to a drawing using a semi-automated process, where the default text of each Dimension (lengths or angles) is based on the geometry of associated objects in the drawing. These *associative* Dimensions are automatically updated if you later modify the drawing.

Considering the selection of units and drawing limits in an example application, if you are producing an electronic printed circuit board (PCB) design then you would be aware that the pins on typical integrated circuits are 0.1 inches apart. It would therefore make sense to use feet and inches as the system of measurement. If we assume that this particular PCB is 3 inches wide and 2 inches high, then we would want the available drawing area to be slightly larger, so that the entire design can be displayed on screen, with room for a margin. A sensible decision therefore would be to set the size of the drawing area – called the *drawing limits* – to be 4 units wide by 3 units high. This is illustrated by Figure 2–13.

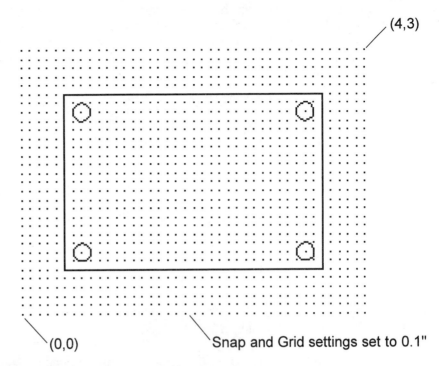

Figure 2–13. Deciding on the screen layout and selecting drawing limits.

As we have just seen, with Release 2 of AutoCAD LT, you can now specify the drawing limits when a new drawing is created. It is also possible to use the LIMITS command at any time, as shown below.

Command: **LIMITS** ↵
Reset Model space limits:

ON/OFF/<Lower left corner><0.0000,0.0000>: ↵   - Accept the default value

Upper right corner <420.0000,297.0000>: **4,3** ↵

At this stage the drawing limits have been set to 4 units horizontally (the X coordinate) by 3 units vertically (the Y coordinate). One thing which tends to confuse newcomers to AutoCAD LT when the LIMITS command has been used, is that nothing seems to have changed – the coordinate display in the Toolbar still shows the <u>old</u> limits as you move the cursor around the graphics area. To complete the operation it is necessary to use the ZOOM command to display the new drawing area. This may be achieved by typing **Z** [Spacebar] **A** [Spacebar] (ZOOM ALL) at the Command prompt.

Next, we must select the required units and display precision. Once again, users of Release 2 can select this option during the creation of a new drawing. Alternatively, you can start the DDUNITS command by typing **DDUNITS** at the Command prompt or by selecting the **U**nits Style... option from the **S**ettings pull-down menu.

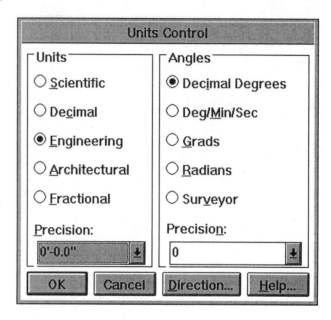

Figure 2–14. The DDUNITS dialogue box.

As you can see from Figure 2–14, the left section of the Units Control dialogue box deals with linear measurements, while the right-hand side is concerned with angles. Notice in each case that it is possible to control the measurement system used and also its precision (the number of decimal places used in decimal measurements for example). We are only interested in linear measurements for the moment so ignore the Angles section of the dialogue box.

The best way to understand the meaning of the different systems of linear measurement is to click on each of the *radio buttons* in turn, while examining the display format in the **P**recision: list box. For the PCB design example being considered here then either the **De**cimal or **E**ngineering settings would seem to be satisfactory, with the precision set to one decimal place.

Now, bearing in mind that all pins in our PCB design will be placed with a 0.1 inch spacing, it would be useful to display a suitably-sized *grid* of dots on the screen. In addition, to assist the user in the accurate placement of *pads* and other PCB layout components, the *snap* setting should be enabled, with the snap spacing equal to that used for the grid. The grid and snap settings may be set during drawing creation in Release 2, or by using the DDRMODES command. The DDRMODES command may be started by picking the **D**rawing Aids... option from the **S**ettings pull-down menu, by clicking the appropriate button on the Toolbar (see margin), or by typing **DDRMODES** at the Command prompt. The Drawing Aids dialogue box, together with the required settings for PCB design are shown in Figure 2–15.

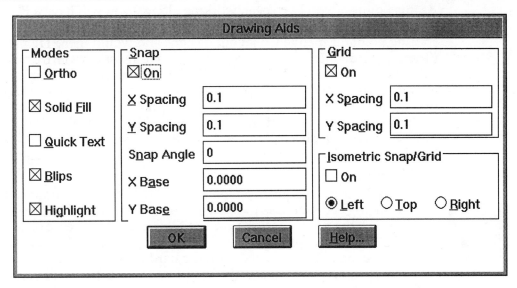

Figure 2–15. The Drawing Aids dialogue box and settings for PCB design.

Notice that both the snap and grid settings have been enabled (their check boxes are on), and that the X and Y spacings have all been set to 0.1. (An important conclusion which can be drawn here is that the grid and snap settings do not <u>have</u> to be the same!). When you click **OK**, a grid of dots will appear and the snap button in the Toolbar area should appear 'depressed'. Now use the LINE and CIRCLE commands to create a PCB outline, such as that shown in Figure 2–13.

Tutorial 3   Drawing Setup and Prototype Drawings

The aim of this exercise is to create a prototype drawing which is suitable for printed circuit board (PCB) design.

1.   Click the New Drawing icon in the Toolbar to create a new drawing (which will later be called PCBPROTO).

2.   Set the drawing limits to 4 by 3 units.

3.   Set the drawing units to feet and inches, with a precision of 1 decimal place.

4.   Set the snap and grid to a spacing of 0.1 units, with both enabled.

5.   Use the LINE and CIRCLE commands to create a basic PCB outline, similar to that shown in Figure 2–13.

6.   Click the Save drawing icon (SAVE) in the Toolbar to save your drawing with the filename PCBPROTO.

7.   As a test, click the New drawing icon in the Toolbar and create a new PCB design called LAYOUT1, using the file PCBPROTO as the prototype drawing.

Now consider how you could use prototype drawings in your own work.

At this point – if you have been working along – you will have a PCB layout on screen similar to that shown in Figure 2–13. This drawing would be a basic starting point for many PCB layout designs and would therefore make an ideal prototype drawing. To create a prototype, we must save our drawing with a suitably descriptive name, such as PCBPROTO (remember filenames can have up to eight characters). What happens next depends on whether or not you have previously 'named' your drawing. If you cannot remember, look at the Title bar at the top of the screen. If it shows 'AutoCAD LT - UNNAMED' then your drawing has not yet been given a filename. Otherwise, the current filename will be shown in place of 'UNNAMED' in the Title bar area. There are three possibilities:

1. The drawing was given a filename of PCBPROTO (or similar). To save the drawing either choose the Save Drawing icon in the Toolbar (see margin), or pick the **Save...** option from the **File** pull-down menu, or type **SAVE** at the Command prompt. The file will be automatically saved. (You may notice the LED associated with the hard disk become illuminated briefly, and you may hear disk activity, but you will not see a dialogue box.)

2. The drawing was given a name other than PCBPROTO. To save the drawing as PCBPROTO either pick the **Save As...** option from the **File** pull-down menu, or type **SAVEAS** at the Command prompt. The Save Drawing As dialogue box of Figure 2–16 will be displayed, at which point you should type **PCBPROTO** in the **File Name:** edit box and either click **OK** or press ⏎.

3. The drawing is currently unnamed. To save the drawing choose either the Save Drawing icon in the Toolbar (see margin above), pick the **Save...** (or **Save As...**) option from the **File** pull-down menu, or type **SAVE** (or **SAVEAS**) at the Command prompt. When the Save Drawing As dialogue box is displayed, type **PCBPROTO** in the **File Name:** edit box and either click **OK** or press ⏎.

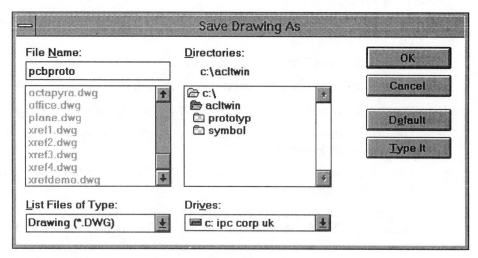

Figure 2–16. The Save Drawing As dialogue box.

Now, to check that your prototype drawing has been saved correctly, start a new PCB layout drawing by clicking the New Drawing icon in the Toolbar. At the displayed dialogue box, select PCBPROTO as the prototype drawing. When you click the OK button, you should see an identical copy of the PCBPROTO drawing on screen.

Note: If you have installed the utility diskette supplied with this book, then a directory called C:\ACLTWIN\PROTOTYP should exist. (Look at the **Directories** section of Figure 2–16 to see where this directory name will appear, if it exists.) The existing file called PCB in the PROTOTYP directory may be used as the prototype drawing if you have for some reason failed to create PCBPROTO. If this is the case then click on the **Prototype...** button in the Create new Drawing dialogue box. At the displayed dialogue box, double-click on the PROTOTYP entry in the **Directories:** list box, which should cause a list of possible protype drawing files to appear in the **File Name:** list box. Either double-click on the PCB entry or highlight PCB and then click **OK**.

In the next section we will introduce several new drawing and editing commands, and use these to produce the PCB layout shown in Figure 2–17 below. To complete the first chapter we will then save our work and obtain a printout of our design at a scale of 1:1.

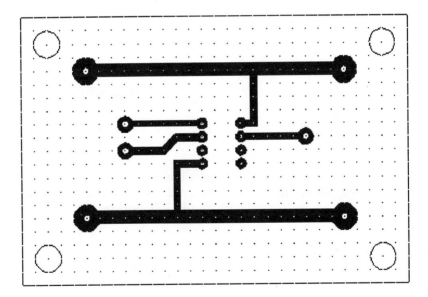

Figure 2–17. The final PCB layout.

Note: Although this is simply a drawing exercise, in the 'real world' an electronic engineer could use the *artwork* produced here to manufacture a fibre-glass PCB, with copper *tracks* forming connections between electronic *components* which would be soldered to each of the circular *pads*. (A photographic process is used here, which explains the need for an accurately scaled printout.)

Step 1   The PLINE and DONUT Commands

The PCB layout of Figure 2–17 is constructed from a series of circular pads, which are joined together by tracks. Looking more closely, you should be able to see that there are two different track widths and three different sizes of pad. The AutoCAD LT commands used to create these objects – PLINE (Polyline) and DONUT (Doughnut) – are quite similar in operation to the LINE and CIRCLE commands which we have already seen. The main difference in this case is that Polylines and Doughnuts can be given a property called *thickness*. Consider firstly a typical command dialogue for the DONUT command, which can be started either by picking the **Donut** option from the **Draw** pull-down menu, by clicking the Doughnut icon in the Toolbox (see margin), or by entering **DONUT** (or **DO**) at the Command prompt.

Command: **DONUT** ⏎	– Or you can type **DO** or **DOUGHNUT** here.
Inside diameter<0'-0.5">: **0.03** ⏎	– Specify the size of the 'hole'.
Outside diameter <0'-1.0">: **0.08** ⏎	– Give the outside diameter.
Center of doughnut:	– Use the mouse to indicate a centre coordinate.
Center of doughnut:	– Repeat the last step for each doughnut.
Center of doughnut: ⏎	– Press ⏎ to finish.

Now try to recreate the three sizes of doughnut and create a layout of pads similar to that shown in Figure 2–17. You may also want to save your work, just in case you encounter problems with the PLINE command!

The PLINE command is very similar in operation to LINE, although it can seem rather complex due to the large number of options which are presented to the user. We will only look at a <u>single</u> option here – the *width* setting – in order to keep things relatively straightforward. To begin the PLINE command, either pick the **Polyline** option from the **Draw** pull-down menu, click the Polyline button in the Toolbox (see margin), or enter **PLINE** (or **PL**) at the Command prompt.

A typical command dialogue is shown for the PLINE command is given on the next page.

Command: **PLINE** ⏎   - (Or you can type **PL** here.)

From point: - Indicate a start coordinate using the
                                       mouse (i.e. click ⌐ᵗₕ in the graphics area).
Current line width is 0'-0.0"
Arc/Close/Halfwidth/Length/Undo/Width/<Endpoint of line>: **w** ⏎

Starting width<0'-0.0">: **0.1** ⏎   - Give the <u>start</u> width for the next segment.

Ending width<0'-0.1">: ⏎   - Give the <u>end</u> width for the next segment.

Arc/Close/Halfwidth/Length/Undo/Width/<Endpoint of line>:

                               - Use the mouse to indicate each endpoint.
                               - Press **U** ⏎ to undo the last segment.
                               - Press **C** ⏎ to *close* the Polyline and exit.
                               - Press ⏎ to exit from the command.

Examine the above sequence of operations carefully. In particular, notice that you must indicate a <u>start coordinate</u>, before any of the other PLINE options become available. Also, when specifying the width of the next segment (not segments which have already been drawn), you must enter the <u>start</u> and <u>end</u> width for the next segment. This width setting then remains in force until a new value is entered. (Thus it is possible to draw complex shapes with tapered sections using the PLINE command – more on this later.)

Next we will use Polylines to produce the track layout and then erase any mistakes using suitable editing commands.

Notice in Figure 2–17 that all pads have been placed on the 0.1 inch snap grid – so the snap button in the Toolbar must have been <u>on</u> when pads were placed using the DONUT command. Once potential problem with using this same snap setting when drawing tracks is that if the tracks are drawn 'over' the pads, then part of the hole will be obscured. To overcome this problem, use the SNAP command to set the snap increment to a smaller value (0.025 for example), before drawing the PCB tracks. It is then a simple matter to ensure that the end of each track overlaps the pad slightly, without obscuring the central hole.

If you are working along, first set the snap increment to 0.025 and then use the PLINE command to draw the interconnecting tracks, as shown in Figure 2–17.

Step 2   Using Display Control Commands

When working on a design which has fine detail (such as a PCB layout), it can be useful to 'zoom in' on a small section of the design so that small features can be added or modified. As you might expect, this may be achieved using the ZOOM command. All AutoCAD LT drawing commands work as normal when a magnified portion of the drawing is displayed, so this feature can prove very useful. Figure 2–18 shows the use of the ZOOM command to produce a magnified view of one section of the PCB.

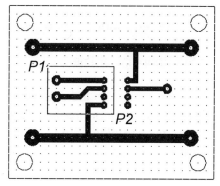

a) Indicating a window.

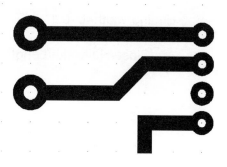

b) The resulting 'magnified' display.

Figure 2–18. Using ZOOM WINDOW to magnify one area of the drawing.

Once the Zoom command has been activated, the usual method of operation is to indicate two points (P1 and P2 above) which define a rectangular window. A typical command dialogue for the ZOOM command is shown below.

Command: **ZOOM** ⏎   - (Or you can use the abbreviation **Z** here.)

All/Center/Extents/Previous/Window/<Scale(X/XP)>:

                                            - Indicate points *P1* and *P2* with the mouse.

Having zoomed in on a small section, the previous display can easily be retrieved by selecting the ZOOM PREVIOUS option (**Z** [Spacebar] **P** [Spacebar] for example). Similarly, the ZOOM ALL command may be used to display the entire drawing, which may be shortened to **Z** [Spacebar] **A** [Spacebar]. (The meaning of the remaining command options will be discussed later.)

Note: When zooming into a small section of the drawing with the snap feature enabled, be aware that the cursor will always jump from one snap increment to the next. This can make it appear that the cursor has 'frozen', when in fact it is just a combination of large snap setting, relative to the screen size. The 'cure' is to either disable the snap feature, or reduce its increment.

Step 3   Correcting Mistakes and Modifying Your Design

At this stage in the design, you are almost certain to have made some mistakes which will need to be corrected! AutoCAD LT provides a sophisticated range of commands which allow existing objects to be modified, and new objects to be constructed, based on existing drawing geometry (hence the names of the **Modify** and **Construct** pull-down menu areas). For new users, who are not yet familiar with the available range of editing commands, the simplest approach is to <u>erase</u> any incorrect features, prior to <u>redrawing</u> them. (Bear in mind that, as you gain experience, you may discover less drastic ways of achieving the same goal!)

With the majority of editing commands, the first step is to select the object(s) which will be affected by the command (these will appear *highlighted* on screen). This group of objects is referred to as the *selection set* and this stage in the command dialogue is indicated by the 'Select Objects:' prompt, which will be displayed in the Command area, and by the fact that an object selection *pickbox* appears at the centre of the crosshairs.

Individual objects may be selected by positioning the pickbox over the object and then clicking ⌐. Ideally, you should arrange that only one object passes through the pickbox, to ensure that the correct object is selected. In difficult cases, it may help to zoom in prior to making a selection, or you may wish to alter the size of the pickbox, as shown below. You can also select a group of objects in one operation by drawing a window which encloses the required objects. Before trying to indicate a window using the ERASE command, first check that the **Implied Windowing** feature is enabled, and that a suitable pickbox size has been selected, as shown in the dialogue box of Figure 2–19.

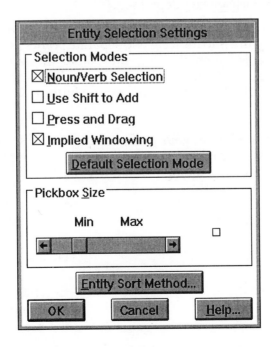

Figure 2–19. The DDSELECT command dialogue box.

To cause the Entity Selection dialogue box to be displayed, either type **DDSELECT** at the Command prompt or select **Sele̲ction Style...** from the **S̲ettings** pull-down menu.

The significance of the *implied windowing* feature is that if you point to an area of the screen which does not contain an object, then AutoCAD LT will assume that you are indicating the first corner of a rectangular object selection window. Most users find that this simplifies the process of selecting objects. You may also wish to experiment with some of the other operating modes which may be enabled or disabled from the DDSELECT dialogue box. The significance of each feature is given below.

❑ **Noun/Verb Selection.** If this feature is enabled then some (but not all) editing commands will allow you to select a group of objects <u>before</u> you choose the actual command. This contrasts with the more normal sequence where the command is first chosen, after which the selection set is constructed. (If the object selection pickbox appears at the cursor position when the Command prompt is displayed, then this feature may already be enabled. However note that the 'grips' feature – which will be considered later – <u>also</u> causes a pickbox to appear at the intersection of the crosshairs when the Command prompt is displayed.)

❑ **U̲se Shift to Add.** With this mode enabled, it is necessary to hold down the ⌗Shift⌗ key when adding new objects to the selection set. If ⌗Shift⌗ is not depressed then selecting one object, causes any previously selected object(s) to be removed from the selection set. It is also possible to remove single objects from the selection set by clicking ⌕ on a previously highlighted item with the ⌗Shift⌗ key depressed.

❑ **P̲ress and Drag.** When using the ZOOM WINDOW command, the normal procedure is to indicate two separate points using the mouse. If this feature is enabled then the user must hold the left mouse button down after indicating the first point and then 'drag' the cursor to the second point, before finally releasing the mouse button.

Having decided upon your preferred method of selecting objects, you can now use the ERASE command to remove any errors, prior to redrawing those sections. A typical command dialogue is shown below.

Command: **ERASE**	- (Or you can type **E** here.)
Select objects:	- Do so.
Select objects:	- Enter a command separator to complete the command and erase the previously selected objects.

Step 4   Saving Your Work

Earlier in this chapter (see p. 26) we created a new drawing, based on the prototype drawing PCBPROTO. Assuming that you have been working along with the PCB design exercise, you should now save your work. To do this, follow the same procedure as when the prototype drawing was saved, but name the drawing as LAYOUT1 in the Save Drawing As dialogue box. (You should notice some brief 'disk activity' as your file is saved.)

Tutorial 4   Customizing Object Selection Using DDSELECT

This exercise encourages you to experiment with different methods of <u>selecting objects</u>, particularly when working with editing commands, such as ERASE.

Note: If you are not yet familiar with the use of 'grips' then – to avoid confusion – temporarily disable this feature by selecting the **Grips Style...** option from the **Settings** pull-down menu. Ensure that the **Enable Grips** checkbox is <u>disabled</u> before continuing.

1.   Use typical drawing commands to create at least 20 objects on screen (which will be erased shortly).

2.   Use the DDSELECT command to enable *noun/verb* entity selection. When the Command prompt is displayed (press [Ctrl] + [C] if necessary), you should notice that a rectangular pickbox appears at the cursor position. Click on several objects and then type **E** [Spacebar] to erase these previously selected items. Now press [Spacebar] again to repeat the last command (ERASE) and at the 'Select objects:' prompt, indicate several objects. Press [Spacebar] to complete the command.

3.   Enable the **Use Shift to Add** checkbox in the Entity Selection Settings dialogue box. Start the ERASE command and, at the 'Select objects:' prompt use the mouse to select individual entities. Notice that holding down the [Shift] key allows new objects to be <u>added</u> to the selection set, or previously selected objects to be <u>removed</u>. Press [Spacebar] to complete the command.

4.   Enable the **Press and Drag** option, as explained above. Start the ZOOM command and move the cursor to the top left corner of the area which is to be magnified. Press ⏚ and, while holding this button down, move the cursor to the bottom right corner of the desired window, before finally releasing the button. Now return to the previous display usng either ZOOM ALL or ZOOM PREVIOUS. Disable the **Press and Drag** checkbox and repeat the above process by specifying two separate points which define the window.

5.   Use the DDSELECT command and enable the **Implied Windowing** checkbox. Start the ERASE command. Notice when selecting objects, that an object selection window is automatically started if no object is found at the indicated point. Now disable the above setting and repeat the exercise. (You can still force a *window* selection by entering **W** [Spacebar] at the 'Select objects:' prompt.)

Step 5   Producing a Plot

One of the main purposes of using a CAD system is to produce a high quality printout (or 'plot') of your design. A key advantage of using a computer over paper and pencil is the ease with which corrections can be made to the design, after which you can produce another perfect copy of your drawing.

 Before proceeding to produce a plot, ensure that the drawing LAYOUT1 is currently loaded. If not then select the **Open...** option from the **File** pull-down menu, or click the Open drawing icon in the Toolbar (see margin). A dialogue box similar to Figure 2–16 will appear, at which point the appropriate filename should be entered or selected from the displayed list.

 To start the PLOT command pick the **Print/Plot...** option from the **File** menu or click the Plot drawing icon in the Toolbar (see margin). At this point the dialogue box of Figure 2–20 should be displayed.

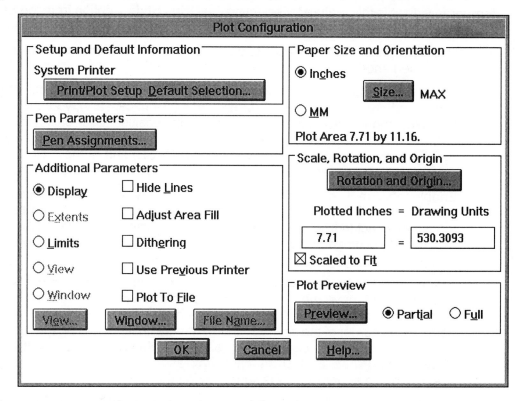

Figure 2–20. The Print/Plot drawing dialogue box.

As you can see from the complexity of this dialogue box, the plot facility is a very powerful feature! In fact we will be returning to this dialogue box several times during the course of this book. For the moment we will concentrate on obtaining a basic printout of the information which appears on the display screen.

The first step is to ensure that your printer has been correctly initialized. By default, AutoCAD LT will use your normal Windows printer setup so if you regularly use your printer with other Windows applications, there should be no problem here. To check the current setup, click the **Print/Plot Setup & Default Selection...** button and then press the **Print/Plot Setup...** button in the displayed dialogue box. At this point you should see a dialogue box similar to Figure 2–21.

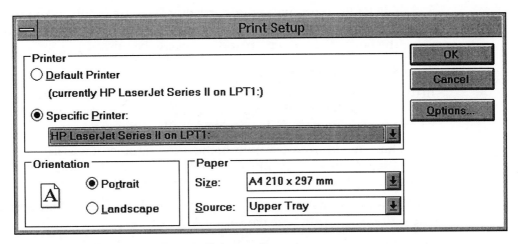

Figure 2–21. The Print Setup dialogue box.

At this stage you can either select the default printer or select a new printer from those currently installed.

Note: If your printer is not visible then you may need to run the *Control Panel* program, whose icon is normally found in the Main program folder. Click on the *Printers* button to see a list of currently installed printers/plotters. You can then modify the configuration of existing printers (port connection etc.), add new printers or change the identity of the default printer.

Having ensured that the printer is correctly configured, the next stage is to select the required plot parameters, after which we will preview the plot as a final check before producing our printout.

1.   We simply require a copy of the 'display' as our hardcopy, so ensure that the **Display** option is selected at the left of the dialogue box and that all other options in the Additional Parameters section are as shown in Figure 2–20.

2.   Check that the paper size is correct, as indicated at the top right of the dialogue box. (If not then click the **Size...** button and select the correct option.)

3.   To ensure that the printout will <u>fill</u> the available paper area, regardless of the actual drawing size (larger or smaller), ensure that the **Scaled to Fit** checkbox is selected.

4. In the Plot Preview section, click the **Full** radio button and then press the **Preview...** button. You should now see a preview of your drawing as it will be arranged on the paper. If the drawing does <u>not</u> fill the available area then click the **Rotation and Origin** button and make the necessary changes before returning to the print preview display. Once everything is satisfactory then you can proceed to the final stage.

5. Click **OK** to produce your hardcopy. You are finally asked to ensure that your printer/plotter is ready before proceeding. (This message appears at the bottom of the screen and can easily be missed.)

Step 6   Leaving the Program

In this chapter we have created a simple drawing from scratch, saved it for future reference and then produced a printout. It only remains to leave the AutoCAD LT program in an orderly fashion to complete your first session.

If you have made any alterations to the drawing since it was last saved, then you should save your work before leaving the program. (If AutoCAD LT detects that changes have been made then you will be prompted to save these prior to exiting.)

Having ensured that your work has been saved, choose the **Exit** option from the **File** pull-down menu to leave AutoCAD LT.

Note: It is also important to realise that you should <u>not</u> turn off the power until you have properly exited from AutoCAD LT and have left the Windows environment itself. Failure to obey this simple routine can result in temporary files being left on your hard disk, or even worse, may mean that your drawing file will not be properly saved.

3   Drawing Techniques

Introduction

A range of drawing commands and techniques will be introduced in this chapter. The drawing methods presented here form a solid foundation, which will enable you to grasp the more advanced topics to be presented in later chapters. Once again, the emphasis is on encouraging you to develop your own fast and effective drawing style, while at the same time highlighting aspects of good drawing practice.

Drawing Setup

The previous chapter introduced several commands which were particularly useful when starting a new drawing project. This section briefly summarizes these commands and reminds you of their purpose!

1. The PREFERENCES command displays a dialogue box which contains a number of general AutoCAD LT settings. Changes here will affect <u>all</u> subsequent drawing sessions (not just the current drawing), so it is worth checking these settings from time to time.

2. The NEW command starts a new drawing session and selects a range of drawing settings, as well as the name of the prototype drawing, if any. With AutoCAD LT Release 2, it is now possible to set the drawing limits, unit conventions and drawing aids during the creation of a new drawing. These features may be accessed at other times using the commands given below.

3. The size of the drawing area in drawing units may be specified using the LIMITS command. It is normal practice to enter drawing information using <u>actual</u> sizes, so that the drawing is an accurate representation. Any scaling of the drawing – to fit the drawing onto a sheet of paper for example – is performed by the PLOT command.

4. Conventions used by AutoCAD LT to represent lengths and angles are controlled by the DDUNITS command. (Modification of the display format and the numeric precision can be particularly useful when creating Dimensions, as will be seen in Chapter 6.)

5. The DDRMODES command displays a single dialogue box which controls a wide range of drawing settings, including the *ortho*, *snap* and *grid* features, each of which will be considered shortly.

Drawing Techniques and Commands

AutoCAD LT drawings are constructed using a range of 'building blocks', each of which is created using an associated drawing command. The previous chapter introduced several of these commands including the creation of Lines, Arcs, Circles, Doughnuts and Polylines. The present chapter builds on this experience, while also introducing several new drawing commands. More advanced topics (such as dimensioning, hatching and 3D drawing commands) will be considered later. Table 3.1 lists commonly used drawing commands, their minimum command abbreviation and the type of AutoCAD LT object (or *entity*) created.

Table 3–1. Basic Drawing Commands.

Command	Abbreviation	Entity Type
ARC	A	Circular arc
CIRCLE	C	Circle
DLINE	DL	Double line
DONUT	DO	Doughnut
DTEXT	T	Text
ELLIPSE	EL	Ellipse
PLINE	PL	Polyline
POINT	PT	Point
POLYGON	PG	Polygon
RECTANG	RC	Rectangle
SOLID	SO	Solid filled area

When tackling a new drawing project, in addition to the wide range of drawing commands which is available, there is also considerable flexibility in the methods which may be used to specify the drawing geometry. In this section we will consider four different approaches to drawing creation, including:

❑   freehand drawing;

❑   ortho and snap;

❑   typed input;

❑   object snap.

Once again, we will leave some of the more advanced techniques such as user coordinate systems, isometric drawing and true 3D drawing for later!

Freehand Drawing

Where absolute accuracy is not vital, the simplest drawing technique is to use AutoCAD LT as a freehand drawing tool. To do this, first ensure that the snap and ortho buttons in the Toolbar are in the 'off' position, as shown in Figure 3–1 below.

Figure 3–1. Disabling ortho and snap during freehand drawing.

At this point you can use typical AutoCAD LT drawing commands such as LINE, ARC or CIRCLE to create a simple freehand sketch. Now try the following drawing exercise.

Drawing Exercise 1   Freehand Drawing

Use AutoCAD LT drawing commands to produce a simple freehand sketch. You can choose any topic. (A possible Idea might be a house and its surrounding garden.)

Obtain a plot of your drawing and examine it carefully. Notice particularly the accuracy of any junctions between drawing features.

As you should be able to see if you have tried the above exercise, one of the main drawbacks of freehand sketching is the lack of accuracy in the final drawing. This is particularly obvious where Lines and Arcs fail to meet at junctions, as intended.

There are several ways to overcome these problems, including the use of *snap*, and *object snap* which will be considered shortly. Another useful technique makes use of the fact the <u>default</u> start position (and direction in some cases) of any new Line or Arc is defined by the endpoint of the most recently drawn object of a similar type. By carefully choosing the order with which a drawing is completed (so that objects are joined 'end to end'), the accuracy of the resulting sketch may be greatly improved. As a general rule, to cause the current object to begin where the most recently drawn object ended, simply press ↵ at the 'Start point:' or 'From point:' prompt.

Note: Recall also that the CLOSE option may be used to cause the <u>last</u> point of a Polyline (or a series of individual Lines) to be joined to the <u>first</u> point entered.

Tutorial 5   Using the 'Continue from Last Point' Option with Lines and Arcs

This exercise demonstrates that Lines and Arcs may be blended together, simply by pressing ⏎ at the 'From point:' or 'Start point:' prompts. (Before proceeding, ensure that the snap and ortho features are disabled.)

1.   First draw a single Line. Next, start the ARC command and press ⏎ at the 'First point:' prompt. Notice that the start point and starting direction of the Arc has been 'inherited' from the previously drawn Line. Now indicate an endpoint for the Arc.

2.   Press ⏎ to restart the ARC command. Press ⏎ again at the 'First point:' prompt and notice once again that the start direction and starting point of the Arc are taken from the most recently drawn Arc. Now complete the ARC command by specifying an endpoint.

3.   Start the LINE command and then press ⏎ at the 'From point:' prompt. You should notice that the Line starts at the endpoint of the most recently drawn ARC, and that the direction of the Line is tangential to this same Arc endpoint. In fact, the command prompt changes to 'Length of line:' at this stage, so you have the option of typing the required Line length, rather than using the mouse.

4.   Now have another go at the previous drawing exercise, using the 'continue from last point' option to improve the quality of any junctions. (Another possible subject for this drawing exercise would be a side view of a motorcar.)

Ortho and Snap

When enabled, the *ortho* button forces AutoCAD LT drawing commands to align newly created objects either horizontally or vertically. This greatly simplifies the task of drawing horizontal or vertical Lines when using freehand drawing techniques, and may also be used to accurately set the starting or ending direction of Arcs. Thus, simply by clicking the ortho button in the Toolbar area, you can switch between orthographic and freestyle methods of entering geometrical data.

The *snap* button in the Toolbar area (when enabled), causes coordinates which are indicated using the mouse to be aligned with an imaginary rectangular grid. The spacing and alignment of this grid is determined by settings in the Drawing Aids dialogue box, which may be modified using the DDRMODES command (see margin for the appearance of the DDRMODES command's icon). The snap feature is particularly useful when drawing information must be entered accurately, in cases where the majority of lengths are <u>multiples</u> of the snap spacing.

For example, if the snap spacing is set to 10 units and the snap feature has been enabled, a horizontal Line of length 70 units may easily be drawn. With snap enabled, you should notice that the coordinate display alters in increments of 10 units, while the crosshairs jump from one snap position to the next in the drawing area. Thus by moving the cursor away from the first entered point until the X coordinate has increased by 70 units, the required endpoint may be identified quite simply.

In fact, you can eliminate the need to perform this type of mental arithmetic by causing AutoCAD LT to display the <u>relative</u> displacement of the crosshairs from the first indicated point, rather than the 'absolute' position of the cursor. To do this, having entered the first Line endpoint, repeatedly press function key F6 until the coordinate area contains a 'length and angle' display of the form '70<0'. With this type of display, the first number indicates the <u>distance</u> of the cursor position from the previously indicated point, while the second number specifies the <u>direction</u> in degrees. By default, angles are measured in an anticlockwise direction, with 0° corresponding to a movement to the right (so 90° is vertically upwards, for example).

At this stage, it may be useful to summarize the various AutoCAD LT operating modes which may be selected using single and multiple key combinations. These are shown in Table 3–2 below.

Table 3–2. AutoCAD LT keyboard short-cuts and key significance.

Key	Operation performed
F1	On-line help.
F2	Switch to or from text only display.
F5	Select next isometric drawing plane.
F6	Coordinate display mode toggle.
F7	Grid on/off toggle.
F8	Ortho on/off toggle.
F9	Snap on/off toggle.
Ctrl + B	Snap on/off toggle.
Ctrl + C	Cancel current command.
Ctrl + D	Coordinate display mode toggle.
Ctrl + E	Select next isometric drawing plane.
Ctrl + G	Grid on/off toggle.
Ctrl + O	Ortho on/off toggle.
Ctrl + V	Select next active viewport.
Esc	Cancel dialogue box or pull-down menu.
⌐	Pick indicated coordinate.
⌐	Command separator (see Spacebar and ↵).
Shift + ⌐	Display cursor menu.
Ctrl + ⌐	Display cursor menu.
Spacebar	Command separator.
↵	Command separator.

The *grid* facility, which was briefly introduced in the previous chapter, may also be used as a visual indication of the snap grid spacing. The normal method is to use the Drawing Aids dialogue box (see the DDRMODES command on pages 24–25) to set the snap and grid spacings to be the same. Both settings may be enabled from this same dialogue box, or you can use the appropriate key combinations (see Table 3–2) to toggle individual settings while drawing.

When deciding whether a particular drawing project may be tackled using ortho and snap, the question to ask is 'Do the majority of defining points lie on a rectangular grid, and if so, what is the spacing between these points?' If, for example, a particular drawing consists mostly of horizontal and vertical Lines, and most lengths are found to be multiples of 5 drawing units, then ortho and snap may be the easiest method to use. (A value of 5 would be the setting used for the snap and grid increments in this case.) On the other hand, a design containing lengths such as '32.71' and Lines drawn at awkward angles, would be better tackled using *typed input*, which will be considered next.

Drawing Exercise 2   Ortho and Snap

The illustration below shows three views of a simple engineering component. Produce an accurate copy of this drawing (omitting the Dimensions), using the snap, ortho and grid settings only.

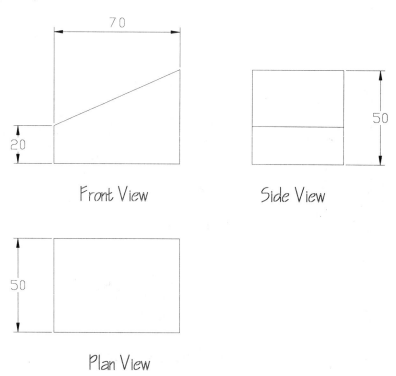

Typed Input

So far we have used freehand drawing techniques where absolute accuracy was not important, and have used the snap facility when defining points were aligned with an imaginary grid. In cases where these techniques are not readily applicable, *typed input* may be the best option.

Note: In this section, consideration of typed input is restricted to 2-dimensional coordinates. 3-dimensional drawing will be introduced in Chapter 6.

If you start a new drawing and then move the crosshairs down to the bottom left corner of the drawing area, you should notice that the coordinate display in the status area shows (0,0) (or something similar). Moving the cursor to the right causes the X coordinate to increase, while moving the crosshairs upwards increases the Y coordinate. This behaviour is summarized in Figure 3–2.

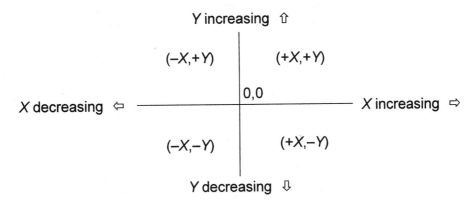

Figure 3–2. The Cartesian coordinate system used by AutoCAD LT.

It is important to realise that drawing commands (such as LINE or CIRCLE) will accept typed input as an alternative to the direct use of the mouse to specify coordinates. AutoCAD LT really doesn't care <u>how</u> data is specified – its the information itself that matters!

The simplest form of typed input is where AutoCAD LT requests a *scalar* value, such as the radius of a Circle, or the length of a Line. (Scalar values have 'size' only, unlike *vectors* which have both 'length' and 'direction'.) With the input of scalar values, simply type the required number and press ⏎.

Several methods exist for the specification of coordinates using typed input. An *absolute* coordinate specifies a <u>unique</u> location on the 2-dimensional drawing plane, which tends to be useful when specifying features whose position does not depend on other items in the drawing. *Relative* coordinates, on the other hand, are used where it is more convenient to indicate a position as the distance from an existing feature. When drawing a series of joined Lines for example, it would be normal to specify the startpoint of the Line as an absolute coordinate, and then each endpoint in turn as the relative distance from the last point specified. Thus relative and absolute coordinates are complementary.

In addition to Cartesian coordinates, where the X and Y axes are at right-angles to each other, it is also possible to define a coordinate in *polar* form using a length and angle (or a distance and direction). Once again, such a coordinate may be *absolute*, if measured from the drawing *origin* (0,0), or *relative* if it is based on the most recently entered point. To summarize, AutoCAD LT will accept typed input of coordinates in four basic forms, as shown in Table 3–3.

Table 3–3. Basic forms of typed input and their appearance.

	Absolute	Relative
Cartesian	50,100	@50,100
Polar	50<30	@50<30

As can be seen from the above table, Cartesian coordinates are entered as two numbers, separated by a comma. Relative displacement is indicated by preceding the coordinate with an '@' symbol (pronounced 'at').

Example

The following command sequence demonstrates the use of typed input to draw a rectangle 100 × 80 units in size, with its lower left corner at the absolute coordinate (50,50).

Command: **LINE** ↵	- Start the LINE command.
From point: **50,50** ↵	- Specify the absolute coordinate 50,50.
To point: **@100,0** ↵	- Draw to the right by 100 units (relative).
To point: **@0,80** ↵	-Draw vertically up by 80 units (relative).
To point: **@–100,0** ↵	- Draw to the left by 100 units (relative).
To point: **@0,–80** ↵	- Draw vertically down by 80 units (relative). - (Or type **C** here, to 'close' the rectangle.)

Polar coordinates are much more suitable for use where the length and angle of a particular feature are both known, but not the actual coordinate of the endpoint. For example, an equilateral triangle may be drawn much more easily using polar coordinates, compared with a 'Cartesian' approach.

When using polar coordinates, it is important to remember the angular conventions which are used by AutoCAD LT. By default, positive angles are measured in an anticlockwise direction, with 0° being horizontally to the right (at 3 o'clock in other words).

The conventions used for angular measurements may be displayed or altered using the DDUNITS command, which was introduced in the previous chapter. Once the command is activated, a dialogue box is displayed (refer back to Figure 2–14), the right hand side of which is used to control the system of angular measurement. Notice that the **Direction...** button allows another dialogue box to be displayed, which controls the direction and starting angle used for angular measurements.

Example

The following command dialogue demonstrates the use of polar coordinates to define an equilateral triangle of side 50 units, with the lower left corner at the absolute coordinate 100,40.

Command: **LINE** ↵   - Start the LINE command.

From point: **100,40** ↵   - Specify the absolute coordinate 100,40.

To point: **@50<0** ↵   - Draw to the right by 50 units (relative – polar).

To point: **@50<120** ↵   -Draw the second side (relative – polar).

To point: **@50<240** ↵   - Draw the final side (relative – polar).
             - (Or type **@50<–120** to using a negative angle.)
             - (Or type **C** here, to 'close' the triangle.)

Note: A new feature in AutoCAD LT Release 2 is the use of *direct distance entry* to specify relative displacements. To use this method, simply move the cursor away from the last point in the required <u>direction</u>, and then enter the actual <u>distance</u> as a scalar value using the keyboard. (This is commonly combined with ORTHO.)

Drawing Exercise 3 Relative and Absolute Coordinates

This exercise demonstrates the various forms of typed input which may be used with drawing commands.

1. Begin a new drawing. Start the LINE command and enter the absolute coordinate 100,60 at the 'From point:' prompt. Now enter suitable relative coordinates to draw a rectangle of width 80 units and height 55 units.

2. Start the LINE command and draw an equilateral triangle of side 65 units, with its lower left corner at the absolute coordinate 200,100. Use relative polar coordinates wherever possible.

3. Start the LINE command once again and give a start coordinate of 300,100. Then use the direct distance entry method (with ORTHO enabled) to draw a rectangle of width 47 units and height 54 units.

Object Snap

As the name suggests, *object snap* is used where you require that a new drawing feature should be based in some way on an <u>existing</u> object. For example, you may want to draw a Line from the *midpoint* of an existing Line and then to the *endpoint* of another. Using previously considered methods, it would be necessary to know, or to be able to calculate, the coordinates of the two Line endpoints. Using object snap, you simply select the required object feature (the *midpoint* or *endpoint* of an existing Line for example) and then 'pick' the object of interest. AutoCAD LT then uses the indicated coordinate as the command input.

Object snap is not <u>just</u> for cases where a particular coordinate is unknown. Complex geometrical constructions may be achieved easily using combinations of object snap settings. For example you can draw a Line which begins at the *intersection* of two existing objects and which ends as a *tangent* to an existing Circle or Arc. Another Line could then be drawn from the *centre* of that Circle (or Arc), which ends *perpendicular* (or 'normal') to an existing Line, Circle or Arc. Object snap settings may also refer to the *insertion* point of Blocks, or of Point entities.

There are basically <u>two</u> different ways of using object snap.

❑ *Single point override.* As the name suggests, this mode allows a particular object snap mode to be activated for a single drawing operation, after which the object selection method reverts to its default behaviour. Use this mode where object snap is only required on an occasional basis.

❑ *Running object snap.* This method allows one or more object snap modes to be enabled using a dialogue box. Once selected, these settings remain in force until cancelled. Thus, running object snap is particularly suitable where you know that a particular snap mode will be needed several times in succession.

To select a single point override, click Ctrl + ↖ (or Shift + ↖) at the appropriate point in the command dialogue, which will cause a *Cursor* menu to appear, close to the current cursor position, as shown in Figure 3–3.

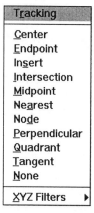

Figure 3–3. The AutoCAD LT Cursor menu.

Almost any situation where AutoCAD LT expects the entry of a coordinate is suitable for the use of object snap. With the LINE command, for example, the 'From point:' or 'To point:' prompts could both be applicable. Having chosen a single point override, you should notice that AutoCAD LT adds the suffix 'of' to the existing command line, meaning that you should now indicate the object of interest by carefully positioning the object selection box (or *aperture*), as close as possible to the feature of interest. The following command dialogue illustrates this process.

Command: **LINE** ↵	- Start the LINE command.
From point: Ctrl + ⌐	- Select **Endpoint** from the cursor menu.
From point:_endp of ⌐	- Pick an existing Line or Arc, as close as possible to the required endpoint.
To point:	- Continue as required.

There are several points which should be noted here, related to object snap.

❑ There is a possible source of confusion in the above example, due to the fact that an existing Line or Arc actually has two endpoints. AutoCAD LT overcomes this difficulty by assuming that you are referring to the endpoint which is closest to the indicated point. Thus, when selecting objects, you should ensure both that the object passes through the object selection box, and that the indicated point is as close as possible to the feature of interest.

❑ Although the above example refers to a 'drawing' command, many editing commands will also accept object snap. For example, the action of moving or copying existing objects can sometimes be simplified by using these same techniques. (MOVE and COPY will be considered in Chapter 4.)

❑ One alternative to using the Cursor menu to select a single point override is to type the required object snap option. Thus you could have typed **endpoint** Spacebar directly at the 'From point:' prompt. If this seems rather tedious, you may prefer to enter the first three letters only, as an abbreviation. (Thus, for example, **endpoint** can be shortened to **end**.)

❑ The second row of the Toolbox offers a series of object snap buttons, which may be used to control running object snap and select single point overrides. Referring back to the second row of Figure 2–9, from left to right these buttons are, DDOSNAP (running object snap), endpoint, intersection, midpoint, perpendicular, centre, tangent, quadrant, insertion point, node, nearest and none.

Table 3–4 (overleaf) gives a full list of these object snap overrides, their minimum keyboard abbreviations, and their main areas of application.

Table 3–4. Object snap settings and some possible applications.

Operating mode	Keyboard abbreviation	Possible applications
Center	Cen	Centre of a Circle or Arc.
Endpoint	End	Endpoint of a Line, Arc or Polyline segment.
Insert	Ins	Insertion point of a Block (or symbol).
Intersection	Int	Intersection of any two objects.
Midpoint	Mid	Midpoint of a Line or Arc.
Nearest	Nea	<u>Nearest</u> point on an object to the indicated coordinate.
Node	Nod	Insertion point of a Point entity.
Perpendicular	Per	At right angles to the indicated Line, Arc or Circle.
Quadrant	Qua	The closest quadrant point on an Arc or Circle, to the indicated coordinate (i.e. 0, 90, 180 or 270°).
Tangent	Tan	Tangential to the indicated Arc or Circle.
None	Non	Cancels any previously activated object snap mode.

As mentioned previously, it is also possible to select a default or 'running' object snap method, where the same option is likely to be required several times in succession. To do this, select the DDOSNAP command by picking the **Object Snap...** option from the **Assist** pull-down menu, type **DDOSNAP** (or **OS**) at the Command prompt, or click the appropriate button in the Toolbox (see margin). The dialogue box of Figure 3–4 will then be displayed.

This dialogue box displays currently selected object snap setting(s), and allows individual modes to be enabled or disabled. Notice here that it is possible to enable more than one object snap mode at any time, although this may cause confusion in some circumstances. It is also possible to modify the size of the object snap 'aperture' from the same dialogue box (which should not be confused with the object selection 'pickbox', used by ERASE and other editing commands).

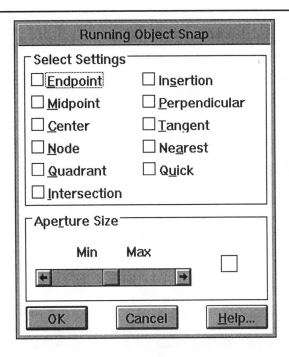

Figure 3–4. The DDOSNAP (Running Object Snap) dialogue box.

Drawing Exercise 4   Object Snap

This exercise demonstrates the use of object snap to form simple geometrical constructions.

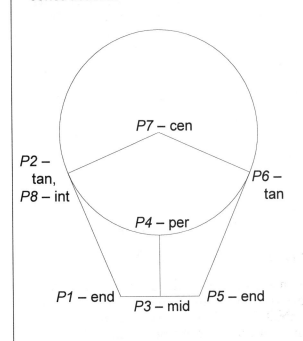

1.   Draw a Circle of radius 50 units and 30 units below this, draw a horizontal Line of length 40 units. Now ensure that the snap, ortho and grid settings are all disabled, before continuing.

2.   Draw a Line from points 1–2 using the *endpoint* and *tangent* object snap modes.

3.   Draw a Line from points 3–4 using the *midpoint* and *perpendicular* object snap options (or *midpoint* and *quadrant* if you prefer).

4.   Draw a Line from points 5–6, as shown above. Continue this Line to point 7 using the *center* option, before using the *intersection* option to end at point 8.

Observant readers may notice slight differences between the object snap modes offered by the AutoCAD LT cursor menu (Figure 3–3) and by the DDOSNAP command dialogue box (Figure 3–4). As you would expect, the **None** option, offered by the Cursor menu is equivalent to cancelling all of the checkboxes in the running object snap dialogue box. The dialogue box also offers a **Quick** option which is not offered by the Cursor menu, and which cannot be entered from the keyboard. When object snap is active, AutoCAD LT searches the zone indicated by the 'aperture' box, looking for possible object snap points. If 'quick' mode is active, this search finishes when the <u>first</u> suitable target is identified. With this mode disabled, AutoCAD LT continues to search until <u>all</u> possible object snap points (inside the aperture zone) have been found. The chosen point is then taken to be the one which is closest to the centre of the aperture area. The latter method is generally preferred, due to its greater accuracy of selection, but it can be significantly slower than 'quick' mode in some circumstances.

Further Drawing Commands

The range of drawing commands introduced so far has been deliberately limited, to allow basic concepts to be understood, without overloading the reader with a barrage of new information. Remaining AutoCAD LT drawing commands will now be considered, and some of the more powerful aspects of Polylines (introduced in Chapter 2) will also be discussed.

Rectangles

Of course, it is simple enough to draw a rectangle using either the LINE or PLINE commands, but the RECTANG command makes this task a little bit easier, hence speeding up the drawing process. Having started the command, it is only necessary to give the coordinates of two opposite corners, in order to define a rectangle uniquely, as shown in Figure 3–5. (The rectangle is assumed to be aligned horizontally)

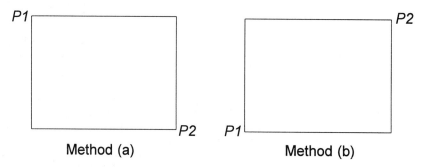

Figure 3–5. Using the RECT command to draw a rectangle.

Note: The rectangle is actually drawn as a closed Polyline, rather than as a series of individual Lines. This means that the rectangle may be erased as a single object, and that it can be edited using the PEDIT (Polyline edit) command, or by using the *grips* feature – both of which are considered in the next chapter.

Single Points

The POINT command may be used to insert one or more Point entities into the drawing. By default, a Point is drawn as a single coloured 'dot' or pixel, which can seem rather unimpressive amongst a cluttered screen display – to the extent that you may fail to notice that anything has been drawn at all!

To overcome this problem, you should select an appropriate Point display format, prior to actually drawing Points with the POINT command. To do this, select the **Point Style...** option from the **Settings** pull-down menu, or type **DDPTYPE** at the Command prompt. The dialogue box of Figure 3–6 will then be displayed.

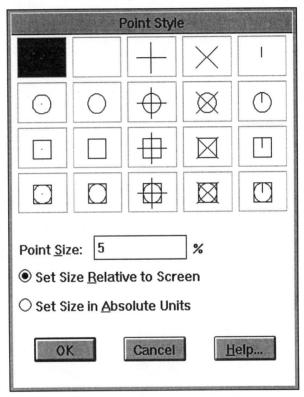

Figure 3–6. Selecting the display format used by Points.

If you examine the structure of the above 'matrix', certain patterns should become evident. Thus, the columns select the shape of the object which is placed in the centre of the Point, while the rows determine what, if anything, surrounds the central region.

Now that a suitable display format has been selected, the POINT command may be activated by selecting the **Point** option from the **Draw** pull-down menu, by typing **POINT** (or **PT**) at the Command prompt, or by pressing the appropriate button in the Toolbar (see margin).

Note: To update the appearance of existing Points, type **REGEN** [Spacebar].

Ellipses

If you view a Circle from an angle (not from directly above), then it will appear to be 'flattened' along one axis, thus forming an ellipse. As you would expect, the ELLIPSE command is used to create this type of object.

Before actually creating an ellipse, it is useful to understand the three methods which may be used to define the geometry of an ellipse, as shown in Figure 3–7.

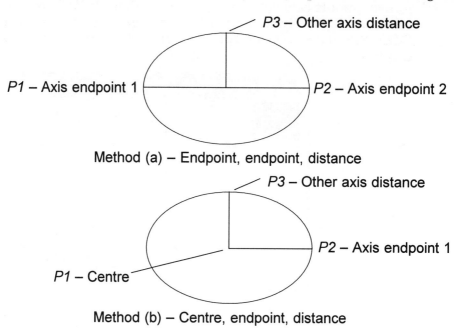

Method (a) – Endpoint, endpoint, distance

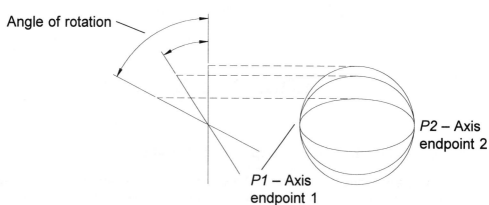

Method (c) – Endpoint, endpoint, angle of rotation

Figure 3–7. The three methods used to define ellipses.

To start the ELLIPSE command, type **ELLIPSE** (or **EL**) at the Command prompt, choose the **Ellipse** option from the **Draw** pull-down menu, or press the appropriate button in the Toolbox area (see margin).

Polygons

The POLYGON command is used to create regular closed shapes having any-where between 3 and 1024 sides. (The term 'regular' here means that all sides are of equal length, and that all internal angles are the same.)

There are two basic methods which may be used to define a polygon, which are both illustrated by Figure 3–8.

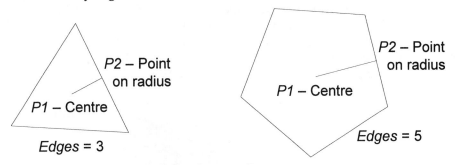

Method (a) – Number of edges, centre and radius

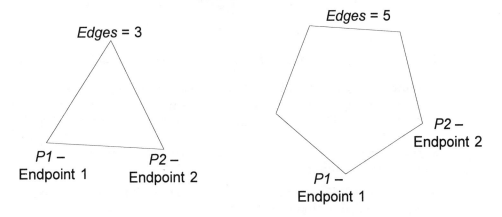

Method (b) – Number of edges, segment endpoint, segment endpoint

Figure 3–8. The two methods used to define polygons.

The number of sides is first requested, which is common to both approaches. In method (a) the polygon is then defined by specifying the centre, followed by the position of the midpoint of one of the polygon segments. In method (b), the endpoints of a single segment are indicated, assuming here that the polygon will be drawn in an anticlockwise direction.

To start the POLYGON command, type **POLYGON** (or **PG**) at the Command prompt, select the **Polygon** option from the **D**raw pull-down menu, or press the appropriate button in the Toolbox (see margin).

Solids

In some circumstances, you may wish to define an irregularly shaped area which must be completely <u>filled</u> with the current drawing colour. The SOLID command is generally the easiest approach to use in these situations, although alternative methods do exist, include hatching (with a very small line spacing), and the use of the *width* setting with the PLINE command.

The command dialogue used by the SOLID command is reasonably straightforward, consisting of prompts for the coordinates of each vertex defining the area. The main thing to remember here is the <u>order</u> with which these points must be defined, to avoid creating a 'bow-tie', rather than the intended four-sided polygon. This correct sequence is shown in Figure 3–9.

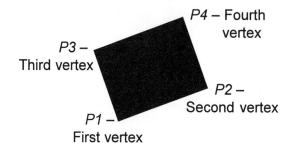

Figure 3–9. Using the SOLID command to create a 4-sided filled region.

Having drawn one Solid, as shown above, you should notice that the prompt changes to 'Third point:', rather than returning to 'Command:', as you might expect. AutoCAD LT assumes that you will want to continue drawing Solids and uses the last two vertices (*P3* and *P4*) of the previous Solid to form the first two vertices of the next. If you do not wish to continue drawing Solids then press ⏎ to finish the command.

To start the SOLID command, type **SOLID** (or **SO**) at the Command prompt, or select the **Solid** option from the **Draw** pull-down menu area.

Note: It is also possible to draw three-sided Solids, simply by pressing ⏎ (or any other command separator) at the 'Fourth point:' prompt.

Drawing Exercise 5   Creating Filled Areas with Solids

Use the SOLID command (four times) to create the following filled region. (All drawing sizes are at your discretion.)

Double Lines

As the name suggests, the DLINE command is used to draw pairs of parallel Lines (or parallel Arcs). This ability proves particularly useful when drawing plan views of building layouts, where the inner and outer edge of walls must be separately represented, as shown in Figure 3–10.

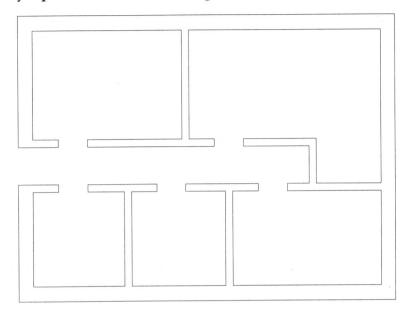

Figure 3–10. Using the DLINE command to produce a plan view of a building.

The sheer number of command options which are available with the DLINE command can make it seem rather confusing to the beginner, but rest assured that most of these are set to sensible default values and are unlikely to require modification. As you will soon see, the DLINE and PLINE commands have quite a lot in common, so an understanding of the double-line command dialogue will also prove useful when the PLINE command is considered, in the next section.

When the DLINE command is entered, the following command options are presented.

Command: **DLINE** ↵
Break/Caps/Dragline/Offset/Snap/Undo/Width/<start point>:   - Click ↺

Once the start coordinate has been given, this dialogue changes slightly, as shown below.

Arc/Break/CAps/CLose/Dragline/Snap/Undo/Width/<next point>:

Before entering any further coordinates, the spacing between the two Lines would normally be specified by choosing the *Width* option. For example, if the required line separation is 10 units then **W** ⏎ **10** ⏎ would be entered at the Command prompt. At this stage a series of double-line segments may be entered by indicating coordinates using the mouse in the normal way. Several points should be noticed.

❑   The *Close* option causes the last segment to be joined to the start point.

❑   The *Undo* option erases the last segment drawn.

❑   By default, indicated coordinates are defined as being along an imaginary centre line, with the two Lines being drawn on either side at equal distance. The *Dragline* option allows this behaviour to be modified, offering options of *Left*, *Right* or *Center* (the default). Experiment to see the effect.

❑   When you finish drawing a double-line, the *CAps* option determines whether Lines or 'caps' are automatically drawn across the two open ends. Several options are available, with the *Auto* (automatic) option being selected by default.

❑   If you start or end a double-line in close proximity to another Line or double-line segment, the *Break* option determines whether a gap should be created at the junction. Break is enabled by default.

❑   When *Snap* mode is enabled, the DLINE command terminates automatically when an endpoint is found to be in close proximity to an existing Line or double-line segment. The actual snap distance (in pixels) may also be set using this option. Whether or not a gap is created at this junction depends on the Break option setting.

❑   The Offset option (which is only available prior to indicating the start point) allows the <u>actual</u> start point and starting direction of the double-line to be specified as an offset (i.e. direction and distance) from an indicated point.

The DLINE command may be started in several different ways, according to personal preference. Either Type **DLINE** (or **DL**) at the Command prompt, select the **Double Line** option from the **Draw** pull-down menu area, or click the appropriate button in the Toolbox (see margin).

Note: Double-lines are actually drawn as a series of individual Lines.

Drawing Exercise 6   Using the DLINE Command

Use the DLINE command to create a plan view of your home or workplace.

(Ensure that you use the <u>full</u> range of DLINE options during the course of this exercise.)

Polylines

As we have already seen in the previous chapter, the PLINE command proves particularly useful where lines having a particular <u>width</u> must be drawn. (Recall that we used Polylines to produce 'tracks' of different thicknesses on a printed circuit board layout.) In fact, Polylines may be used to create objects which are much more complex than those previously seen, some examples of which are shown in Figure 3–11.

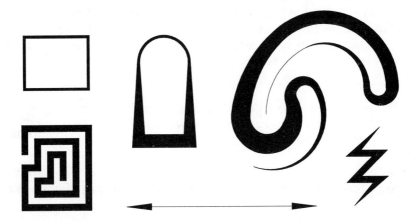

Figure 3–11. Some examples of Polylines.

By examining the above illustration, you should be able to see examples of 'open' and 'closed' Polylines. (The first and last points are connected in a closed Polyline.) There are also Polylines which consist entirely of lines or Arcs, or a mixture of the two. Finally, notice the varying line widths and the use of tapering line or arc segments.

 The PLINE command may be started by typing **PLINE** (or **PL**) at the Command prompt, by selecting the **Polyline** option from the **Draw** pull-down menu, or by pressing the Polyline button in the Toolbox (see margin). Once you have given the start point of the Polyline, the following range of command options becomes available.

Arc/Close/Halfwidth/Length/Undo/Width/<endpoint of line>:

By default, the PLINE command expects to receive a series of coordinates, each of which is taken to be the endpoint of the current segment, and the startpoint of the next. A 'null' entry (entering a command separator by itself) terminates the command.

The Polyline is treated as a <u>single</u> object by AutoCAD LT so, for example, if you attempt to use the ERASE command to delete a single segment, you will find that the entire Polyline will be erased. For this reason, a special command (PEDIT or 'Polyline edit') has been provided to allow detailed modification of Polylines.

If you examine a typical engineering drawing carefully, you should notice that more than one line width has been used! It is common practice to use a thicker line to emphasize the boundary of an object, with a thinner line width being used for internal detail. Typically a 2:1 ratio of pen widths is used, with 0.7 mm and 0.35 mm line widths being popular. Clearly, the ability to set different line widths when drawing Polylines has considerable application with this type of drawing.

Note: There is another way to achieve this effect with a CAD system. If a pen plotter is being used as the output device, then place two pens into the carousel, with each pen having a different line width. You can configure AutoCAD LT so that objects drawn with particular colours are printed using different plotter pens – and hence with different line widths! (The selection of different drawing colours will be covered shortly.)

To create a Polyline segment which has differing starting and ending line width, you must enter two different line widths (before drawing the next segment) by selecting the *Width* option, as shown below.

Arc/Close/Halfwidth/Length/Undo/Width/<endpoint of line>: **W** ⏎

Starting width <0.000>: **5** ⏎

Ending width <5.000>: **10** ⏎

The *Halfwidth* option – which defines the distance from the centre of the Polyline to an edge – may also be used here. Notice also that, having entered a starting width for the next segment (5 units in this case), that the default ending width is taken from this value.

Of the remaining command options, selecting the *Length* option causes a new segment of the specified length to be added, continuing in the direction of the previous segment, while *Close* joins the first and last points of the Polyline (and also exits the command).

Lastly, the *Arc* option switches from drawing lines to arcs, as you might expect. At this stage, there are significant changes to the options provided by the PLINE command, as shown below.

Angle/CEnter/CLose/Direction/Halfwidth/Line/Radius/Second pt/Undo/ Width/<endpoint of arc>:

Notice here that the *Arc* option has now disappeared, and has been replaced by *Line*. Thus you select Arc to switch to drawing arc segments, and *Line* to return to your original drawing mode. The remaining options allow the next arc segment to be defined using several different methods – not unlike those offered by the ARC command itself.

- ❑ The *Angle* option specifies the included angle of the next arc segment, which is measured in an anticlockwise direction by default.

- ❑ *CEnter* allows the coordinate of the centre of the next segment to be given, which therefore defines the starting direction and the radius of the arc.

- ❑ By default, the starting direction of the next arc segment is taken from the ending direction of the last. The *Direction* option allows you to explicitly define this starting direction.

- ❑ The *Radius* option defines the radius of the next arc segment.

- ❑ The next segment may be defined as a three-point arc by selecting the *Second pt* option.

Text and Text Styles

The DTEXT or *dynamic text* command allows textual information to be placed onto a drawing. The term 'dynamic' here refers to the fact that you actually get to see the text drawn on screen as you enter the text, rather than having to press the ↵ key first. (The related TEXT command does not display the Text on screen until you press ↵. Another difference between the two commands is that the TEXT command terminates after creating a single line, while DTEXT can produce multiple lines of Text.)

Although the DTEXT command is quite straightforward in use, there are a number of advanced concepts which will need to be understood, to allow complete mastery of this powerful feature. These include the use of *fonts, character sets,* 'special' characters, *text styles* and *justification*. Before launching into an examination of these advanced options, consider the basic use of the DTEXT command, which may be started in several different ways.

To begin using the DTEXT command either type **DTEXT** (or **DT**), select the **Text** option from the **Draw** pull-down menu, or press the appropriate button in the Toolbox area (see margin). A typical command dialogue is given below.

Command: DTEXT ↵

Justify/Style/<Start point>: 🖑   - Indicate the start point.

Height<3.5000>: **20** ↵   - Specify the height of the text.

Rotation angle<0.000>: ↵   - Accept the default angle (0°).

Text: **Enter your text line here** ↵   - Enter your text here.

Text: ↵   - Press ↵ on an empty line to end.

Drawing Exercise 7   Text Sizes and Rotation Angles

Use the DTEXT command to reproduce the following drawing, making particular use of the *Height* and *Rotation angle* command options.

5 units high

10 units high

15 units high

20 units high

0 degrees
45 degrees
90 degrees
135 degrees
180 degrees
225 degrees
270 degrees
315 degrees

Note: If you notice a mistake while entering text, then press the ⌫ (backspace) key to delete the incorrect character(s) and then continue typing. For the moment, if you notice a mistake <u>after</u> pressing ↵, then use the ERASE command to remove the entire line, prior to resuming the DTEXT command. (In the next chapter we will learn how to use the DDEDIT command to modify an existing line of text, and the CHANGE and DDMODIFY commands to alter Text properties, such as height, rotation angle or text style.)

Having mastered the basic entry of textual information, you may be wondering how to achieve effects such as underlining, or to print unusual characters such as the 'degree' symbol (i.e. $0°$) or the 'diameter' symbol (ϕ). AutoCAD LT allows these effects to be achieved by inserting *control sequences* into the text string, which take the form %%<effect>. Table 3–5 shows the available range of control sequences, while Tutorial 6 gives some examples of their use.

Table 3–5. Text control sequences and their applications.

Sequence	Function
%%o	Enable or disable overscore (line above text) mode.
%%u	Enable or disable underscore (line below text) mode.
%%d	Draw 'degree' symbol (°).
%%p	Draw 'plus or minus' symbol (±).
%%c	Draw 'diameter' symbol (φ).
%%%	Draw 'percentage' symbol (%).
%%nnn	Draw the character whose ASCII code is 'nnn', where 'nnn' is normally in the range 128–255. (This function is used to access non standard ASCII characters.)

Tutorial 6   Using Text Control Sequences

This tutorial demonstrates the use of control sequences to obtain effects such as underscore, overscore, and to print unusual characters like 'φ', or '±'. Use the DTEXT command and enter the text shown to obtain the required effect.

%%oOverscored	O̅v̅e̅r̅s̅c̅o̅r̅e̅d̅
%%uUnderscored	U̲n̲d̲e̲s̲c̲o̲r̲e̲d̲
%%oOver%%o, %%uunder%%u, and %%o%%uboth	O̅v̅e̅r̅, u̲n̲d̲e̲r̲ and b̲o̅t̲h̅
54.2%%dC	54.2°C
%%p5	±5
%%c50	⌀50
45%%% (or 45%)	45%
%%128	Ω

So far, we have seen how to place text of various heights and rotation angles, and we have been able to incorporate effects such as underlining, and to print unusual characters. The next step is learn how to select different *fonts* and to control the appearance of the Text using *text styles*. Figure 3–12 shows a few of the fonts which are available with AutoCAD LT, and how their appearance may be modified using text styles.

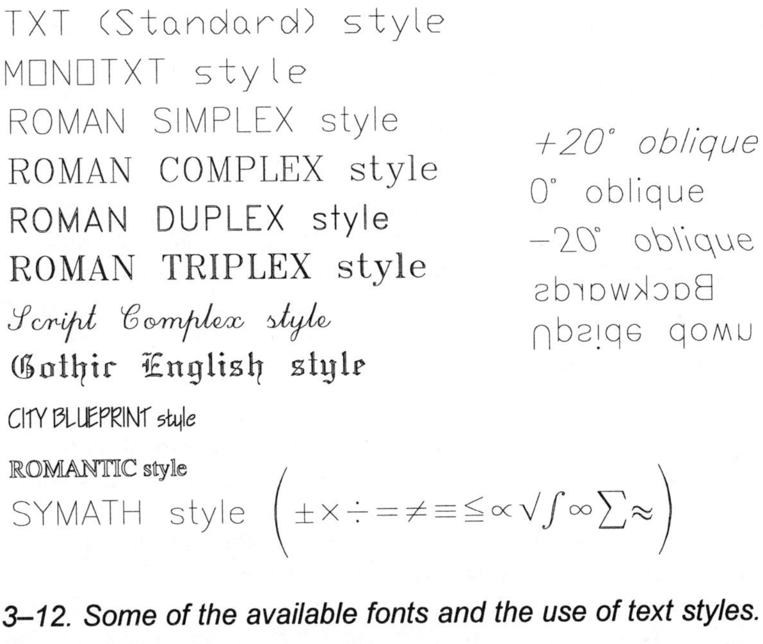

TXT (Standard) style
MONOTXT style
ROMAN SIMPLEX style
ROMAN COMPLEX style
ROMAN DUPLEX style
ROMAN TRIPLEX style
Script Complex style
𝕲𝖔𝖙𝖍𝖎𝖈 𝕰𝖓𝖌𝖑𝖎𝖘𝖍 𝖘𝖙𝖞𝖑𝖊
CITY BLUEPRINT style
ROMANTIC style
SYMATH style $\left(\pm \times \div = \neq \equiv \leqq \propto \sqrt{} \int \infty \sum \approx \right)$

+20° oblique
0° oblique
−20° oblique
sbɔɒwʞɔɒ𐐒
∩bsᴉpǝ ɓoɯu

Figure 3–12. Some of the available fonts and the use of text styles.

After examining Figure 3–12 carefully, you might conclude that the study of the appearance and style of printed text (known as *typography*) is an art in its own right! In fact, once you begin to notice the many subtly-different styles of presentation of textual information, you may find yourself looking at the appearance of the words on a page, as much as their meaning!

In printing terminology, a *font* (or *fount*) is a set of printing-type of a certain size and appearance. A particular font is likely to be classified as either *monospaced* or *proportionally spaced*. In a monospaced font, each character occupies a horizontal space which is of equal width – thus the letter 'i' occupies the same space as a 'w'. Monospaced fonts are commonly used for printing computer program listings and are useful where characters must be aligned accurately in vertical columns (tables). Proportionally spaced fonts are much easier to read and for this reason are used wherever possible. From Figure 3–12, you should be able to see that MONOTXT is a monospaced font (as the name suggests), while ROMAN SIMPLEX is proportionally spaced.

Another font classification is based on the presence or absence of *serifs*, which are the slight 'projections' at the extremities of printed letters. (The letter 'T' here makes use of a serif font, while 'T' is non serif.) Thus MONOTXT, ROMAN SIMPLEX, ROMAN DUPLEX and CITY BLUEPRINT are examples of non serif fonts, while ROMAN COMPLEX, ROMAN TRIPLEX and GOTHIC ENGLISH all have serifs. As a rule, non serif fonts are easy to read and are thus ideal for applications where clarity is essential. Typical applications would include titles, labels and tables (and CAD drawings in general). The use of a serif font tends to suggest 'authority', and is typically used for the main body of written work (such as a book).

Fonts which simulate handwriting (such as SCRIPT COMPLEX) or give the impression of 'olde worlde' writing (as in GOTHIC ENGLISH) are classified under the general heading of *novelty* fonts. These would be unlikely to find application in an engineering drawing, but might be used in specialist applications such as advertising or promotional materials. (In general, to avoid giving your design a confused or cluttered appearance, you should make a deliberate effort to minimize the number of different fonts which are used.)

The SYMATH font is an example of a *utility* font, whose purpose is to provide a range of symbols for a particular specialist application. As the name suggests, SYMATH provides mathematical symbols which would prove useful if you needed to use AutoCAD LT to draw an equation. (Other utility fonts are available within AutoCAD LT covering applications such as astronomy, mapping, meteorology and music.)

A final point regarding the use of fonts is that AutoCAD LT uses *outline* or *vector* fonts internally, which are fundamentally different from the solid (filled-in) fonts used by Windows (and by printers in general). This stems from the historical development of CAD systems where the main output device was likely to be a pen plotter, rather than a dot matrix, inkjet, or laser printer. AutoCAD LT does currently provide some support for *Postscript* fonts (and hence for Postscript compatible printers), and is likely to allow the use of the *Truetype* fonts in future versions of the software (*Truetype* is the main font format used by Windows).

When creating text style which will be used with any newly created Text, the first step is select the **Text Style...** option from the **Settings** pull-down menu, which causes the following dialogue box to appear.

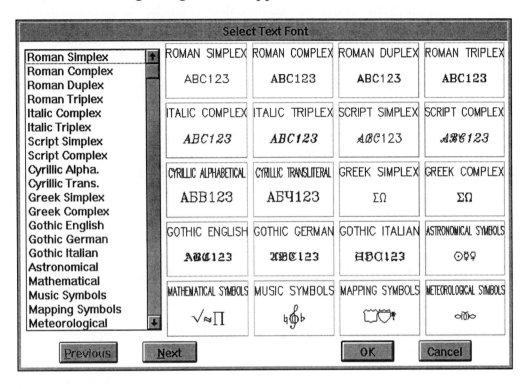

Figure 3–13. The Select Text Font dialogue box (Icon menu).

Use the **Previous** and **Next** buttons to cycle through the range of available fonts. (Notice that a sample of each font is shown in each of the icon boxes.) Having highlighted the required font, click **OK** and proceed to answer the questions, as shown in the following command dialogue.

Font file <txt>:italict   - It is assumed here that ITALIC TRIPLEX has been selected.

Height <0.000>: ⏎   - Accept the default at each stage.

Width factor <1.000>: ⏎

Obliquing angle <0> ⏎

Backwards? <N>: ⏎

Upside down? <N>: ⏎

Vertical? <N>: ⏎
ITALICT is now the current text style.

The combination of text font, together with the parameters (such as width factor and obliquing angle) specified by the user, define a *text style*. You are allowed to create as many styles as you need, and then switch between these styles, as appropriate. One restriction here stems from the fact that the <u>name</u> of the text style is automatically taken from that of the selected text font. (However, you can use the DDRENAME command to change the name of <u>existing</u> text styles.)

It is worth experimenting with the various text style options to see the effect in each case (a few examples were given in Figure 3–12). The height option should normally be left unaltered at 0.000, which will then allow the height of the Text to be varied using the DTEXT command.

Note: If you redefine a text style, existing Text objects which were drawn using the same style name are <u>not</u> normally updated. However, you can use the CHANGE command (covered in the next chapter) to update text properties, including the text style name.

To change the name of the currently active text style, select the DTEXT command's Style option, as shown below.

Justify/Style/<Start point>: **S** ↵   - Select the style option.

Style name (or ?)<Standard>: **?** ↵   - List currently defined styles.

Text style to list <*> ↵   - Press ↵ to list all styles.

......   - Text style information is listed here.

Justify/Style/<Start point>: **S** ↵   - Now select the style option again.

Style name (or ?)<Standard>: **ITALICT** ↵   - Enter your chosen style name.

......   - Continue with the DTEXT command.

Drawing Exercise 8   Using Utility Text Fonts

This exercise demonstrates the use of utility text fonts such as SYMATH to create special text effects.

1.   Create a text style based on the SYMATH font.

2.   Use the DTEXT command to create the equation shown.

$$\frac{1}{N} \sum_{r=1}^{N} x\, r$$

The current text style may also be selected or examined using the DDEMODES command, which allows a range of entity properties to be controlled using dialogue boxes. To display the main Entity Creation Modes dialogue box, enter **DDEMODES** (or **EM**) at the Command prompt, select the **Entity Modes...** option from the **Settings** pull-down menu, or click the appropriate button in the Toolbar (see margin). The dialogue box of Figure 3–14 is then displayed.

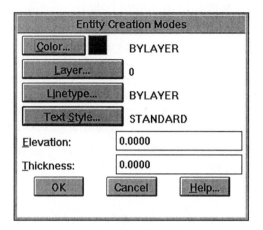

Figure 3–14. The Entity Creation Modes dialogue box.

Note: The **Color...** and **Linetype** options will be considered in the next section. *Layers* and the 3D drawing properties *elevation* and *thickness* will be left until Chapter 6.

Now press the **Text Style...** button, which will cause the dialogue box of Figure 3–15 to be displayed.

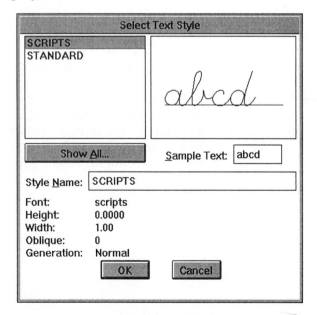

Fig. 3–15. The Select Text Style dialogue box.

The Select Text Style dialogue box may be used to select the current text style, from the list of previously defined styles. It can also be used to check detailed settings such as width factor or height, or to preview the appearance of the text font itself. If you enter your own sequence of characters into the **Sample Text:** edit box (and then press ⏎), the associated font preview window will be updated. As an alternative, clicking the **Show All...** button causes the entire font to be displayed in a separate dialogue box.

The DTEXT command also offers a Justify option, which will now be considered. In typography, *justification* is the adjustment of the width and/or position of a block of text, so that it fills the space available. Right-justified text, for example, is adjusted so that a neat margin is generated at the right-hand side of the page. At other times, it might be desirable to align text against the left-hand margin, or to evenly space the text about an invisible centre line. The width or size of the text may also be altered in order to 'fit' a line of text between the two margins.

As you would expect, AutoCAD LT offers options to allow all these effects to be achieved, as shown in Figure 3–16.

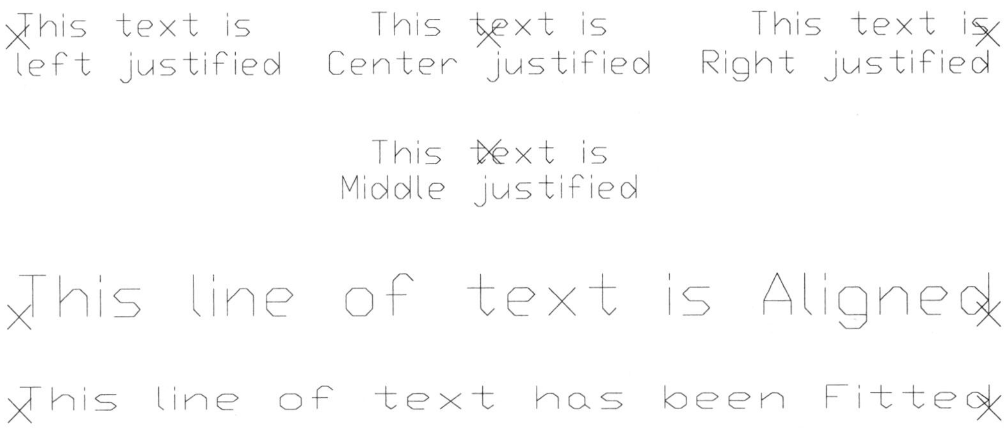

Figure 3–16. Text justification styles available with AutoCAD LT.

Left justification is selected by default, in which case the start point is taken to be the lower left corner of the first line. The Center and Right command options are similar and cause the text to be centred or right-justified respectively, while the Middle option is a slight variation on Center. Notice that the defining point used here is vertically <u>and</u> horizontally centred, rather than being on the baseline of the text.

The remaining two justification options are Align and Fit. In each case, you are required to indicate two defining points which specify the left and right margins (and a rotation angle if these points are not horizontal). With aligned text, the overall size of the text is adjusted so that it fills the available space. (The ratio of width to height remains constant – the text simply becomes bigger or smaller, as required.) When text is 'fitted', the height of the text is specified by the user, and AutoCAD LT adjusts the *width factor* of the current style to fill the available space.

Note: You can *paste* text from other Windows applications using the DTEXT command. To do this, in the application which is to be the source (*Notepad* for example), highlight the text and copy it to the *clipboard*. Then switch to AutoCAD LT and start the DTEXT command. At the 'Text:' prompt, select the **Paste Command** option from the **Edit** menu to paste the text.

Selecting Drawing Colours

Until now, all drawing operations have been performed using a single colour. This is fine if the drawing is intended to be printed on a monochrome printer, but might be prove restrictive if a multiple pen plotter, or a colour printer is the intended destination.

The selection of a new drawing colour is quite straightforward. Simply start the DDEMODES command (as explained on p. 65), which will cause the Entity Creation Modes dialogue box to be displayed. Then click the **Color** button, which will produce a dialogue box similar to that shown in Figure 3–17.

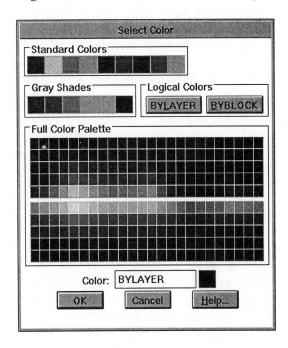

Figure 3–17. The Select Color dialogue box.

To select a new drawing colour, click one of the coloured squares in the Standard Colors, Gray Shades or Full Colour Palette regions. When the appropriate colour name (or colour number) appears in the edit box then click **OK**, which will activate this drawing colour. At this stage, you should notice that the appearance of the Colour Display button in the Toolbar has changed, to reflect the active drawing colour. If you now start a drawing command, the new drawing colour will be used (existing objects remain unchanged).

Note: At this stage you may be wondering how to alter the colour associated with <u>existing</u> objects. This operation may be performed using the DDCHPROP command (Change Properties), which will be explained in the next chapter.

Although the selection of drawing colours seems very straightforward, newcomers to AutoCAD LT frequently experience problems with the use and control of colours. The explanation is that several <u>different</u> approaches to the use of colour are available, not all of which are compatible! If you inadvertently 'mix' these techniques, the end result may be unpredictable, and sometimes frustrating. Precise details of these other methods will be given in the appropriate sections, but the following brief explanations may be useful.

❑   Each AutoCAD LT object has an associated drawing *layer*, which in turn has a <u>default</u> drawing colour. A useful analogy is to think of these layers as transparent plastic sheets, onto which the individual objects have been drawn. Layers may be selectively enabled or disabled, which is equivalent to inserting or removing individual plastic sheets. Any objects on a particular layer which have been drawn with the *logical* colour BYLAYER, are displayed using the default colour for that layer. Where the drawing colour has been explicitly defined (using DDEMODES for example), this <u>overrides</u> the layer's default colour. (If this is not the intended behaviour, then use the DDCHPROP command to set the colour of affected objects back to BYLAYER.)

❑   It is possible to produce drawings in a modular fashion, by inserting pre-defined *Blocks* or symbols into the drawing. This approach is particularly suitable in applications such as electronic design, where circuits are constructed using a library of standard elements. Objects <u>inside</u> Blocks may sometimes be given the logical colour BYBLOCK, which causes them to be drawn with the currently active drawing colour when they are inserted into a drawing, rather than with the colour associated with the layer on which they were created. Also, objects within Blocks which have been drawn on the 'special' layer '0' are always drawn on the currently-active layer, thus inheriting the colour associated with that layer.

❑   When adding Dimensions to a drawing, the currently active *dimension style* may have specific colours associated with the *dimension line, extension line* and *dimension text* sections of the Dimension. (The default colour is BYBLOCK in each case.) If so defined, then these colours will override the currently active drawing colour, or the colour associated with the active drawing layer.

Selecting Linetypes

In a similar manner to the use of colours in drawings, it is also possible to specify a *linetype* which will be used when new objects are drawn. The availability of different linetypes is particularly useful in engineering drawings, where features such as hidden detail, or centre lines must be shown.

When a new drawing is started, the default linetype is set to CONTINUOUS. (As the name suggests, this is simply an unbroken line.) Two other (logical) linetypes called BYLAYER and BYBLOCK are also available, whose functions are analogous to those previously discussed with the use of colours. Other linetypes must first be <u>created</u> or (more likely) <u>loaded</u> from a linetype definition file, prior to use.

Two linetype files are supplied, called ACLT.LIN and ACLTISO.LIN, which differ slightly in their content (see later in this section for more details). Table 3–6 shows linetypes which are typically available and their appearance.

Table 3–6. Available linetypes in ACLT.LIN and ACLTISO.LIN files.

Name	Appearance
BORDER	
BORDER2	
BORDERX2	
CENTER	
CENTER2	
CENTERX2	
DASHDOT	
DASHDOT2	
DASHDOTX2	
DASHED	
DASHED2	
DASHEDX2	
DIVIDE	
DIVIDE2	
DIVIDEX2	
DOT	
DOT2	
DOTX2	
HIDDEN	
HIDDEN2	
HIDDENX2	
PHANTOM	
PHANTOM2	
PHANTOMX2	

To load a new linetype definition, select the **Linetype Style** option from the **Settings** pull-down menu, which will cause a *cascading* menu to appear, as shown in Figure 3–18 overleaf. (An alternative is to type **LINETYPE** or **LT** at the Command prompt.)

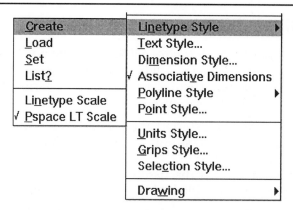

*Figure 3–18. Controlling linetype styles using the **Settings** pull-down menu.*

At this point, to load a new linetype definition, select the LINETYPE command's Load option and at the 'Linetype(s) to Load:' prompt (in the Command area), enter the required linetype name. (Recall that available linetype names were given in Table 3–6, and that CENTER and HIDDEN are amongst the most commonly used.) A file selection dialogue box will then be displayed, listing those files in the default directory with an extension of '.LIN'. Select the required file (which must contain the named linetype for this operation to succeed), before clicking the **OK** button.

The next step is to make the newly available linetype 'current'. To do this, click the Color display button, at the left of the Toolbar, which will activate the DDEMODES (Entity Creation Modes) command. As previously seen, the dialogue box of Figure 3–14 will be displayed. Now click the **Linetype...** button, which will show a dialogue box similar to Figure 3–19 below.

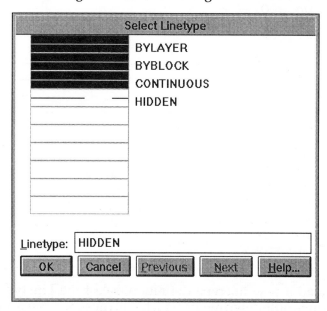

Figure 3–19. Selecting a linetype style using the DDEMODES command.

The newly loaded linetype (HIDDEN in this example) should appear in the Select Linetype dialogue box. To select this linetype, either type the linetype name in the edit box, or click the appropriate linetype icon. Finally, click **OK** to complete the selection.

At this stage you may wish to draw one or two Lines, or other objects, to confirm that the chosen linetype has been loaded and selected without error. If you do not see the expected pattern of dots and dashes then do not panic, as there is a perfectly logical explanation, as you will soon discover!

An AutoCAD LT linetype definition consists of a series of Line segments and spaces, each of which has a defined length in drawing units. When a particular linetype is used, the line is generated by drawing a repeating sequence of lines and spaces, based on the linetype definition. If the linetype definition is very small compared to the size of the displayed portion of the drawing, then the linetype may appear to be a solid line because the individual gaps between segments are too small to see. Similarly, if the linetype definition is too coarse, then it may not be possible to draw even part of the dot-dash sequence, and a solid line may be drawn in its place. Thus, if a continuous line appears, rather than the expected linetype sequence, the most likely explanation is that the linetype definition is either too large, or too small.

As you may already have guessed, a linetype scaling factor is available, which may be used to correct these 'errors of scale'. The LTSCALE setting contains a global multiplier, which affects the size of all linetypes, including those already drawn. Specifying a value less than unity causes linetypes to become smaller, while values larger than one make linetypes appear larger. To modify the linetype scale factor, either type **LTSCALE** at the command prompt, or select the **Linetype Scale** option, as shown in Figure 3–18.

At this stage, it is useful to study the main differences between the two available linetype definition files – ACLT.LIN and ACLTISO.LIN. (This can be achieved by loading each file into the Notepad text editor, after setting the default filetype to '*.LIN'.) For example, the HIDDEN linetype in the ACLT.LIN file consists of line segments of length 0.25 units, each separated by a space of 0.125 units. In contrast, the same linetype definition in the ACLTISO.LIN file has lines and spaces of length 6.35 and 3.175 units respectively. A moment's reflection here will show that the latter linetype definition is larger by a factor of 25.4, which is simply the conversion factor between inches and millimetres!

Thus, it would make sense to use definitions from ACLT.LIN when working in inches. This would be particularly true if the current drawing is based on the ACLT.DWG prototype, which has drawing limits of 12 by 9 units. In contrast, drawings based on the ACLTISO.DWG prototype, which has drawing limits of 420 by 297 units, would be more suited to the coarser linetype definitions found in the ACLTISO.LIN file. (Note that an A3 drawing sheet is 420 by 297 mm.)

Note: It is only necessary to load a particular linetype definition <u>once</u> during the creation of a particular drawing. After this, the linetype will always appear in the DDEMODES command's Select Linetype dialogue box. A previously loaded linetype may also be selected by choosing the **Li<u>n</u>etype Style**, followed by **<u>S</u>et** options from the **<u>S</u>ettings** pull-down menu, as shown in Figure 3–18.

It is also possible to assign a linetype when drawing Polylines. This can be useful where a linetype must be drawn with an increased <u>thickness</u>. Examples here include the use of a thick CONTINUOUS linetype to indicate visible outlines, or a thickened CENTER linetype for surfaces which must meet special require-ments. Cutting planes for sections also use a modified CENTER linetype, with thickened lines at the ends, and at changes of direction. This effect can also be produced using Polylines, although it is slightly more difficult.

When an individual Line or Arc is drawn with a particular linetype, the endpoints are <u>always</u> drawn as solid lines, rather than as spaces. This ensures that the <u>true</u> endpoints of the object are evident in the drawing, regardless of the linetype or linetype scale chosen. A single Polyline consists of a series of line or arc segments, so the question arises of whether or not to modify the linetype generation so that junctions between Polyline segments are also solid.

The PLINEGEN setting is used to control the appearance of the linetype at Polyline junctions. A value of 1 gives continuous linetype generation along the Polyline (with the possibility of a gap in the Linetype coinciding with a vertex), while a value of 0 causes each segment to be treated as an individual Line or Arc. To modify this setting, either type **PLINEGEN** at the Command prompt, or from the **<u>S</u>ettings** pull-down menu, choose the **<u>P</u>olyline Style** option, followed by **<u>L</u>inetype Generation** from the displayed child menu. Figure 3.20 illustrates the two effects of the PLINEGEN setting.

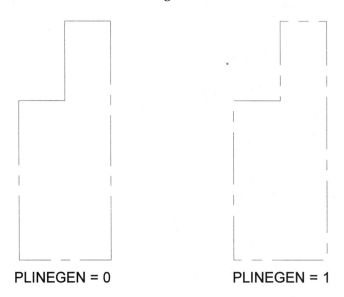

PLINEGEN = 0   PLINEGEN = 1

Figure 3–20. The effect of the PLINEGEN setting when drawing Polylines.

Tutorial 7 Indicating Cutting Planes using Polylines and Linetypes

The drawing below shows a *cutting plane*, such as that used to indicate a section on a drawing. The aim of this tutorial is to draw the cutting plane as a <u>single</u> Polyline.

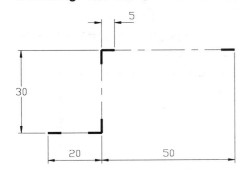

1. Load the CENTER linetype from the ACLT.LIN file, and use DDEMODES to make this the current linetype style.

2. Set LTSCALE to 10 and PLINEGEN to 0.

3. Enable snap and set it to 5 units.

4. Use the PLINE command to draw the cutting plane. Draw each of the thickened sections as a separate segment, using a drawing width of 0.7 units.

Plotting to Scale

In this chapter we have learned how to draw accurately using techniques such as snap, object snap and typed input. We have also discovered several new drawing commands, and have been able to control the appearance of the drawing using features such as text styles, colours and linetypes.

Having created an accurate representation of your design from within AutoCAD LT, you may then wish to produce a scaled printout or plot of the drawing. Once again, the PLOT command is used for this purpose (which was first introduced in Chapter 2).

As we have already seen, drawing information is normally entered in AutoCAD LT at natural size, so that the computer contains an accurate representation or model. Thus a line of length 100 mm or 100 inches would be entered as 100 drawing units – perhaps using snap or typed input. When the Plot Configuration dialogue box is displayed (see Figure 2–20), the user may then specify that the active unit is either **In<u>c</u>hes** or <u>**MM**</u> by clicking the appropriate radio button.

The next step would be to select the paper size by clicking the **Size...** button in the Paper Size and Orientation section of the dialogue box. Thus, for example, if the active unit is set to mm and a paper size of A4 is used, the available paper dimensions will be 297 × 210 mm. (It is important to realise here that not all of the paper area is available for actual drawing, due to the requirement for a margin around the edge of the paper. The minimum size of this margin will depend on the printer or plotter being used.)

To produce an accurately scaled printout, the **Scaled <u>t</u>o Fit** checkbox should first be disabled, after which an appropriate scale factor may be entered in the 'Plotted Inches = Drawing Units' section of the dialogue box. Thus to produce a life-sized printout (paper size permitting) a 1:1 ratio should be entered. Similarly, by specifying that 2 mm is equivalent to 1 drawing unit, the size of all printed lengths will be doubled.

Drawing Exercise 9   Producing an Accurately scaled Printout

Use the techniques presented in this Chapter to produce an accurate copy of the drawing given below (omitting Dimensions). Then produce a 1:1 scaled printout on A4 paper, assuming that all sizes are in mm.

Note: The exact size and design of the border is at your discretion. Remember to allow room for a margin around the border for printing purposes.

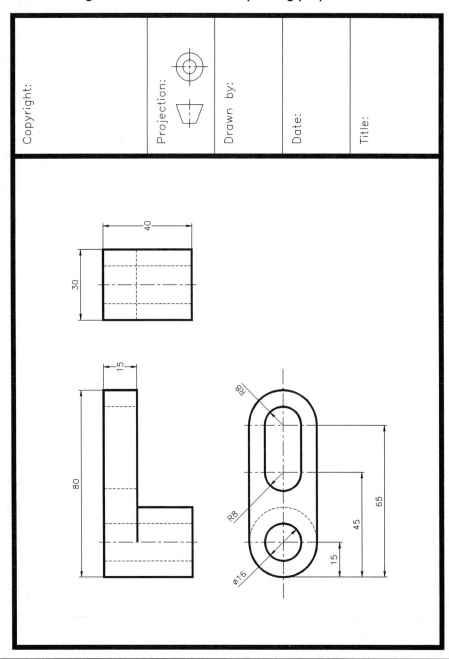

4   Modifying Your Drawing

Introduction

Until now, the approach used to deal with the inevitable errors which occur during the creation of drawings has been to erase the offending object(s) and then to repeat the command. This is not always the best approach, as it is often quicker and easier to modify the offending item(s), using one of the wide range of available commands.

Using the methods described in this chapter you will learn how to:

❑   selectively reverse the effect of one or more drawing or editing commands;

❑   interactively select a group of objects upon which an editing command will operate;

❑   erase, move, rotate, scale (re-size), or stretch (distort) existing objects;

❑   customize the object selection methods used by AutoCAD LT;

❑   tidy-up junctions between two or more objects;

❑   change object properties such as linetype, layer, colour or text style;

❑   correct spelling mistakes in existing Text;

❑   modify features of existing Polylines;

❑   use 'grips' to move, rotate, scale or stretch objects;

❑   remove unused drawing features, such as text styles, from a drawing.

UNDO and REDO

As we have already seen, drawing commands such as LINE, DLINE and PLINE have an *undo* option which may be used to remove the most recently drawn line or arc segment. This feature is particularly convenient when drawing, as it allows a mistake to be corrected without the need to leave – and subsequently resume – the current drawing command.

It may come as something of a surprise to learn that AutoCAD LT actually 'remembers' every drawing and editing operation that you perform during the current editing session, even including details of any deleted objects! This information may be used to 'step backwards' through a drawing session, undoing successive operations until the effects of an unwanted series of commands have been totally reversed. If you inadvertently go too far, the REDO command may be used to revert back to the previous state.

There are actually <u>two</u> different commands which may be used to undo the effect of successive drawing or editing operations, one of which is a simplified version of the other! The U command is the simpler of the two and is similar in appearance to the Undo option offered by the previously mentioned drawing commands. The only difference in use is that you would enter **U** ⏎ at the <u>Command</u> prompt, rather than during a drawing command dialogue.

In fact, Release 2 of AutoCAD LT also allows the U command to be accessed by clicking the appropriate button in the Toolbar (see margin), or by selecting the **<u>U</u>ndo** option from the **<u>E</u>dit** pull-down menu.

To understand the operation of the U command, imagine that the most recently used commands have been LINE, ERASE, CIRCLE and ARC – in that order. Clicking the U button will erase the most recently drawn Arc. Repeatedly pressing this button will cause each Arc to disappear, followed by any Circles. Undoing the effect of any erase operations causes the previously deleted Lines to reappear briefly, prior to being erased once again as the effect of the LINE command is itself reversed. Finally, you will be informed that 'Everything has been undone', at which point you will be left with a blank drawing.

Note: At each stage, you are given the name of the command whose effect has been reversed. This can be helpful if you loose track of the point reached.

The UNDO command is more powerful than U, at the expense of being slightly harder to use. A typical command dialogue is given below.

Command: **UNDO** ⏎   - (or enter **UN** as an abbreviation).

Auto/Back/Control/End/Group/Mark/<number>:

The default response is simply to type a number, which defines the number of commands to be undone (so **UNDO 4** is equivalent to entering the U command four times in succession). While this option is clearly more convenient than repeated use of the U command, you may be uncertain as to the number of operations to be reversed. If you go too far back, then the REDO command may be used to reverse the effect of the most recent undo operation, but <u>only</u> if the REDO command is started <u>immediately</u> after UNDO.

The REDO command may be started in several different ways according to personal preference. Users of AutoCAD LT Release 1 may type **REDO** (or **RE**) at the Command prompt, while users of Release 2 (or later) may additionally select the **<u>R</u>edo** option from the **<u>E</u>dit** pull-down menu, or click the appropriate button in the Toolbar (see margin).

The following command dialogue shows how the UNDO and REDO commands may be used interactively to determine the number of commands to be undone.

Command: **UNDO 10** ⏎   - Undo the last 10 commands.

Command: **REDO** ⏎   - Too many so try 8 next time!

Command: **UNDO 8** ⏎   - Correct.

Note: Remember to issue the REDO command immediately after the last undo operation, if you wish to reverse its effect. Also, be aware that this limitation means that you cannot repeat the REDO command several times in succession!

Tutorial 8   Using the UNDO, U and REDO commands

This exercise examines the use of the UNDO, U and REDO commands to selectively reverse the effect of drawing and editing commands.

1.   Start a new drawing. Use a range of drawing commands in sequence to create a fairly complex drawing. As part of this sequence, use the ERASE command to remove several objects, before resuming drawing.

2.   Type **U** ⏎, to undo the last command. Notice that pressing ⏎ alone causes the last command to be repeated, thus undoing one command at a time.

3.   Enter **UNDO 5** to undo the five most recent operations. Then use the REDO command to reverse the effect of the UNDO command. Experiment until you are confident in the use of these commands.

Note: These techniques are often used to recover a drawing after potentially disastrous modifications have been made to it, provided that the changes have not actually been saved to disk. Some operations, such as saving files or printing drawings cannot be undone!

When an existing drawing is opened for further editing, AutoCAD LT creates a 'backup' drawing file (with the file extension '.BAK'). This file contains the drawing as it was at the end of the last drawing session. If disastrous changes to a drawing have been saved, it may still be possible to reload this backup file! To do this, return temporarily to DOS and rename the backup file so that it has an extension of '.DWG'. For example, to make the backup file TEST.BAK available as a drawing file, you could type **REN TEST.BAK RECOVER.DWG**. Finally, return to AutoCAD LT and proceed in the normal way to open the backup drawing file.

The remaining options offered by the UNDO command are explained in Table 4–1 overleaf.

Table 4–1. Options offered by the UNDO command.

Option	Description
Auto	An on/off toggle. When enabled, complex sequences of operations (menu macros) which are selected from the pull-down menu, will be treated as a single operation by the UNDO command.
Back	If the *Mark* option has previously been used, then this option will undo all operations carried out subsequently to the mark.
Control	Displays several control options. The *All* option enables full undo operation, which is enabled by default, while *None* disables the undo feature completely. The *One* option allows the last operation (only) to be undone, and causes the UNDO command to display a simplified range of command options. (Bear in mind that implementation of the <u>full</u> undo feature may require considerable quantities of memory in some circumstances.)
End	Marks the <u>end</u> of a sequence of instructions (started by the *Group* option), which will be treated as a single operation by the UNDO command.
Group	Marks the <u>start</u> of a sequence of instructions, which will be treated as a single operation by the UNDO command. The sequence is terminated by the *End* option. (Group and End are mainly intended for use within automated sequences of commands, such as menu macros or script files.)
Mark	Places a 'marker' in the command sequence which may later be used by selecting the *Back* option. The *Mark* option is unavailable if a *Group – End* sequence is in progress.
Number	Entering a number causes the specified number of operations (or groups) to be undone. Pressing ⏎ at the command prompt causes the most recent operation to be undone.

Object Selection Methods

When using editing commands such as ERASE or COPY, you have considerable flexibility in the methods which may be used to select the objects upon which the command will operate. Recall that the process of forming such a *selection set* was first introduced in Chapter 2 (p. 31–2) in relation to the ERASE command, although these principles are applicable generally. The use of the DDSELECT command to customize the object selection process was also discussed.

In general, AutoCAD LT displays a 'Select objects:' prompt in the command area at the appropriate stage in the command dialogue, and an object selection *pickbox* appears at the cursor position. At this stage you can pick individual objects by placing the pickbox over the object and clicking ᐔ. Alternatively, if the *implied windowing* feature has been enabled (using DDSELECT) you can draw an object selection window which will allow several objects to be selected in a single operation.

There are actually <u>two</u> basic types of object selection window. A *window* box selects only those objects which are entirely within the box, while a *crossing* box selects objects which are wholly or partly within the object selection window. You can easily identify the type of object selection box which is active because window selection boxes are drawn with a solid border, while crossing boxes have a dotted outline.

To force a window selection, you can type **W** [Spacebar] at the 'Select objects:' prompt, prior to giving the two corners of the box. Alternatively, if implied windowing is enabled, indicating the two corners of the object selection box from left to right will always make a window selection.

Similarly, entering **C** [Spacebar] at the 'Select objects:' prompt, or selecting the two corners of the object selection box from right to left (using implied windowing) will cause objects to be selected using a crossing box.

Tutorial 9   Using Crossing and Window Object Selection Techniques

This tutorial demonstrates the selection of objects using crossing and window object selection boxes. Visual differences between the two methods are also highlighted.

1.   Start a new drawing. Draw several Lines or other objects at randomly selected locations in the drawing area.

2.   Use the DDSELECT command to enable the *implied windowing* feature.

3.   Start the ERASE command. At the 'Select objects:' prompt, use the mouse to pick the first point of the object selection window (ensuring that the pickbox does <u>not</u> touch an existing object). Notice that moving the cursor to the left of the first point causes the window to be drawn with a dotted outline, while moving it to the right draws a solid border.

4.   Experiment with the erasing of objects with both types of window. (Use the UNDO command to retrieve previously deleted objects.)

5.   Repeat the ERASE command and explicitly force a crossing or window selection by entering **C** [Spacebar] or **W** [Spacebar] at the 'Select objects:' prompt. Notice that the position of the two defining points of the window are no longer significant in defining the type of object selection box.

Up to now, objects have been selected by enclosing them within a rectangular object selection window. In some cases, the proximity of other objects may make it difficult to select the required objects in isolation. In this case, it may be more convenient to use an object selection *polygon*.

As you would expect, there are <u>two</u> varieties of object selection polygon! The CPOLYGON option selects a crossing polygon (minimum abbreviation **CP**), while WPOLYGON selects a window polygon (normally abbreviated to **WP**). Having entered the appropriate option at the 'Select objects:' prompt, simply indicate the vertices of the polygon using the mouse. Entering a command separator causes the first and last points to be joined, thus closing the polygon.

Where window or Polygon selection boxes are not appropriate, the *fence* option may be used. With this method, having entered **FENCE** or **F** at the 'Select objects:' prompt, objects are selected by drawing a series of connected lines which <u>pass</u> <u>over</u> the required objects. Any objects which 'touch' the object selection fence are added to the selection set. Figure 4–1 summarizes the use of window, polygon and fence object selection techniques.

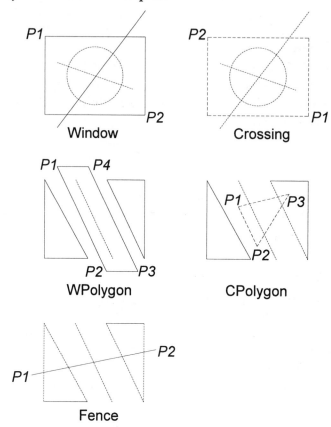

Figure 4–1. Object selection using window, polygon and fence techniques.

Many editing operations will quite naturally be carried out on the most recently created object. (This is particularly true where a drawing error needs to be corrected.) A quick way to select this object is to select the *Last* option at the 'Select objects:' prompt (which may be abbreviated to **L**).

The *Previous* option is another time saving feature (minimum abbreviation **P**). This option allows the most recently defined selection set to be reselected for use by the current editing command. This can be useful where several commands must operate on the same group of objects, or an editing command needs to be repeated for some reason.

Finally, the *Add* and *Remove* operating modes allow the selection set to be constructed by adding or removing objects from the selection set respectively. Additive mode is selected by default as indicated by the 'Select objects:' prompt. Entering **REMOVE** ⏎ (minimum abbreviation **R**) at this prompt causes the message 'Remove objects:' to be displayed. Objects may then be removed from the selection set using any of the methods previously described. The ability to switch between these modes can be useful where you wish an editing command to operate on <u>most</u> of the objects in the drawing. This would be achieved by selecting the *All* objects option (minimum abbreviation **A**), prior to removing unwanted objects from the selection set.

Basic Drawing Modification

This section introduces several commands and techniques which may be used in the modification of an existing drawing.

ERASE, UNDO and OOPS

The ERASE command was first introduced in Chapter 2 (page 32) and you should by now be more than familiar with its use! Recall also that we have used the UNDO command to retrieve previously deleted objects, if these have been erased by mistake.

The ERASE command may be started in several different ways. Either Type **ERASE** (or **E**) at the Command prompt, select the **E**rase option from the **Modify** pull-down menu, or click the appropriate button in the Toolbox (see margin). The options considered in the previous section are all available when the 'Select objects:' prompt is displayed.

The OOPS command is an alternative to UNDO, which may be preferable in some circumstances. OOPS causes any objects which were erased by the most recent command (ERASE perhaps) to be redrawn. Unlike the UNDO command, OOPS only keeps track of these most recently erased objects so it is not possible to 'step back' through the drawing.

To start the OOPS command enter **OOPS** (or **OO**) at the Command prompt, or select the **O**ops option from the **Modify** pull-down menu.

Another application of OOPS is to recover objects which have been automatically erased by other commands, without undoing the command itself. An example is the creation of a Block using the BLOCK command, where the original objects are erased after creation of the Block. The OOPS command simply redraws the deleted objects, while UNDO would also erase the newly created Block definition. (The creation and use of Blocks is considered in Chapter 6.)

MOVE

As its name suggests, the MOVE command is used to move one or more objects to a new location. Unlike the COPY command (which will be discussed in the next chapter), the original group of objects are <u>erased</u>, prior to being redrawn in their new location.

The MOVE command may be started either by entering **MOVE** (or **M**) at the Command prompt, by selecting the **Move** option from the **Modify** pull-down menu, or by clicking the appropriate button in the Toolbox (see margin).

Having selected the objects on which the command is to operate, you are then asked to indicate a 'Base point or displacement', followed by the 'Second point of displacement'. Perhaps the best way to understand the significance of these two values is to think of them as forming the two ends of a *displacement vector*.

This displacement vector specifies the distance and direction by which every object must be moved (or translated), as shown in Figure 4–2.

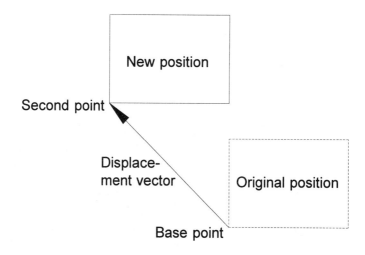

Figure 4–2. Understanding the dialogue used by the MOVE command.

Although the command dialogue seems quite straightforward, there are many subtly different ways in which the base point and second point options may be specified, each of which have their own areas of application. Bear in mind that snap, object snap and typed input – which were originally introduced in association with <u>drawing</u> commands – may also be used here!

Probably the simplest application is where the selected objects must be moved through a distance whose exact value is known. The following command dialogue demonstrates the use of typed input to specify the displacement.

Base point or displacement: **50,0** ⏎	- Move selected objects 50 units to the right.
Second point of displacement: ⏎	- A null response causes the previous value to be inter- preted as a <u>displacement</u>.

(Bear in mind that the displacement could also have been specified as a polar coordinate, if this was more convenient.) Another way to achieve the same result would be to specify a base point of 0,0 (absolute), followed by a second point of 50,0 (absolute). In this case it is the <u>difference</u> between the two coordinates which defines the displacement vector. Yet another variation would be to pick <u>any</u> point in the drawing area using the mouse, and then to enter a relative coordinate of @50,0 as the second point.

Alternatively, the snap feature could have been enabled, thus allowing the base point and second point to be defined using the mouse.

Finally, object snap may be used to force the base point and/or second point to align to an existing drawing feature. This is useful where the object to be moved has an easily identified reference point, which must be moved so that it coincides with another existing feature. (So you would press ⟨Shift⟩ + ⌐ at the base point or second point prompt, to call up the Cursor menu. Then select the desired object snap feature before pointing at the object of interest with the mouse and click ⌐.)

Tutorial 10 Combining MOVE with Snap and Object Snap

This tutorial demonstrates the use of the MOVE command to align a previously drawn group of objects with the snap grid. (A possible application is where several views of an engineering component must be accurately aligned, to produce a neat drawing.)

1.   Start a new drawing. Use the DDRMODES command to set the snap and grid spacings to 10 units, and then <u>disable</u> both features by clicking the appropriate check boxes, prior to leaving the command.

2.   Produce a simple drawing using Lines or Polylines. Now enable the grid by pressing function key ⟨F7⟩ and confirm that your drawing does <u>not</u> align to the grid.

3.   Now start the MOVE command and select the previously drawn objects (you can enter **ALL** to select all objects in the drawing). At the 'Base point or displacement:' prompt, click ⟨Shift⟩ + ⌐ to display the cursor menu and select the Endpoint option from the displayed list of object snap modes. Now use the mouse to pick an endpoint which is to act as the base point.

4.   At the 'Second point of displacement:' prompt, press ⟨F9⟩ to enable the snap feature. Now use the mouse to point to the desired destination coordinate (which should automatically snap to the visible grid).

ROTATE

As its name suggests, the ROTATE command is used to rotate existing objects. The initial command dialogue is similar to that of other drawing modification commands, requiring the selection of objects upon which the command will operate. This is then followed by the specification of a base point, which is taken to be the centre of rotation.

To start the ROTATE command, enter **ROTATE** (or **RO**) at the Command prompt, select the **Rotate** option from the **Modify** pull-down menu, or click the appropriate button in the Toolbox (see margin).

Once the selection set and the base point have both been given, the command dialogue continues as shown below.

Command: <Rotation angle>/Reference: - type an angle or enter **R** ⏎ to select the Reference option.

The default response is simply to type an angle, which is taken to be the angle of rotation. (Recall that AutoCAD LT normally measures positive angles in an anticlockwise direction. You can alter this setting using the DDUNITS command, if you wish.) Thus, for example, typing **90** ⏎ at the above prompt would cause the selected objects to be rotated through 90° anticlockwise.

The Reference option allows a base or *reference* angle to be given followed by the *new* angle. The selected objects are then rotated through an angle which is the result of subtracting the new and reference angles. (So, if the reference angle is given as 30° and the new angle is 45°, the selected objects will be rotated through 15° in a positive direction.) A particular application of this Reference option is where the object has a datum edge which must be drawn at a specific angle. Using this option, the two endpoints of the datum line are first given (typically using object snap techniques). These two points define the *Reference angle*. Next the *New angle* is entered, which causes the object to be rotated so that the datum edge is aligned at the desired angle. This process is illustrated by Figure 4–3.

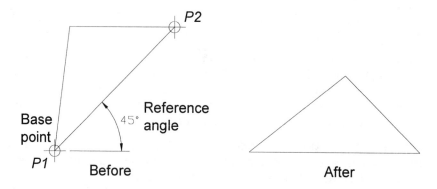

Figure 4–3. Using the Reference option with the ROTATE command.

Tutorial 11   Rotating Objects using the Reference Option

This tutorial demonstrates how the ROTATE command may be used to align a previously drawn group of objects to a specified angle (horizontal in this example).

1.   Draw a triangle, so that its base lies at an angle (as shown in Figure 4–3).

2.   Start the ROTATE command. Select the object(s) to be rotated and use object snap to pick the lower left vertex as the base point.

3.   At the '<Rotation angle>/Reference:' prompt, enter **R** ⏎ to select the Reference option. Once the 'Reference angle:' prompt is displayed, press Ctrl + ⏷ to activate the Cursor menu and select the Endpoint option. Now use the mouse to pick the lower left vertex of the triangle as the first point on the datum line (point *P1* in Figure 4–3). In response to the 'Second point:' prompt, use object snap once again to select point *P2* as the other end of the datum line.

4.   Finally, at the 'New angle:' prompt, enter the required angle of rotation (i.e. **0** ⏎).

SCALE

The SCALE command is used to re-size previously drawn objects, which can be a useful and time-saving alternative to redrawing the affected items.

To start the SCALE command, type **SCALE** (or **SC**) at the Command prompt, select the **Sc**ale option from the **Modify** pull-down menu, or click the appropriate button in the Toolbar (see margin).

As with the ERASE, MOVE and ROTATE commands considered earlier, the command dialogue begins with the selection of objects, followed by the specification of a base point. With the SCALE command this base point is the 'focus' of the expansion or contraction. In other words, selected objects move away from or towards this focus as they are resized. The command dialogue then continues as shown below.

<Scale factor>/Reference: - Type a number or enter **R** ⏎ to select the
                                      Reference option.

If a number is entered at the above prompt, this is taken to be the scale factor. Values larger than unity cause selected objects to be enlarged, while numbers less than one give a reduction in size. The scale factor acts as a 'multiplier' so for example, a scale factor of 2 will cause the size of each selected item to double.

The *Reference* option has some similarity with the option of the same name offered by the ROTATE command. In this case, you are prompted to enter a reference length, followed by the new length (so angles are replaced by lengths in the SCALE command's dialogue).

A possible application for the Reference option would be where the size of an existing feature is known, and also its intended size after rescaling. (As with ROTATE, it is also possible to use object snap techniques to pick two existing points, thus defining the reference length.)

Drawing Exercise 10   Resizing Objects using the SCALE Command

This exercise involves resizing an existing object, as an alternative to erasure, prior to redrawing.

1.   Draw a rectangle of length 84.2 units and height 63.7 units, with the lower left corner positioned at the absolute coordinate 50,50.

2.   Use the SCALE command (and the Reference option) to resize the rectangle so that its base is now 100 units in length, while its lower left corner remains at the same coordinate.

3.   Confirm using the Grid that the resulting object is correctly positioned, and of the specified size.

STRETCH

The STRETCH command is fundamentally different from other drawing modification commands already considered, in that it is used to selectively <u>distort</u> the drawing. There are many similarities – both functionally and in the command dialogue – with the MOVE command.

In normal use, objects are selected using a *crossing window* or *crossing polygon* selection. Thus objects may be <u>completely</u> within the selection box, <u>partly</u> within the selection box, or <u>entirely</u> outside of the selection box. The effect of the STRETCH command on objects which are completely inside or entirely outside of the selection box is indistinguishable from that of the MOVE command, with the selected objects being shifted to their new location, or left unaltered respectively. The major difference (assuming a crossing window selection) is that those objects which lie partly inside of the selection box are 'stretched' so as to maintain contact with the relocated objects. This is shown in Figure 4–4.

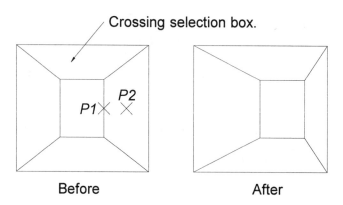

Before   After

Figure 4–4. Distorting an object using the STRETCH command.

To start the STRETCH command, type **STRETCH** (or **S**) and the Command prompt, select the **Stretch** option from the **Modify** pull-down menu, or click the appropriate button in the Toolbox (see margin).

Note: When the STRETCH command is started from the pull-down menu, a crossing window selection is selected automatically (as indicated by the dotted appearance of the selection window). When using the keyboard, remember to type **C** [Spacebar] or **CP** [Spacebar], at the 'Select objects:' prompt, to force a crossing window or polygon selection, or draw the selection window from <u>right</u> <u>to</u> <u>left</u>.

Drawing Exercise 11   Changing Lengths using the STRETCH Command

The illustration below shows a section of wall which has been drawn using the DLINE command. Use the STRETCH command to change the length of the wall from 60 to 80 units.

Changing Properties

When an object is drawn using AutoCAD LT, it inherits certain *properties* which are active at the time when the object is drawn. We have already seen that objects may have different colours and linetypes, and that certain types of object have specialized properties. For example, a line of Text has properties which include the text style, height, rotation angle, obliquing angle and the actual text itself.

This section shows how the properties associated with existing objects may be altered, and describes how named features such as linetypes and text styles may be renamed.

DDCHPROP

The DDCHPROP command is used to modify basic object properties such as *colour*, *layer*, *linetype* or *thickness*. This command is straightforward in use, due to the extensive use of dialogue boxes. It may also be used to modify the properties of several selected objects in a single operation. Thus DDCHPROP is the preferred method of altering <u>basic</u> object properties. Where more advanced properties must be altered, the CHANGE command may be used.

Note: The DDMODIFY command is also available to users of AutoCAD LT Release 2 (or later). This advanced editing command allows the properties associated with a <u>single</u> selected object to be modified using a dialogue box. The exact appearance of the dialogue box depends on the type of object selected.

To start the DDCHPROP command, type **DDCHPROP** (or **DC**) at the Command prompt, select the **Change Properties** option from the **Modify** pull-down menu, or press the appropriate button in the Toolbox (see margin).

The first step is to select the object(s) upon which the command is to operate. Having done this, the dialogue box of Figure 4–5 is displayed.

From this main screen, subsidiary dialogue boxes may be accessed by pressing the **Color...**, **Layer...** and **Linetype...** buttons, (two of which have already been encountered).

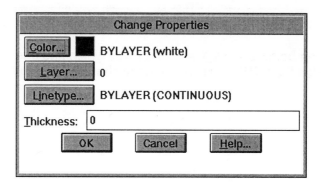

Figure 4–5. The DDCHPROP command's main dialogue box.

Note: In the above figure, the colour and linetype are both set to the logical colour BYLAYER, so these settings are taken from the layer upon which the objects were originally drawn. This is layer '0', which is drawn with a white, continuous linetype here. As we saw earlier, you can explicitly set these properties, thus overriding the default values associated with this layer.

Editing Text with DDEDIT

In drawings which contain significant amounts of textual information, it is frequently necessary to correct spelling mistakes in existing Text. The DDEDIT command allows this task to be performed very simply, while the CHANGE command (considered next) allows other Text properties to be modified. (Users of Release 2 or later may also use the DDMODIFY command to modify Text properties, as will be seen later in this section.)

Release 2
icon

To start the DDEDIT command, type **DDEDIT** (or **ED**) at the Command prompt, select the **Edit Text** option from the **Modify** pull-down menu, or press the appropriate button in the Toolbox (see margin). The following command options are then displayed.

Release 1
Icon

<Select a TEXT or ATTDEF object>/Undo:

Once a line of text has been selected, the dialogue box of Figure 4–6 appears.

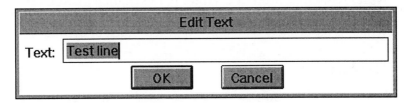

Figure 4–6. Editing Text using the DDEDIT command.

Notice here that the entire line appears highlighted in the edit box, so typing any new text will cause the old text to be <u>replaced</u>. (This behaviour is standard in Windows-based applications, where a block of text is first highlighted by 'dragging' the mouse over the region, prior to being replaced by typing any new text.) If the editing process is required to be less 'drastic', then use the cursor keys or the mouse to move the text insertion point to the required location, prior to inserting or erasing individual characters. Table 4–2 lists commonly used text editing keystrokes and the actions performed.

Table 4–2. Commonly used text editing keystrokes and their functions.

Key	Function
[Home]	Move to the start of the line.
[End]	Move to the end of the line.
[←]	Move cursor 1 position to the left.
[→]	Move cursor 1 position to the right.
[Ctrl] + [←]	Move cursor 1 word to the left.
[Ctrl] + [→]	Move cursor 1 word to the right.
🖱	Move cursor to new position.
[Shift] + [Home]	Highlight to the start of the line.
[Shift] + [End]	Highlight to the end of the line.
[Shift] + [←]	Highlight 1 position to the left.
[Shift] + [→]	Highlight 1 position to the right.
[Shift] + [Ctrl] + [←]	Highlight 1 word to the left.
[Shift] + [Ctrl] + [→]	Highlight 1 word to the right.
🖱 + drag	Highlight region.
[←]	Delete character at cursor position (or block).
[Delete]	Delete character to the right of the cursor (or block).
ABC 123 etc.	Insert text at cursor position.

Once the required modifications have been made, click **OK** to accept the changes, or **Cancel** to leave the Text unaltered.

Note: As will be seen in Chapter 6, the DDEDIT command may also be used to modify *Attributes*. (An Attribute is a specialized form of textual information which is associated with a pre-defined Block or symbol.)

CHANGE

The CHANGE command may be used to modify object properties from the command line, where it offers a more advanced range of options than the DDCHPROP command. Alternatively, it can be used as a simple method of tidying up drawings – for example, where Line endpoints have failed to meet at a junction, as intended.

To start the CHANGE command, type **CHANGE** (or **CH**) at the Command prompt or select the **Change Point** option from the **Modify** pull-down menu. You are then asked to select the objects upon which the command will operate, after which the following command options are presented.

Properties/<Change point>:   - Type **P** ↵ to display available properties or give a coordinate in the normal way.

The behaviour of the 'Change point' option depends on the type of object selected, as shown in Table 4–3.

Table 4–3. Types of object and features modified by the 'Change point' option of the CHANGE command.

Object type	Feature modified
Line	Position of selected endpoint.
Circle	Radius (Circle passes through new point).
Block	Insertion point, rotation angle.
Text	Base point, text style, height, rotation angle, new text.

As mentioned above, a typical application is to force the endpoints of two or more Lines to meet at a particular point, as shown in Figure 4–7.

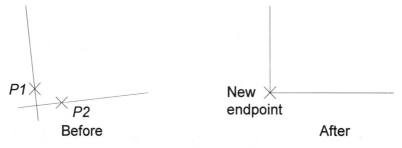

Figure 4–7. Using the CHANGE command to tidy a junction between Lines.

With this example, the two Lines are first indicated at the 'Select objects:' prompt (making sure that the selected point is as close as possible to the required endpoint). The entry of a command separator terminates the object selection stage. Finally, the new endpoint may be specified, using any preferred method.

If the *Properties* option is selected, the following range of properties is displayed in the Command area. A particular option may be chosen for alteration by entering the capitalized letters, followed by a command separator (i.e. **LT** ↵ for linetype).

Change what property (Color/Elev/LAyer/LType/Thickness) ?

DDMODIFY

A major introduction for AutoCAD LT Release 2 is the DDMODIFY command, which allows advanced editing of the properties of <u>single</u> objects. DDMODIFY is surprisingly easy to use, because the appearance of the dialogue box varies intelligently, based on the type of object selected

A basic set of object properties is provided for all types of object. These include colour, linetype, layer and thickness (as with DDCHPROP considered earlier). Other properties may also be modified, depending on the type of object. Objects which may be edited using DDMODIFY include

❑ Arcs   ❑ Attributes

❑ Block insertions   ❑ Circles

❑ External references ❑ Lines

❑ Points   ❑ Polylines

❑ Solids   ❑ Text

Note: This version of DDMODIFY is slightly simplified, when compared to that available in the full version of AutoCAD. In particular, 3D Faces, Dimensions, Shapes, Traces and Viewports cannot be edited using DDMODIFY.

To start the DDMODIFY command, either type **DDMODIFY** at the Command prompt, or select the **Modify Entity** option from the <u>M</u>odify pull-down menu. You are then asked to 'Select an object to modify:', at which point the appropriate dialogue box will be displayed.

Tutorial 12   Modifying Object Properties Using DDMODIFY

This tutorial is intended to provide practice in the use of the DDMODIFY command with various types of object.

1.   Draw <u>one</u> of each of the following: Arc, Circle, Line, Point, Polyline, Solid and Text.

2.   Use the DDMODIFY command to modify properties of each type of object.

DDRENAME

During the creation of a drawing, several different types of <u>named</u> object may be either created or used. (We have already encountered the use of named *linetypes* and *text styles*, and several other varieties of named object will be encountered in subsequent chapters.) The DDRENAME command provides a convenient method for renaming these objects, should you need to do so.

To start the Command, type **DDRENAME** (or **DR**) at the Command prompt, or select the **Re̲name** option from the **M̲odify** pull-down menu. The dialogue box of Figure 4–8 will then be displayed.

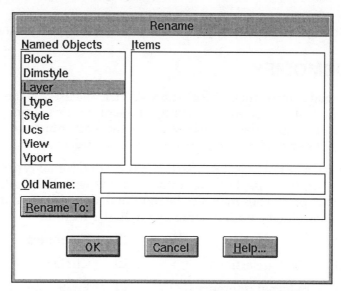

Figure 4–8. Renaming named objects using the DDRENAME command.

In general, to rename an existing object, begin by selecting the type of object from the **Named Objects** list box. At this point, a list of existing named objects of the specified type will appear in the **I̲tems** list box. Now use the mouse to click on the required item, which will cause its name to appear in the **O̲ld name:** edit box (or simply type the item name here). Now type the new item name in the lower edit box and then press the **Rename To:** button.

Notes:

1. Some types of object cannot be renamed. Examples are the CONTINUOUS linetype and layer 0.

2. You can use the wildcard characters such as '*' (match any group of characters) and '?' (match any single character) to rename several objects in a single operation. For example '?BC' would match 'ABC' or '3BC', while 'L_*' would match 'L_001' or 'L_00345'. A detailed list of available options is given in the *AutoCAD LT User's Guide*.

Using BREAK, EXTEND and TRIM to Tidy Drawings

These three commands offer a powerful and complementary range of drawing modification commands, which are particularly suited to the tidying of existing drawings. In fact, they are so easy and quick to use that you may find yourself producing drawings using fast 'construction line' techniques, in the knowledge that unwanted detail can easily be removed at a later stage!

BREAK

The BREAK command allows the removal of an unwanted section from an existing object, simply by the indication of two points on the object. Some example applications of BREAK are shown in Figure 4–9.

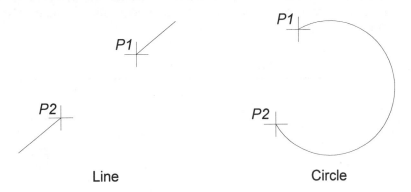

Line   Circle

Figure 4–9. Using the BREAK command to remove unwanted sections.

To start the BREAK command, type **BREAK** (or **BR**) at the Command prompt, select the **B**reak option from the **M**odify pull-down menu, or press the appropriate button in the Toolbox (see margin). A typical command dialogue is given below.

Command: **BREAK** ↵   - (Or enter **BR** here.)

Select object: - Do so (at the first break point if possible).

Enter second point (or F for first point): - Do so, or enter **F** ↵ to enter the first break point, followed by the second.

Under normal circumstances, the selection of the object is combined with the indication of the first break point. It is then only necessary to indicate a second point to complete the command. However, in order to make an unambiguous object selection, it may be necessary to indicate a point which is different from the first break point. In this case, use the 'F' option to show that the first break point has not yet been chosen.

Notes:

1. When removing part of a Circle or Arc, the <u>order</u> in which the two points are entered is important! These features are normally drawn by AutoCAD LT in an anticlockwise direction, so the defining points should be entered in the same manner (as shown in Figure 4–9).

2. You can use *object snap* when entering the first and second break points. However, if these points are intersections with other objects then the TRIM command may be an easier alternative.

EXTEND

If an existing object, such as a Line or Arc, finishes short of an intended boundary then this command may be used to extend the selected object so that a neat intersection is produced. Typical applications of the EXTEND command are shown in Figure 4–10.

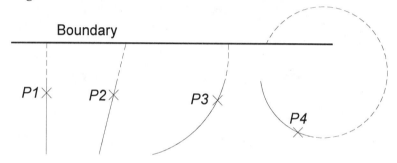

Boundary

P1   P2   P3   P4

Figure 4–10. Using the EXTEND command to join objects at a boundary.

To start the EXTEND command, enter **EXTEND** (or **EX**) at the Command prompt, select the **Ex**tend option from the **Modify** pull-down menu, or click the appropriate button in the Toolbox (see margin). The command dialogue then proceeds as shown below.

Command: **EXTEND** ⏎   - (Or enter **EX** here.)

Select boundary edge(s)...
Select objects: - Pick one or more <u>boundary</u> objects.

Select objects: ⏎   - Press ⏎ to end boundary selection.

<Select object to extend>/Undo: - Click on each object in turn, or enter **U** ⏎ to undo the last extend.

Notice that the above dialogue consists of <u>two</u> distinct phases. The first step is the selection of one or more boundary objects. You must enter a command separator at the 'Select objects:' prompt before selecting the object(s) to be extended.

Note: When selecting the object to be extended, pick the defining point to be as close as possible to the endpoint from where the extension is to take place. (Study the position of points *P3* and *P4* in Figure 4–10 to see the effect.)

TRIM

The TRIM command is similar to BREAK, in that it is used to remove a section from an existing object. However the TRIM command uses the intersection between the object and one or more *cutting planes* to define the break points. This is illustrated in Figure 4–11.

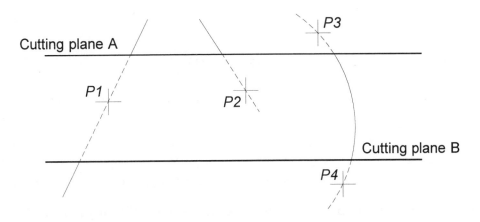

Figure 4–11. Using 'cutting planes' with the TRIM command.

 To start the TRIM command, type **TRIM** (or **TR**) at the Command prompt, select the **Trim** option from the **Modify** pull-down menu, or press the appropriate button in the Toolbox (see margin).

The command dialogue is very similar to that used by the Extend command, as shown below.

Command: **TRIM** [↵]   - (Or enter **TR** [↵] here.)

Select cutting edge(s)...   - Pick one or more <u>boundary</u> edges.
Select objects:

Select objects: [↵]   - Press [↵] to end boundary selection.

<Select object to trim>/Undo: - Click on each object to be trimmed, or press **U** [↵] to undo the last trim.

Once again, you must follow the command dialogue carefully, as it begins with the selection of boundary objects, followed by the indication of the objects to be trimmed!

Notice also from Figure 4–11 that it is the portion of the object which is to be discarded, that is indicated.

Example

This example demonstrates a typical application of the TRIM command, in which the intersection between two Lines must be tidied by removal of any excess. The sequence of events is shown in Figure 4–12 below.

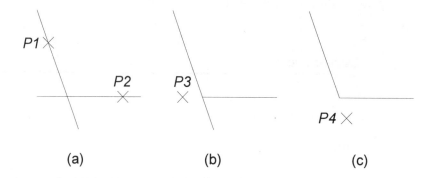

(a)   (b)   (c)

Figure 4–12. Trimming to an intersection using the TRIM command.

First, the two cutting planes are selected by indicating points *P1* and *P2*. Then the horizontal Line is trimmed by pointing to the unwanted side at point *P3*. Lastly, the Line which is inclined at an angle is trimmed by indicating point *P4*.

Note: You can also trim to an intersection by using the FILLET command, with the fillet radius set to zero, as will be seem in the next chapter.

Editing Polylines

Polylines are amongst the most complex of objects which may be created by AutoCAD LT. As we have already seen, a single Polyline may consist of a series of linked line and arc segments, each of which may have its own starting and ending line widths.

A Polyline is treated as a single object by editing commands, such as MOVE, COPY or ERASE, so an obvious question arises – How can we edit the individual details of a Polyline, without the need to erase and then redraw the entire object?

The inevitable answer is that AutoCAD LT provides a purpose designed Polyline editing command called PEDIT. Using this command, you can alter the width of the entire Polyline, or of individual segments; you can insert, move or delete vertices; you can even draw a smooth curve based on the original Polyline definition.

On the down side, the provision of this wide range of options can make the PEDIT command seem overcomplex to new users. We will therefore consider each of the PEDIT command's options separately, thus leading to an overall understanding.

The PEDIT command may be started in several different ways, according to personal preference. Either select the **Edit Polyline** option from the **Modify** pull-down menu, or type **PEDIT** (or **PE**) at the Command prompt. You are first asked to select the Polyline to be edited, after which the following range of options becomes available.

Close/Join/Width/Edit vertex/Fit/Spline/Decurve/Ltypegen/Undo/eXit<X>:

Considering the first command option, recall that when a Polyline is drawn using the PLINE command, you have the option of <u>closing</u> the Polyline by linking the first and last points by using the Close option (which also exits the PLINE command). Thus a Polyline may be defined as either *closed* or *open*, based on the method used to terminate the PLINE command. If a Polyline is currently 'open', then the PEDIT command displays an option allowing it to be 'closed'. Conversely, if the Polyline is already closed, the Open command option is offered in its place.

The Join option allows an existing series of objects to be joined together to form a single Polyline. These objects must be linked 'end to end', or this command option will fail. Having selected the option, simply indicate each object in turn which is to be added to the existing Polyline. (You can use this option to link together Lines, Arcs, or even existing Polylines.)

Note: It is also possible to perform the inverse of the Join option by using the EXPLODE command to break up a Polyline into individual Lines or Arcs. (Any Polyline width information is lost during this process.)

You can set the width of an entire Polyline by using the Width option. (As we will soon see, it is also possible to alter the width of individual segment by selecting the Edit vertex option.)

The Ltypegen option controls the generation of linetype patterns at vertices, determining whether the pattern should be drawn continuously along the Polyline, or starting and ending at each vertex. (Refer to Figure 3–20 and the associated text for a full description of linetype generation issues with Polylines.)

A powerful feature of the PEDIT command is its ability to fit a curve to an existing Polyline. You have the choice of the Fit option, where the curve passes through each vertex, or a B-Spline curve (the Spline option), where the curve is 'guided towards' the vertices, while not actually passing through them. (For most applications the Spline option produces a smoother result.) As its name suggests, the Decurve option is used to remove a fitted curve, or B-Spline, regenerating the original Polyline. There are three system variables or settings which are used to fine tune the behaviour of the curve options. The SPLFRAME setting controls the visibility of the original Polyline or control frame (0 = frame off, 1 = frame on). The SPLINESEGS setting controls the number of individual line segments which are drawn for each spline segment, with higher values producing a more accurate result. Finally, the SPLINETYPE setting controls the type of B-Spline curve which is drawn (5 = quadratic, 6 = cubic). The *cubic* curve will be found to follow the defining points more accurately, but is more complex to calculate (and slower).

The Edit vertex option actually leads to a subsidiary range of options as shown below.

Next/Previous/Break/Insert/Move/Regen/Straighten/Tangent/Width/eXit<N>:

Notice here that choosing the eXit option causes a return to the previously considered range of command options (at which point the eXit option can be entered <u>again</u> to actually leave the command).

The Next and Previous options are used to move the edit point to the desired vertex, which is used by most of the options in this section. (The current position is marked on screen with a cross.)

At this stage, you can choose the Move option to relocate the current vertex, or the Insert option to create a new vertex after the current one. The Width option allows the starting and ending width of the <u>following</u> segment to be modified.

If the displayed Polyline is not updated automatically to reflect the result of an editing operation (such as altering the width of an individual Polyline segment) then the Regen option may be used to refresh the display.

The Tangent option is used to control the direction (the slope or tangent) of a subsequently fitted curve which passes through the current vertex. It thus allows greater control of the curve fitting process (which has just been considered).

Finally, the Break and Straighten options allow a section of the Polyline to be effectively removed. With the Break option, the indicated section is deleted, normally resulting in the creation of <u>two</u> separate Polylines. The Straighten option is slightly less drastic, causing the indicated section to be replaced with a single straight-line segment. With both options you begin by using the Next and Previous options to move to the <u>start</u> position, after which the Break or Straighten option is chosen. At this point the following options are displayed in the Command area. (So you are now at the <u>third</u> level of PEDIT command options!)

Next/Previous/Go/eXit<N>

The Next and Previous options are used to move to the end of the section which is to be erased or 'straightened'. The Go option will then cause the appropriate editing action to be performed. (You can choose the eXit option if you change your mind here, which will return you to the Edit vertex subsection.)

Tutorial 13 Polylines and Polyline Editing

The aim of this tutorial is to create a Polyline based on a series of known coordinate values, and then to use the PEDIT command to fit a curve through these points.

1. Use the PLINE command to draw a Polyline based on the following vertex list (using typed input as the coordinate entry method).

Vertex	X,Y		Vertex	X,Y
1	50,100		8	190,60
2	70,140		9	210,40
3	90,160		10	230,30
4	110,170		11	250,40
5	130,160		12	270,60
6	150,140		13	290,100
7	180,160			

2. Examining the on-screen appearance of the Polyline, it is obviously intended to form a sine wave, but vertex 7 is incorrect. Use the PEDIT command's Edit vertex option to move this vertex to the absolute coordinate 170,100.

3. Use the PEDIT command to draw a smooth curve through these data points. Experiment with the Fit and Spline options to see which gives the best result.

4. Now use the PEDIT command's Width option to set the Polyline width to 0.7 drawing units.

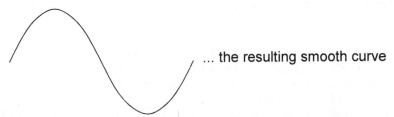

... the resulting smooth curve

5. Experiment with fitting curves to your own Polylines. Try enabling and disabling the control frame using the SPLFRAME setting. Use the SPLINETYPE setting to draw quadratic and cubic Polylines and notice that the cubic curve produces a sharper response to sudden changes in the curve's direction.

Simple Editing Using Grips

When enabled, the grips feature provides a quick method of editing existing objects. In this section we will look at the use of grips to move, rotate, scale or stretch objects, while the next chapter will show that grips may also be used to copy or reflect existing objects.

The first step is to ensure that the grip feature is enabled by using the DDGRIPS command. To do this, select the **Grips Style...** option from the **Settings** pull-down menu, or type **DDGRIPS** (or **GR**) at the Command prompt. The dialogue box of Figure 4–13 will then be displayed.

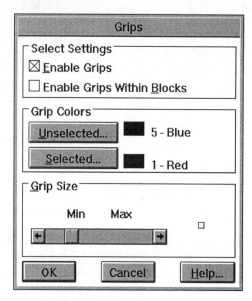

Figure 4–13. The Grips control dialogue box.

To use grips, the **Enable Grips** checkbox must be checked. The remaining options allow you to fine tune the grips feature by altering the colour of selected and unselected grips, as well as their size. (The dialogue box also controls whether individual objects within Blocks may be edited using grips. The use of Blocks will be introduced in Chapter 6.)

One of the first problems most newcomers to AutoCAD LT have with grips is trying to get rid of them! If grips are enabled and you click on an object when the Command prompt is displayed in the Command area, then a series of coloured squares will appear on the indicated object. The first thing to realize is that these grips will disappear automatically if you start any AutoCAD LT command, so there is no need to worry. (As an alternative, pressing Ctrl + C twice will also erase any grips which are being displayed.)

Clicking on an object when the Command prompt is displayed is actually the method used to <u>activate</u> the grips feature, as shown in Figure 4–14.

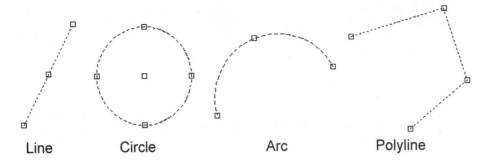

| Line | Circle | Arc | Polyline |

Figure 4–14. Typical objects and their (unselected) grips.

Notice firstly that the position and number of grips depends on the type of object which has been selected. With Lines and Arcs, grips appear at the two endpoints and at the midpoint. Circles display grips at the four quadrant points and at the centre, while Polylines have a grip at each vertex.

At this stage, grips are displayed, but the grips feature is not yet active. To do this you must click on one of the displayed grips, which will cause it to appear highlighted (or *selected*). Pressing the [Spacebar] key repeatedly will now cycle through the available operating modes, as shown below.

STRETCH   — [Spacebar]

MOVE   — [Spacebar]

ROTATE   — [Spacebar]

SCALE   — [Spacebar]

MIRROR   — [Spacebar]

STRETCH   etc.

By default the 'stretch' operating mode is selected, which may actually be used to stretch, move or copy existing objects. At this stage, the Command area offers the following options.

<Stretch to point>/Base point/Copy/Undo/eXit:

The simplest way to move an existing Line or Circle is to select the midpoint or centre grip respectively and then to indicate the new position using the mouse or by typed input. An effect similar to object snap is observed if the selected grip is moved over an existing unselected grip. The object seems to 'jump' to this new location, as if there is a magnetic attraction between the grips!

Selecting other grips such as endpoints of Lines or Arcs, quadrant points of Circles or Polyline vertices allows the object to be stretched as the grip is moved to a new location. Entire objects may still be moved, regardless of the grip selected, if the [Spacebar] is first pressed to select the 'move' operating mode.

Pressing the [Spacebar] again activates the 'rotate' option. By default, the centre of rotation is the selected grip, although you can change this by selecting the Base point option. The angle of rotation may then be given using the mouse or by typed input. (As with the ROTATE command, which was considered earlier, you can also enter a reference angle, followed by the new angle by choosing the Reference option.)

Finally, the 'scale' option may be used to alter the size of the selected object. Once again, the selected grip is normally the focus of the scale option, although a new origin can be given using the Base point option.

Tutorial 14   Basic Editing Using Grips

1.   Produce a drawing which contains a range of objects including Lines, Arcs, Circles, Polylines and Solids.

2.   Enable grips using the DDGRIPS command and then use the grips feature to move, stretch, rotate and scale individual objects.

3.   Experiment with dragging selected grips onto unselected grips. Confirm that the effect is similar to object snap and that several objects may be edited simultaneously if they share a selected grip.

Purging Unwanted (Named) Objects

During the creation, editing and maintenance of a working drawing, there may be an accumulation of unused features such as Block definitions, dimension styles, layers, linetypes and text styles. These named objects occupy space inside the drawing database, even if they are not in current use, and may cause confusion. Visible (drawn) objects can easily be erased using the ERASE command, but the only way to remove the above types of named object is with the PURGE command, which must be started <u>immediately</u> after opening the drawing (using the OPEN command).

To start the PURGE command, select the **Purge** option from the **Modify** pull-down menu or type **PURGE** (or **PR**) at the Command prompt. The following command options are then displayed.

Blocks/Dimstyles/LAyers/LTypes/Styles/All:

Either select the required type of object, or select the All option to remove all unreferenced named objects from the drawing. (You cannot purge layer 0, the STANDARD text style, or the CONTINUOUS linetype.)

5   Object Construction

Introduction

In the previous chapter we looked at methods of <u>modifying</u> existing objects and their associated properties. This chapter examines a range of editing commands which uses existing objects in some way to <u>construct</u> new drawing features. AutoCAD LT distinguishes between these two types of editing command by grouping them under the Modify and Construct pull-down menu areas respectively, as shown in Figure 5–1.

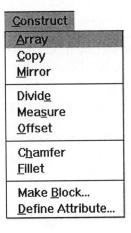

Figure 5–1. The Modify and Construct pull-down areas.

The basic object construction commands are introduced in this chapter, as detailed above. Blocks and Attributes will be considered in Chapter 6.

Copying Existing Objects

One of the advantages of using CAD is the elimination of tedium where a series of identical objects must be drawn. As its name implies, the COPY command provides a quick method of duplicating existing objects in the current drawing.

To start the COPY command, select the **Copy** option from the **Construct** pull-down menu, type **COPY** (or **CP**) at the Command prompt, or click on the Copy button in the Toolbox (see margin). Once the object selection process has been completed, the following command options become available.

<Base point or displacement>/Multiple:

The Base point or displacement option is identical in use to that offered by the MOVE command (introduced in the previous chapter). Thus, you can indicate a displacement vector by giving the two endpoints, or by giving a coordinate and then pressing ⏎ at the Second point of displacement prompt. You can also make multiple copies of the selected objects by selecting the Multiple option. Once multiple copy mode has been activated, the Second point of displacement option repeats, until the ⏎ key is pressed.

Note: The use of Blocks (see Chapter 6) is an alternative to the COPY command, and may lead to savings in the overall size of drawing files. (A Block definition is stored only <u>once</u> in a drawing, followed by details of each individual Block 'insertion'.) Blocks also encourage users to adopt a modular approach to drawing creation, hence encouraging standardization across drawings and between different users.

Creating Rectangular and Circular Arrays

The COPY command is convenient where a drawing feature must be duplicated, but what about situations where large numbers of identical objects must be arranged in regular geometric patterns? Producing individual copies will certainly be faster than drawing each item from scratch, but the process will still be very tedious. In situations like these, the ARRAY command comes into its own, allowing objects to be arranged in a rectangular of circular manner.

To start the ARRAY command, either select the **Array** option from the **Construct** pull-down menu or type **ARRAY** (or **AR**) at the Command prompt.

The initial dialogue is common to most editing commands, requiring you to first select the objects upon which the command will operate. You are then asked to choose a Rectangular or Polar array by typing R or P respectively. These two types of Array are illustrated by Figure 5-2.

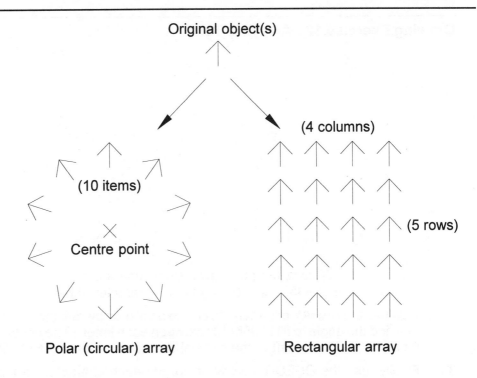

Polar (circular) array   Rectangular array

Figure 5–2. Rectangular and Polar arrays.

Consider the polar array first, as shown in the following command dialogue.

Center point of array: – Indicate the centre coordinate.

Number of items: –10 in the above example (including
                                           the original).

Angle to fill (+=ccw, -=cw)<360>:   – Press ⏎ to select a full circle, or
                                           type an angle to be filled.

Rotate objects as they are copied?<Y> – Yes in the above example.

Notice firstly, that the total number of items <u>includes</u> the original object. Thus in this example, 1 original + 9 copies = 10 objects. The next question asks for the angle to be filled by the arrayed objects, which is normally a full circle (360°). Finally, you must select whether individual objects are rotated as they are copied.

The dialogue for the Rectangular option is different, requiring you to first select the number of rows (horizontal) and columns (vertical), and then give the distance between them. As a short-cut to entering these distances separately, you can give two points specifying the opposite corners of a bounding box, or *unit cell*.

Drawing Exercise 12   Arraying Text

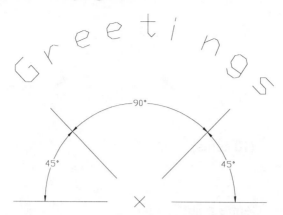

1   Use the DTEXT command to draw a single character. The Text should be at a rotation angle of –45°, as in the rightmost character above.

2.   Now use the ARRAY command to create a polar array. Set the number of objects to 9 and the angle to fill to 90° (10° between each letter). The centre point should be below and to the left of the original character, at an angle of 45°.

3.   Finally, use the DDEDIT command to edit each character so that the above message is produced.

Reflecting Objects with the MIRROR Command

Many objects possess symmetry of reflection, meaning that the object consists of two or more identical parts, with one section being a 'mirror image' of the other. When drawing such objects, a considerable time saving may be made if only one section of the item is drawn, at which point the remaining sections may be generated by reflection. This process is illustrated in Figure 5–3.

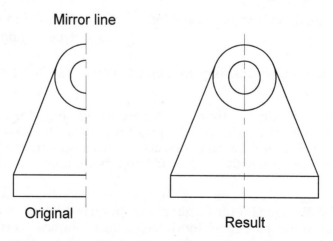

Figure 5–3. Constructing an object by reflection.

The MIRROR command may be started by selecting the **Mirror** option from the **Construct** pull-down menu, or by typing **MIRROR** (or **MI**) at the Command prompt.

Once the objects to be reflected have been selected, the next task is to indicate two points which lie on the mirror line. It is important to realize here that the mirror line may or may not exist. If it does exist, then you may optionally use object snap techniques to accurately identify the mirror line. If it does not exist, then two coordinates may be entered using any of the normal methods.

You are finally asked whether the original objects should be erased or retained. (In the example of Figure 5–3, the original objects <u>are</u> retained.)

Drawing Exercise 13 Constructing Objects by Reflection

| Step 1 | Step 2 | Step 3 |

1.   Use appropriate drawing commands to produce the object shown in step 1.

2.   Reflect this object horizontally, as shown in step 2 above.

3.   Reflect the resulting object vertically to produce the completed object (step 3).

4.   Finally, draw horizontal and vertical centre lines to emphasize the symmetrical nature of the component.

An important aspect of the MIRROR command is how textual information behaves during reflection. Should the reflected Text appear backwards or upside down (or both) after reflection, for example? This behaviour is controlled by the MIRRTEXT setting. A value of 1 causes reflected Text to appear inverted, while a value of 0 gives normal Text, as shown in Figure 5–4.

Figure 5–4. The behaviour of Text during reflection.

Producing Fillets and Chamfers

Fillets and chamfers are common features of engineering components. A rounded corner or *fillet* is often produced at the junction between two edges, particularly with cast components (or where the machine tool used to generate the surface has a rounded profile). Chamfers are often produced when sharp edges are removed from a component, possibly as a result of filing.

AutoCAD LT can automatically generate fillets and chamfers using the FILLET and CHAMFER commands respectively, as shown in Figure 5–5.

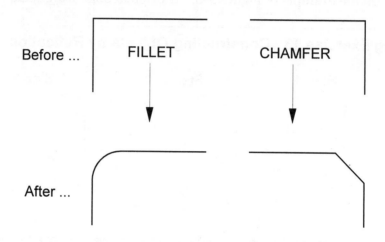

Figure 5–5. Creating fillets and chamfers.

The Command dialogue offered by these two commands is quite similar, as shown below.

Command: **FILLET**   - Or type **F** here.
Polyline/Radius/<Select first object>:

Command: **CHAMFER**   - Or type **CF** here.
Polyline/Distances/<Select first line>:

With the FILLET command, the first step is normally to define the fillet radius. Similarly, with the CHAMFER command, the first and second (i.e. 'horizontal' and 'vertical') chamfer distances are normally given before proceeding further. These values are stored as defaults and are used automatically when objects are subsequently filleted or chamfered.

Note: The FILLET and CHAMFER commands are sometimes used to 'tidy up' junctions between existing objects. The fillet radius or chamfer distances are normally set to zero here, thus giving a sharp corner. These commands also offer the advantage that objects will be <u>extended</u> if necessary to create a junction.

The normal method of operation is to point (using the mouse) to the two objects forming the junction of interest. A fillet or chamfer of the specified size is then generated automatically.

The Polyline option is used to apply fillets or chamfers to an existing Polyline, with each vertex of the Polyline being affected. The result of filleting a closed Polyline is shown in Figure 5–6.

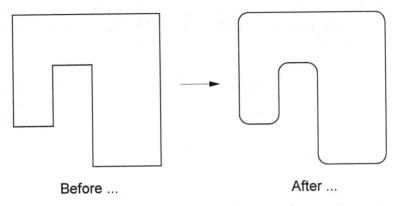

Before ...   After ...

Figure 5–6. Filleting an entire Polyline in a single operation.

Tutorial 15   Geometric Construction using Fillets

The FILLET command is useful where complex objects must be constructed from one or more blended radii. At first glance, it may appear that this type of problem cannot be solved, due to the lack of specific drawing details. In fact, the FILLET command allows the problem to be solved quite easily.

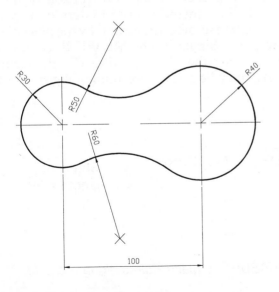

1. Draw two Circles of radius 30 and 40 units respectively, with a distance between centres of 100 units.

2. Use the FILLET command to blend two arcs between these Circles, of radius 50 and 60 units respectively.

3. Remove the unwanted (inner) portions of each Circle, by using the TRIM command.

Note: A similar result may be obtained by using the **CIRCLE TTR** command (Tangent, Tangent and Radius).

Offsetting Existing Objects

The OFFSET command is used to create a new object which runs <u>parallel</u> to an existing object. The command sequence consists of choosing the 'path' to be taken by the new object and then selecting the original object (a Line, Arc, Circle, Donut or Polyline).

To begin the OFFSET command, select the **Offset** option from the **Construct** pull-down menu, or type **OFFSET** (or **OF**) at the Command prompt. The command dialogue then continues as shown below.

Offset distance or Through <Through>:   - Enter a <u>distance</u>, or give a
                                          coordinate, which the new
                                          object must pass <u>through</u>.

Select object to offset: - Do so.

If an offset <u>distance</u> is given, rather than an actual coordinate, then AutoCAD LT asks for further clarification of the new object's position. Simply use the mouse to click (anywhere) on the side of the original, where the new object should be placed.

DIVIDE and MEASURE

DIVIDE and MEASURE are used to place Point objects at regular intervals along an existing object such as a Line, Arc, Circle or Polyline. (These Points are normally used as object snap reference points for the construction of more complex drawing features.) The DIVIDE command is used to divide the perimeter of the selected object into the specified number of sections by the placement of a series of Points (as its name implies). Similarly, the MEASURE command places Points at measured intervals along the given profile. The distinction between these two similar commands may be seen by examining Figure 5-7.

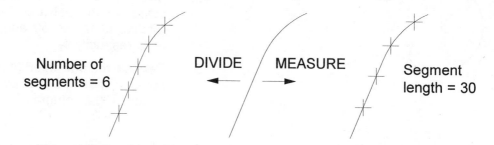

Figure 5-7. Using DIVIDE and MEASURE to place Points along a profile.

Note: DIVIDE and MEASURE are new introductions with AutoCAD LT, Release 2, although they are established features of the full version of AutoCAD.

6   Advanced Drawing Commands

Introduction

In the earlier chapters, basic concepts relating to AutoCAD LT were introduced. This chapter introduces a range of advanced features which enable you to make the most of this powerful CAD system. Topics covered here include:

- ❑   Blocks and Attributes;
- ❑   Layers;
- ❑   Dimensions;
- ❑   Hatching;
- ❑   Isometric drawing;
- ❑   User coordinate systems;
- ❑   Simple 3D drawing;
- ❑   Point filters and tracking;
- ❑   Inquiry commands;
- ❑   Drawing efficiency;

Blocks and Attributes

A basic feature of AutoCAD LT is that it is possible to 'insert' one drawing into another! This principle allows drawings to be created in a modular fashion, with sub-modules being drawn first (as separate drawings) and then assembled later.

There are many advantages to be had from adopting a modular approach, particularly in applications such as electronic design, where standard symbols exist for each type of component. A separate drawing may be created for each form of component, thus allowing the design to be constructed using a building block approach.

These standard symbols would normally be gathered together to form a *symbol library*. The use of such a library speeds up drawing creation, because a particular symbol need only be created once. It can also encourage conformity between different drawings, if a particular set of symbols is adopted as a standard.

AutoCAD LT refers to these symbols or sub-modules as *Blocks*. Closely associated with Blocks are *Attributes*, which are used to hold Textual information linked to a Block definition. These Attributes may be either visible or invisible, and can be either fixed (constant) or variable. Attributes allow the graphical information contained in a Block definition to be associated with the kind of textual data that would normally be found in a computerized database. For example, separate Attributes might be used to hold the description, stock number, and cost of a particular component, while the Block itself provides the graphical symbol. Attributes may be viewed and edited during the Block insertion process, or may be altered at a later stage. It is also possible to extract Attribute values from a drawing to produce a *parts list* or *bill of materials*.

A possible source of confusion regarding the use of Blocks is the wide range of methods which exist for their creation and use. In fact there are two basic possibilities. The Block definition is either stored as part of the current drawing, or as a separate drawing.

If a Block definition exists as a separate drawing, then it may be gathered together with other related Blocks (in a sub-directory perhaps) and used to form a symbol library. These Blocks are then available for use with any future drawing project.

The second method is to store the Block definition as an integral part of the current drawing. Such internally stored Blocks are available within the current drawing only, and cannot be accessed by other drawings. The main advantage of using this approach is a reduction in the size of the drawing database. It is important to realize here that a Block definition is stored only once within a drawing, followed by details of each *insertion* of the Block. This is more efficient than copying a group of objects many times, which results in separate storage of each item.

Once an externally defined Block has been inserted into the current drawing, then it becomes an internally defined Block (an integral part of the present drawing). Further insertions of the same Block make use of the internal Block definition, rather than reading the external drawing file. This is fine where Blocks represent standard components, which are unlikely to change, but it may cause problems where the original Block definition is expected to change over time. Consider an engineering assembly drawing as an example, where separate drawings are used for each component or sub-assembly. If a standard component is altered in some way, then any drawings which use this item must be updated automatically. AutoCAD LT refers to this type of Block as an *External Reference*. External References are not permanently stored in the current drawing. Instead, if a drawing is opened which contains one or more External References, then the associated drawing files are opened automatically, thus ensuring that drawing is up to date. It is even possible to explicitly reload an External Reference, if there is reason to believe that the referenced drawing file may have altered.

Table 6–1 summarizes the range of commands which is available for use with Blocks and Attributes.

Table 6–1(a). Block creation commands.

Command	Description of operation performed
BMAKE	Creates a Block as part of the current drawing (dialogue box).
BLOCK	Creates a Block as part of the current drawing (command line).
WBLOCK	Creates a Block as a separate drawing file.
SAVE	Saves the current drawing. (The BASE command may be used to move the 'insertion point', prior to saving the file, if this is not the origin.)

Table 6–1(b). Block insertion commands.

Command	Description of operation performed
INSERT	Inserts a Block or drawing file into the current drawing (command line).
DDINSERT	Inserts a Block or drawing file into the current drawing (dialogue box).
XREF	The XREF command's Attach option inserts a drawing file into the drawing as an external reference.

Table 6–1(c). Attribute creation and editing commands.

Command	Description of operation performed
ATTDEF	Creates an Attribute (command line).
DDATTDEF	Creates an Attribute (dialogue box).
DDEDIT	Allows basic Attribute (and Text) editing (dialogue box).
DDMODIFY	Advanced Attribute editing (dialogue box).
DDATTE	Edits Block related Attributes after insertion (dialogue box).
ATTEDIT	Edits Block related Attributes after insertion (command line).
DDATTEXT	Extracts Attribute data from a drawing (dialogue box).
ATTEXT	Extracts Attribute data from a drawing (command line).

Table 6–1(d). Miscellaneous Block related commands.

Command	Description of operation performed
BASE	Defines or modifies the drawing's 'insertion point' (used when the current drawing is inserted into another drawing).
EXPLODE	Decomposes a Block into its constituent parts, allowing individual editing (*X*, *Y* and *Z* scales must all be equal).
PURGE	Removes unreferenced Block definitions from the current drawing. (The PURGE command must be issued immediately after opening the drawing.)
XBIND	Causes the specified external reference dependent feature to become a permanent part of the current drawing. (The XREF command offers a Bind option which attaches the <u>entire</u> external reference to the current drawing.)

Table 6–1(e). Block related settings (system variables).

Command	Description of operation performed.
ATTDIA	If Attribute requesting is enabled (see ATTREQ setting), then ATTDIA controls whether this uses the DDATTE command's dialogue box, or command line prompting.
ATTDISP	Controls the visibility of Attributes in the current drawing.
ATTREQ	Controls whether Attribute values are requested automatically during Block insertion, or later (manually) using the DDATTE command.

Creating and Inserting Simple Blocks

This section explains how to create a Block definition as part of the current drawing, or as a separate drawing file. Once a Block definition has been created, the appropriate command is then used to insert the pre-defined Block into a new drawing. The BMAKE, WBLOCK and DDINSERT commands are discussed here, all of which make use of dialogue boxes.

The first step to creating a Block definition is to use normal AutoCAD LT drawing commands to produce the required graphical symbol. At this stage the BMAKE command may be started, which will display the dialogue box of Figure 6–1.

```
┌──────────────────────────────────────────────────┐
│                Block Definition                    │
│                                                    │
│  Block name: [                ]   ☐ Unnamed        │
│  ┌ Base Point ──────────────┐                      │
│  │ ┌──────────────────────┐ │ ┌──────────────────┐ │
│  │ │    Select Point <    │ │ │  Select Objects < │ │
│  │ └──────────────────────┘ │ └──────────────────┘ │
│  │ X:  [ 0        ]          │  Number found: 0     │
│  │ Y:  [ 0        ]          │ ┌──────────────────┐ │
│  │ Z:  [ 0        ]          │ │ List Block Names...│ │
│  │                          │ └──────────────────┘ │
│  └──────────────────────────┘  ☒ Retain Entities   │
│       ┌──────┐  ┌────────┐  ┌────────┐              │
│       │  OK  │  │ Cancel │  │ Help...│              │
│       └──────┘  └────────┘  └────────┘              │
└──────────────────────────────────────────────────┘
```

Figure 6–1. Using BMAKE to store a Block as part of the current drawing.

Next, give the Block a suitably descriptive name, via the edit box at the top of the dialogue box. Then, select the insertion base point by clicking the **Select Point** button, or by manually editing the X, Y and Z areas. (The cross hairs will 'snap' to this point during subsequent insertion of this Block.) Finally, click the **Select objects** button to choose the objects which will form the Block and then click **OK**. (If the **Retain Entities** checkbox is enabled, then the selected objects will still be visible after the Block has been defined.)

The Block now exists as a named Block within the current drawing. If you want to make this Block available to other drawings then the WBLOCK command should be used.

To start the WBLOCK command, use the pull-down menu system to select **File**, **Import/Export** and **Block Out...** in that order, or type **WBLOCK** (or **W**) at the Command prompt.

The command begins by asking you to enter the required drawing filename by using the displayed dialogue box. Once this has been completed, the command continues as shown below.

Block name: - Enter the name of an existing internal Block (as created by the BMAKE command), or press ⏎ here to select objects from the current drawing.

Insertion base point: - Select the insertion base point.

Select objects: - Do so.

At this stage, you should notice some disk activity as the Block is stored as a drawing file, and the selected objects will disappear from the screen.

Notice from the previous command dialogue that you have the choice of selecting currently visible objects to form the Block, or of selecting a previously defined internal Block. Thus you can use WBLOCK to make internal Blocks available to other drawings by saving them as individual drawing files!

The DDINSERT command is used to place a previously defined Block into the current drawing, which will cause the dialogue box of Figure 6-2 to be displayed.

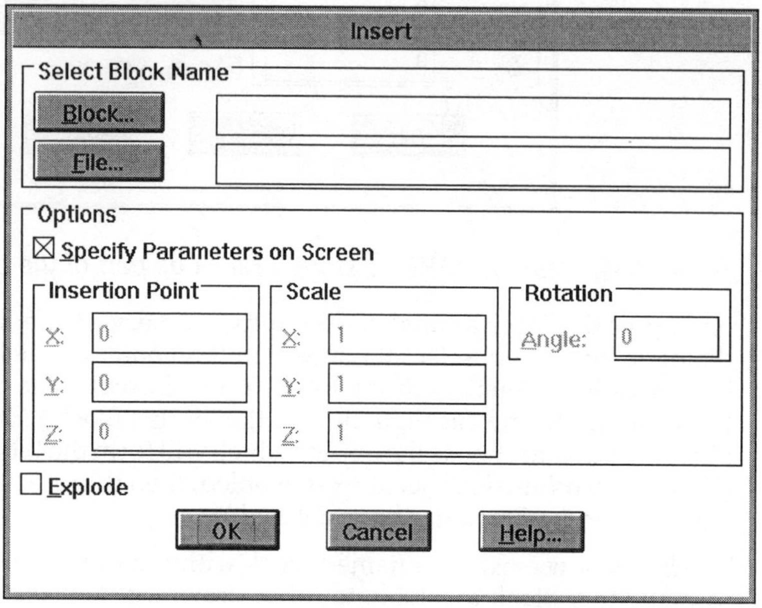

Figure 6–2. The DDINSERT command's dialogue box.

As we have already seen, Block definitions can exist as part of the current drawing, or may be stored as separate drawing files. Thus the first step is to click either the **Block...** or **File...** button, as appropriate, and then make a selection from the displayed subsidiary dialogue box.

The central section allows the Block's insertion point, scale factors and rotation angle to be specified using a series of edit boxes. It is normally quicker to give this information at a later stage, by enabling the **Specify Parameters on Screen** checkbox. (You are then prompted for this information in the Command area.)

Finally, you have the option of 'exploding' the Block during insertion. If this option is disabled (the default), then the Block may be edited as a single object. If it is exploded, then each object forming the Block is treated as a separate item.

Now that you are familiar with the methods used to create simple Blocks, the next step is create and edit Blocks containing Attributes, which is the subject of the next section.

Creating and Editing Attributes

Consider the Block definition of Figure 6–3, which consists of a simple graphical symbol, together with 3 Attributes.

Figure 6–3. A simple Block definition containing graphical and textual data.

This type of Block might be useful for the creation of a diagram showing the organizational structure of a company. Notice here that each Attribute has been given a name which is suggestive of its function. When this Block is inserted into a drawing, these generic labels would need to be replaced with details of real people. We might for example want a dialogue box to appear each time the Block is inserted, which is similar to that shown in Figure 6–4.

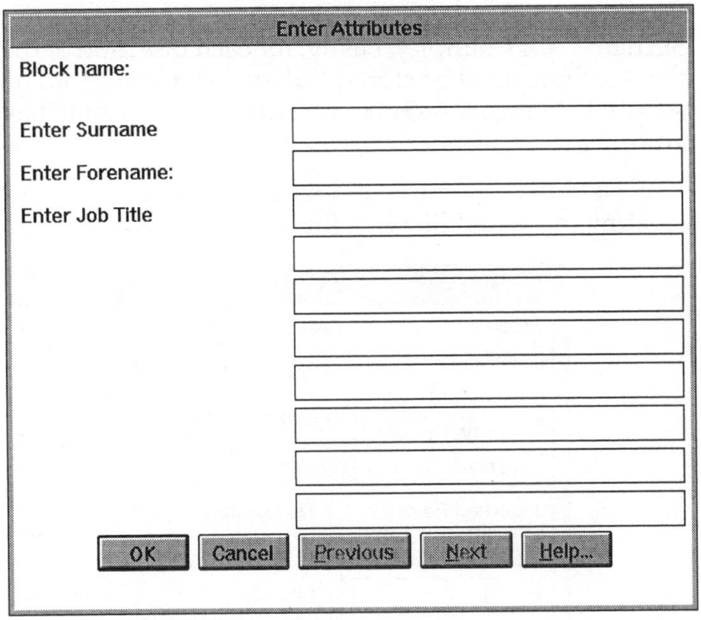

Enter Attributes
Block name:
Enter Surname
Enter Forename:
Enter Job Title
OK   Cancel   Previous   Next   Help...

Figure 6–4. The Attribute request dialogue box.

So, for each of our three Attributes, a suitable question or 'prompt' appears in the left margin. The edit box at the right side allows the user to type in a new value for the Attribute, or view the current (or default) value. In fact, the above dialogue box is available by starting the DDATTE command and then clicking on an existing Block. It also appears automatically when a Block is inserted, if the ATTREQ and ATTDIA settings have both been enabled (1 = on, 0 = off).

Figure 6–5 shows a simple drawing which has been produced by inserting several copies of the previously defined Block.

Figure 6–5. Multiple insertions of a Block with associated Attributes.

Looking at figures 6–3, 6–4 and 6–5, we can see that each Attribute contains three different types of information. Firstly, the Attribute is given a suitably descriptive name when the Block itself is defined. This name – called the *tag* – is normally descriptive of the <u>function</u> of the Attribute (FORENAME, SURNAME and JOB in Figure 6–3). Secondly, a suitable *prompt* must appear when the Edit Attributes dialogue box appears. The prompt must clearly identify the purpose of the Attribute to the user, and the kind of information that is expected ("Enter Surname" for example). Lastly, for each insertion of the Block, the actual *value* of the Attribute must be stored (Julian, Peter, Anne or Patricia for the FORENAME Attribute in Figure 6–5 above). Thus each Attribute has an associated *tag*, *prompt* and *value*.

The DDATTDEF command is normally used to define Attributes, prior to creating the actual Block definition, as shown in Figure 6–6.

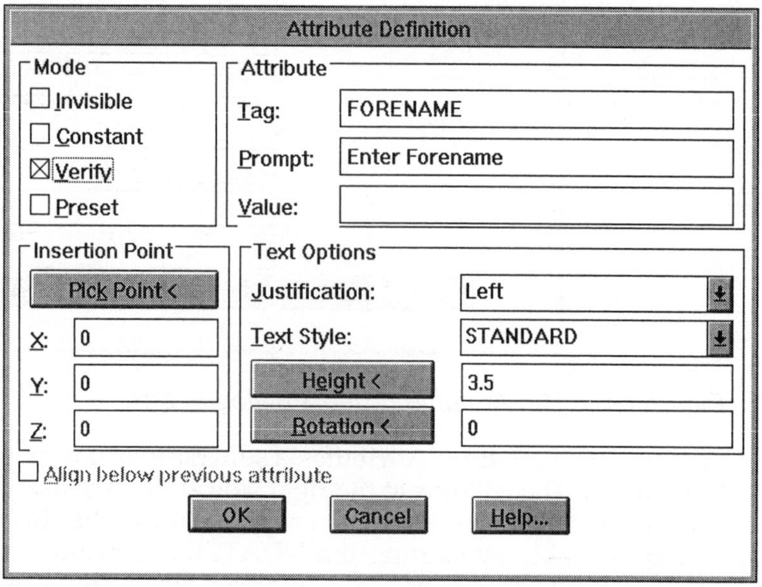

Figure 6–6. The Attribute Definition dialogue box (DDATTDEF command).

The DDATTDEF command may be started by selecting the **Define Attribute** option from the **Construct** pull-down menu, or by typing **DDATTDEF** (or **DAD**) at the Command prompt.

As, can be seen from Figure 6–6, the associated dialogue box consists of four main sections. The upper right area allows the previously discussed tag, prompt and value properties to be defined, while the lower half of the dialogue box controls textual and insertion point options. The upper left area contains four operating modes, which are referred to as Invisible, Constant, Verify and Preset. These modes are defined in Table 6–2 below.

Table 6–2. Attribute operating modes.

Operating Mode	Definition
Invisible	Suppresses the display of the Attribute after Block insertion. Use this option to prevent a cluttered display.
Constant	Causes the Attribute to automatically use the default value. Constant Attributes are not displayed (and hence cannot be altered) by the Edit Attributes dialogue box (DDATTE command).
Verify	Set this option to allow the user to verify or alter an Attribute value during Block insertion.
Preset	Similar to constant, but works only with command line Attribute prompting. (Ignore this mode if you normally use a dialogue box to request Attributes.)

Note: The ATTDISP system variable or setting may be used to control the visibility of Attributes in a drawing. Available options are **ON** – all Attributes visible, **OFF** – all Attributes invisible and **N** – Normal visibility (as controlled by the Invisible property of individual Attributes).

For an Attribute such as a person's surname, for example, it would not be appropriate to have a default value. The Verify operating mode would be used here to cause the Attribute to appear when the Enter Attributes dialogue box is displayed. (The Attribute could also be either visible or invisible, as set by the Invisible property.) Another type of Attribute, such as the stock number of a standard component might be expected to remain constant during its lifetime. In this case, a default value would be specified and the Constant operating mode would be enabled during the creation of the Attribute.

If you need to modify an Attribute after it has been created, then there are several possible approaches. For simple editing of tag, prompt and value properties, the DDEDIT command is the best option. The DDMODIFY command allows more detailed editing of single Attributes using a dialogue box. Finally, the ATTEDIT command permits editing of single or multiple Attributes from the Command line. Figure 6–7 shows the DDEDIT command's dialogue box, as an example.

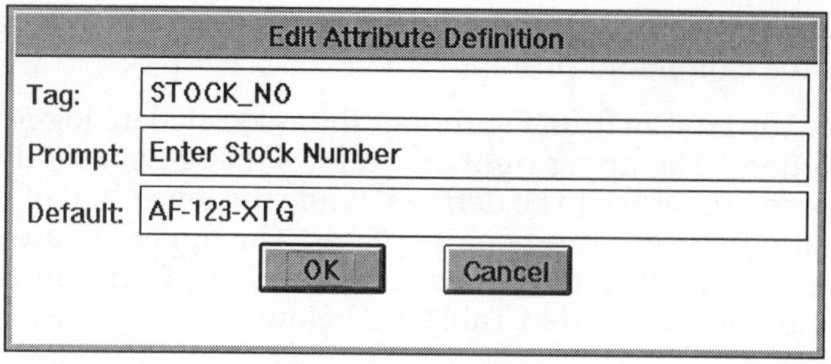

Figure 6–7. Using the DDEDIT command to edit an Attribute definition.

Drawing Exercise 14   Blocks and Attributes (Office Layout)

This drawing exercise demonstrates the creation and use of Blocks and Attributes.

The first stage is to create the two Blocks, as shown below which represent a computer and printer respectively.

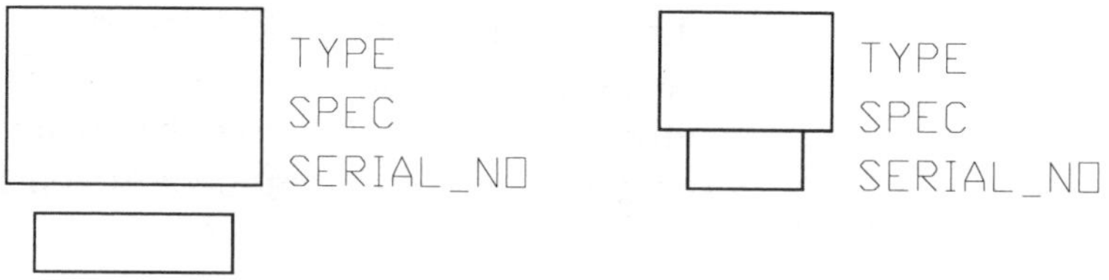

Each Block should have three Attributes. The TYPE Attribute is <u>constant</u> and will contain a description of the object (Computer or Printer). The SPEC Attribute holds the device specification (i.e. '486 DX2-66'), which is expected to vary from one item to the next (so Verify mode should be enabled). Lastly, a unique serial number should be entered for each item using the SERIAL_NO Attribute. The TYPE and SPEC Attributes should be visible, while the SERIAL_NO Attribute should be invisible.

Use your two Block definitions to create a simple office layout for a fictitious company.

Tips

❑   Use normal drawing commands to create the graphical symbol for each Block. (All sizes are at your discretion.)

❑   The DDATTDEF command allows an Attribute to be defined. To edit an Attribute, use the DDEDIT (or DDMODIFY) command.

❑   Use the BMAKE (or WBLOCK) command to create your Block definitions, followed by the DDINSERT command to insert each computer or printer into your office layout.

Working with Layers

When an object is drawn, such as a Line or Circle, it inherits certain *properties* which were in force at the time when the object was created. These properties include the drawing colour and linetype, which are used when the object is displayed on screen or printed.

Another object property is the *layer* on which the object has been placed. Layers are often used to 'group' related items together, thus making it easier to control them. A simple analogy is to imagine several transparent plastic sheets, each containing related items such as drawing information, Dimensions or annotations. The full drawing is visible when all of the plastic sheets (layers) are superimposed, but the visibility of individual layers may easily be controlled by adding or removing sheets. This is illustrated by Figure 6–8.

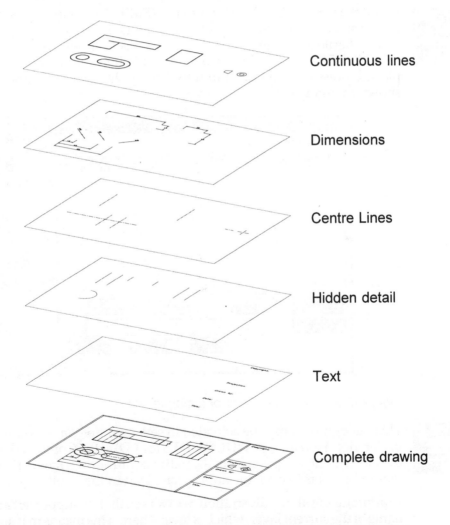

Figure 6–8. The arrangement of drawing information into separate layers.

As well as allowing new layers to be created, AutoCAD LT permits individual layers to have default properties such as colour or linetype. If an object is drawn on a particular layer, then it will normally inherit the linetype or colour which is associated with that layer. This is achieved by setting the default colour or linetype to the value BYLAYER. As an alternative, you can <u>explicitly</u> set an object property to a particular value, which will <u>override</u> the layer's default value.

Note: The control of colours and linetypes is a frequent source of confusion to new users of AutoCAD LT. The key here is to realize that the colour or linetype associated with a particular layer is only a default. This default value will be used <u>only</u> if the appropriate entity property is set to BYLAYER. (Use the DDCHPROP command to examine or alter properties associated with existing objects, or the DDEMODES to control the properties of any subsequently created entities.)

Recall that the DDEMODES command (Entity Creation Modes) was introduced in Chapter 3. This command is used to define basic entity properties, which are then inherited by any newly created objects. (Refer to Figure 3–14 for the DDEMODES command's dialogue box.) When the main dialogue box is displayed, press the **Layer...** button to display the Layer Control dialogue box, as shown in Figure 6–9.

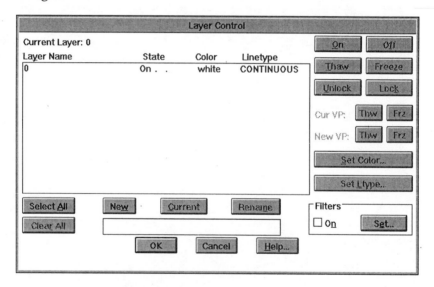

Figure 6–9. The Layer Control dialogue box.

This dialogue box may be activated in several other ways, according to personal preference. You can type **DDLMODES** (or **LD**) at the Command prompt, or select the **Layer Control** option from the **Settings** pull-down menu. Perhaps the easiest method of all is to click the appropriate icon in the Toolbar (see margin).

Examining the above illustration, we can see that the upper left area contains the name of the current layer, which is layer 0 here. This means that any objects which are subsequently drawn will be placed automatically on this layer. In fact, the list box in the central area, shows that the drawing has only <u>one</u> layer at present.

We can see from this single entry in the list box that layer 0 is *on* (meaning that it is visible on screen) and that it is drawn with a white, CONTINUOUS linetype.

To create a new layer, type the required layer name in the edit box (towards the bottom of the dialogue box) and then click the **New** button. A layer name can have up to 31 characters, with letters, digits and the special characters, dollar ($), hyphen (-) and underscore (_) all being allowed. (Spaces are not allowed.)

Once a layer has been created, its properties may then be altered. The first step is to highlight the required layer by clicking on its entry in the list box. Notice here that clicking once on a layer will select it, and that repeating this operation will unselect it. It is also possible to have more than one layer selected, which allows the properties of a group of layers to be altered in a single operation. With the required layer(s) highlighted, you can then modify the desired property, as explained below.

❑ Click the **Rename** button to alter the layer's name to that shown in the edit box.

❑ Click the **Current** button to cause subsequently drawn objects to be created on the selected layer (see the next page for another technique).

❑ Click the **On** or **Off** button to control the visibility of the selected layer in the drawing. (The PLOT command will only plot layers which are visible.)

❑ Click the **Set Color...** or **Set Ltype...** buttons to modify the layer's default colour or linetype respectively. (You must previously have loaded the required linetype using the LINETYPE LOAD command for its name to appear in the Select Linetype dialogue box.)

As well as turning layers on or off (hence controlling layer visibility) layers may also be *thawed* or *frozen*. The visual effect of freezing a layer is the same as turning it off, with the thaw option being equivalent to turning the layer on again. The difference is that objects on a frozen layer are completely ignored when the drawing is regenerated. This may significantly improve AutoCAD LT's performance when dealing with a complex drawing. A frozen layer is indicated by a letter 'F' to the right of the layer name in the dialogue box of Figure 6–9.

Another feature is the ability to *lock* a layer, which prevents users from editing existing objects on that layer. (This feature is intended to prevent accidental erasure or alteration of existing objects.) Bear in mind that it is still possible to create new objects on a locked layer, simply by making the locked layer current. If you subsequently need to edit objects on a locked layer, then highlight the layer and click the **Unlock** button. Locked layers are marked by the letter 'L' to the right of the layer name in the Layer Control dialogue box.

The Filters area of the DDLMODES command's dialogue box controls which layer names are displayed in the Layer Name list box. If the associated check box is enabled then only those layers which match the chosen criteria will be displayed.

We saw on the previous page that the Layer Control dialogue box could be used to make an existing layer current. AutoCAD LT also allows the current layer to be selected using a drop-down list, which is available in the Toolbar area, as shown in Figure 6–10.

Figure 6–10. Using the Toolbar to change the current layer.

To use this facility, you should have previously created the required layers, in the normal way. Having done so, this is certainly the quickest way to change between layers! (Notice, when you try this feature for the first time, that the colour of the Color Display button in the Toolbar changes automatically to reflect the current drawing colour, and that the name of the current layer is stored in a system variable called CLAYER.)

The behaviour of layers associated with Blocks is an important topic, and one which needs some explanation. What happens, for example, if an inserted Block contains objects which have been drawn on layers which are not present in the current drawing? What if the layer <u>does</u> exist in the current drawing, but has a different colour or linetype to that used when the Block was originally defined?

The following points answer these (and other) questions relating to Blocks and layers.

- ❑ Objects originally drawn on layer 0 are inserted into the <u>current</u> layer when the Block is inserted. (Recall that layer 0 is also the only layer which cannot be purged, even if it is unused in the current drawing – see Chapter 4.)

- ❑ Objects drawn with the logical colour or linetype BYBLOCK are drawn with the current colour or linetype respectively when they are inserted into the present drawing.

- ❑ If a Block definition contains a layer which is unused in the current drawing, then that layer is <u>created</u> automatically (inheriting its original colour and linetype). If the layer does exist but has a different colour or linetype, then the layer properties in the current drawing will take precedence.

- ❑ If any of the associated layers are frozen in the current drawing, then regeneration of the <u>entire</u> Block is suppressed.

- ❑ Layers which are dependent on inserted External References are renamed automatically, so that the Xref name precedes the original layer name (so layer CENTER in the Xref DWG would become layer DWG|CENTER).

Drawing Exercise 15   Layers, Linetypes and Prototype Drawings

The aim here is to create a prototype drawing which has the most commonly used drawing colours and linetypes already loaded, and associated with suitably named layers. (The use of this prototype drawing may save time during the creation of subsequent drawings.)

1.   Start a new drawing.

2.   Use the LINETYPE LOAD command to load the linetypes HIDDEN and CENTER into your drawing (linetype CONTINUOUS is available automatically).

3.   Use the DDLMODES command to create layers called CONTINUOUS, HIDDEN and CENTER. Associate an appropriate linetype and colour with each layer.

4.   Save the drawing with a suitably descriptive name (LT_PROTO.DWG for example).

5.   Start a new drawing, using the above prototype drawing, and confirm that you can select each of the layers (and linetypes) using the drop-down list in the Toolbar.

Hatching Enclosed Areas

It is common practice in engineering drawing to indicate sectional or cut-through views of a component, by shading the affected area with an appropriate pattern. The use of different patterns (or variations of the same pattern), is also used to emphasize the boundary between separate sub-components. In other applications, a particular style of hatching may be used to indicate the material from which an object is formed. (This is particularly true in the construction and mapping fields.)

AutoCAD LT Release 2 incorporates a powerful boundary hatch feature, which allows enclosed areas to be hatched, simply by indicating a point which is internal to the desired boundary. (This is a considerable improvement over the hatching capabilities of Release 1, where each object forming the boundary had to be selected individually.) The new boundary hatch facility also simplifies the treatment of internal 'islands' within the boundary, which are intended to be left unhatched.

The first step is use the normal AutoCAD LT drawing commands to create the region to be hatched. This must be an enclosed region, although (unlike Release 1), there is no need for the objects forming the boundary to be joined end-to-end. The BHATCH command may then be started, either by selecting the **Boundary Hatch** option from the **Draw** pull-down menu, by typing **BHATCH** at the Command prompt, or by clicking the appropriate icon in the Toolbox (see margin). The dialogue box of Figure 6–11 will then be displayed.

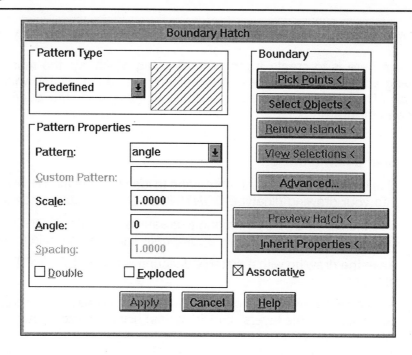

Figure 6–11. The Boundary Hatch dialogue box (BHATCH command).

The above dialogue box allows you to select the desired style of hatching by choosing options from the Pattern Type, Pattern Properties and Boundary areas.

As you would expect, the Boundary area is used to select the boundary (or boundaries) of the hatched area. The **Pick Points** button allows the area to be selected by indicating a point which is <u>inside</u> of the outermost boundary. (This is the preferred method in most situations, but alternatively, the **Select Objects** button may be used to indicate each object which forms the boundary.) In its default operating mode, the **Pick Points** option will automatically detect any internal boundaries or 'islands', which will be left unhatched when the hatch pattern is later applied. These internal boundaries may be removed manually by clicking the **Remove Islands** button and then selecting the highlighted boundary. The two possibilities are illustrated below.

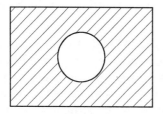

Internal island(s) detected
automatically

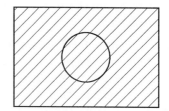

Internal Island(s) removed
manually

Figure 6–12. Controlling the hatching of internal islands.

You can also control how AutoCAD LT deals with internal boundaries by clicking on the **Advanced...** button, which will cause a subsidiary dialogue box to appear. With this dialogue box displayed on screen, the detection of internal islands may be prevented by disabling the **Island Detection** checkbox. A more powerful level of control is provided by the **Style** drop-down list, which allows the *normal, outer,* or *ignore* hatching modes to be selected. In 'normal' mode, all internal boundaries are detected, and these are left alternately hatched and unhatched. As its name implies, the 'outer' operating mode causes the outermost region (only) to be hatched. (This is the area between the two outermost boundaries.) Finally, in 'ignore' mode, all internal detail is disregarded and the entire area is hatched.

The Advanced Options dialogue box provides a graphical display which shows the effect of selecting each hatching mode. This makes it easy to select the correct operating mode for a particular application. Notice from this display that you can select Text as one of the internal boundaries, and that this prevents the Text from being hatched through (which would make it difficult to read).

Clicking on the **Pattern** drop-down list in the Pattern Properties area allows the hatch pattern itself to be selected. Once again, there are three possible operating modes, as selected by the **Pattern Type** drop-down list. These are *pre-defined, user-defined* and *custom.* The 'pre-defined' operating mode is active by default, and this causes hatch patterns to be selected from the standard hatch pattern file (ACLT.PAT or ACLTISO.PAT). With this mode active, the **Scale** and **Angle** edit boxes are used to fine tune the appearance of the selected hatch pattern on screen. The 'user-defined' option creates a simple pattern based on parallel lines with the **Angle** and **Spacing** options being used to control the detail of the hatch pattern. Notice here that selecting the **Double** checkbox causes a second set of lines to be drawn at 90° to the first, when the hatch pattern is applied. The final option allows a 'custom' or special purpose hatch pattern to be loaded. This is expected to exist in a plain or ASCII-only text file, the name of which is given in the **Custom Pattern** edit box. (We will look at the creation of custom hatch patterns in Chapter 8.)

Note: To use the same settings as an existing hatched area, click on the **Inherit Properties** button in the BHATCH command's main dialogue box.

Once the desired hatch boundary and pattern have been chosen, the next step is to see how the selected options will appear on the finished drawing. To do this, select the **Preview Hatch** option, by clicking the button of the same name. At this stage, the Boundary Hatch dialogue box will disappear temporarily, to allow the hatched area to be viewed. Pressing ↵ causes the dialogue box to reappear, at which point you can press the **Apply** button to make the hatch pattern permanent, or modify the hatch parameters, before proceeding further.

The editing of previously hatched areas is an important topic, which needs some explanation. A hatched area is normally treated as a single object (unless you enable the **Exploded** checkbox when the hatched area is created), so if you attempt to erase a single line, this will result in the entire hatched area being erased. (You can also use the EXPLODE command to break up existing hatched areas into separate lines, thus allowing them to be edited individually.)

A new feature in AutoCAD LT Release 2 is the provision of *associative* hatching, (similar in principle to associative dimensioning which is considered in the next section). In earlier releases of the software, a hatched region would remain <u>unaltered</u> if the original boundary was modified in some way. This meant that an alteration to any part of the boundary would normally require the hatched area to be first erased, and then redrawn. With associative hatching, an alteration to any part of the boundary, causes the related hatched area to be re-hatched automatically (based on the <u>new</u> boundary), which provides a considerable saving in editing time. (Be careful to ensure that the boundary itself remains 'closed' during any editing.)

If you need to alter the hatch properties (pattern, scale etc.) of an existing associatively hatched area, then use the HATCHEDIT command. This uses the same dialogue box as the BHATCH command, but with certain options disabled. You can start the HATCHEDIT command by selecting the **Edit Hatch** option from the **Modify** menu, or by typing **HATCHEDIT** at the Command prompt.

Tutorial 16   Associative Hatching using the BHATCH Command

This tutorial demonstrates the hatching of enclosed areas using the BHATCH command.

1.   Use normal AutoCAD LT drawing commands to create a drawing similar to that shown below, minus the hatched areas (with all sizes at your discretion).

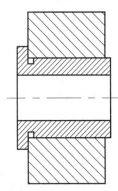

2.   Start the BHATCH command and hatch the uppermost area (only) using a similar pattern and scale factor to that shown. Now reduce the scale factor by 50% and rotate the hatch pattern by 90° before hatching the upper half of the central component.

3.   Use the **Inherit Properties** option from the Boundary Hatch dialogue box to pick up the hatch pattern settings from each of the hatched areas. Using these parameters, hatch the two lower regions.

4.   Use the STRETCH command to alter the width of your drawing and notice that the hatched area is adjusted automatically. (This is associative hatching in action!)

Adding Dimensions to a Drawing

As we have already seen, a basic principle of AutoCAD LT is that the drawing should be entered <u>actual</u> size, with 1 drawing unit being equal to 1 unit of measurement in the design (1 inch, 1 millimetre etc.). Any scaling, such as that required to fit the drawing onto a piece of paper during plotting or printing, is then carried out by the software, rather than by the user.

An important advantage which comes from the accurate entry of drawing geometry is that dimensional information may be added to the design in a semi-automated fashion, with all lengths and angles being calculated by the program, based on the indicated reference coordinates. Thus AutoCAD LT can draw a complete Dimension, including the dimension line itself, the dimension text and any extension lines, based simply on the indicated reference points. These Dimensions are also *associative*, meaning that they are updated automatically if associated objects are edited. Anyone who has produced complex drawings with pencil and paper, will surely appreciate the convenience of AutoCAD LT's automated dimensioning features!

Although dimensioning can seem complex to the newcomer, there are only five basic types of Dimension, as shown in Figure 6–13.

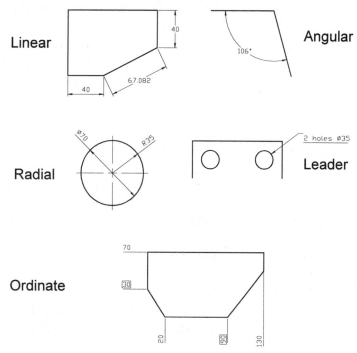

Figure 6–13. The five types of Dimension created by AutoCAD LT.

Dimensions are created using the DIM or DIM1 commands. As its name implies, the DIM1 command creates a <u>single</u> Dimension, after which control is returned to the Command prompt. In contrast, the DIM command allows <u>multiple</u> Dimensions to be created, after entering a special 'dimension mode', where the normal Command prompt is replaced by the prompt 'Dim:'.

Once dimensioning mode has been entered (as indicated by the Dim prompt), a range of dimensioning sub-commands become available. These may be classified into four distinct functional groups:-

❑ creation of new Dimensions;

❑ modification of existing Dimensions;

❑ utility commands;

❑ control of dimension styles.

These sub-commands are summarized in Table 6–3, parts (a) – (d).

Table 6–3(a). Dimension drawing sub-commands.

Sub-command	Function
HORIZONTAL	Draws a linear, horizontal Dimension.
VERTICAL	Draws a linear, vertical Dimension.
ALIGNED	Draws a linear Dimension, which is aligned with the indicated extension line endpoints.
ROTATED	Draws a linear Dimension whose baseline is rotated through a specified angle (0° is equivalent to the Dimension being horizontal and below).
BASELINE	Draws successive linear Dimensions directly beneath the original, with each Dimension sharing a single datum edge.
CONTINUE	Draws successive linear Dimensions in a chain, the end of one Dimension marking the start of the next.
ORDINATE	Dimensions either the X, or Y coordinate of a particular feature, relative to the drawing origin (or UCS origin).
DIAMETER	Indicates the diameter of a Circle, or circular Arc.
RADIUS	Indicates the radius of a Circle or circular Arc.
CENTER	Marks the centre of a Circle or Arc with either a centre mark (a small cross), or a pair of centre lines, as controlled by the current dimension style.
LEADER	Draws an arrowed line (or series of linked lines) with an associated textual message.

Table 6–3(b). Dimension modification sub-commands.

Sub-command	Function
TEDIT	Alters the position and angle of the text associated with a Dimension.
HOMETEXT	Returns the text associated with a Dimension to its default or *home* position.
NEWTEXT	Changes the text string associated with the current Dimension.
TROTATE	Alters the angle of the text associated with one or more Dimensions.
OBLIQUE	Causes extension lines to be drawn at an oblique angle, rather than perpendicular.
UPDATE	Updates the selected Dimension(s), using the settings associated with current dimension style.

Table 6–3(c). Utility dimensioning commands.

Sub-command	Function
EXIT	Exits dimensioning mode and restores the Command prompt. (Pressing Ctrl + C has the same effect.)
REDRAW	Redraws the current viewport.
STYLE	Changes the current text style, (which is used when a Dimension is created, or updated).
UNDO	Reverses the effect of the previous dimension sub-command.

Table 6–3(d). Control of dimension styles.

Sub-command	Function
OVERRIDE	Allows the value of one or more settings (dimension variables) associated with the selected Dimension(s) to be overridden.
RESTORE	Sets the values of all dimension variables to be those associated with a selected dimension style.
SAVE	Creates a new (named) dimension style, based on the current values of all dimension variables (or settings).
VARIABLES	Displays the values of all dimension variables associated with the current dimension style.

Dimensioning sub-commands which actually <u>create</u> new Dimensions may be activated by selecting the appropriate option from the **Draw** pull-down menu. (This is much simpler than trying to remember the name of the appropriate dimensioning sub-command.) Similarly, sub-commands which <u>edit</u> existing Dimensions are available under the **Ed<u>i</u>t Dimension** option of the **<u>M</u>odify** pull-down menu.

Dimension *styles* and dimension *variables* are closely related. AutoCAD LT uses a series of internal system variables to control the appearance of Dimensions on screen. These variables control every aspect of the Dimension, from the height, position and orientation of the textual message, to the size of any arrows (if used). Each Dimension variable has a unique name which begins with the letters 'DIM'. (The variable DIMTXT for example, controls the height of dimension text – Other dimension variables are listed in the *AutoCAD LT User's Guide*.)

A typical AutoCAD LT drawing may contain several named dimension styles, each of which is associated with a particular set of dimension variable values. At any time, <u>one</u> of these named dimension styles is *current*. When a new Dimension is drawn, it inherits the values of all dimension variables in the current dimension style, which in turn controls the <u>appearance</u> of the Dimension.

Related groups of Dimensions will share the same basic appearance, if they are drawn with the same dimension style. Thus, the careful use of dimension styles in a drawing, encourages uniformity in dimensioning practice. (It is even possible to store dimension styles in prototype drawings...)

AutoCAD LT provides a range of dimensioning sub-commands which control the use of dimension styles. However, most users will prefer to use the DDIM command, which performs the same function using a series of dialogue boxes. The DDIM command will be examined shortly, but first we must consider the creation of the five basic types of Dimension (first encountered in Figure 6–13).

Note: The widespread use of dialogue boxes in AutoCAD LT means that you are more likely to interact with internal system variables by changing *settings* in a dialogue box, rather than by using the command line. This is particularly true with dimensioning, where the DDIM command is the preferred method of controlling dimension styles. (In addition, most CAD users do not have a background in computer programming, where the use of *constants* and *variables* has its origin.) This book therefore uses the term *setting* in preference to *system variable*, wherever possible.

Linear Dimensions

Linear Dimensions are used to measure the distance between two points along a particular measurement axis. These Dimensions are further subdivided, based on the orientation of this measurement axis, as shown in Figure 6–14.

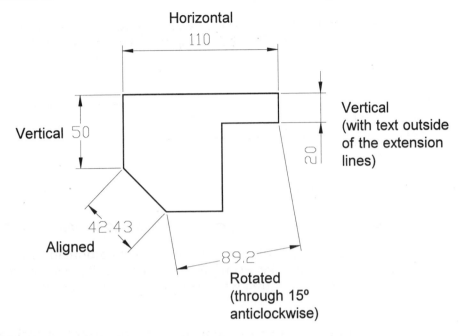

Figure 6–14. The four types of linear Dimension.

These types of Dimension are available from a sub-menu, which is displayed when the **Linear Dimensions** option is selected from the **Draw** pull-down menu. A typical command dialogue would be

Command: **DIM1**	- Draws a single Dimension.
Dim: **HORIZONTAL**	- Select a linear horizontal dimension type.
First extension line origin or RETURN to select:	- Indicate point *P1*.
Second extension line origin:	- Indicate point *P2*.
Dimension line location (Text/Angle):	- Indicate point *P3*.

The first thing to notice is that you have the choice of manually indicating the two extension line origins (the points where the Dimension seems to 'touch' the object being dimensioned), or you can press ↵ to select a <u>single</u> existing object, such as a Line or Arc. If you decide to manually indicate these two extension line origins, then it is important to use snap or object snap to accurately align these points!

Note: A common mistake made by beginners is to fail to use object snap when indicating extension line origins. This can result in the default dimension text showing values such as 18.98 (for example), rather than the expected value (of 20 in this case).

The next step is to indicate the position of the dimension line itself, which also controls the length of the extension lines. This process is illustrated by Figure 6–15.

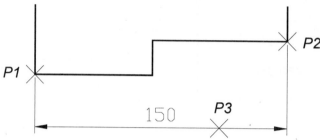

Figure 6–15. The control points used to create a simple Dimension.

Notice that the default text value is obtained automatically by measuring the <u>horizontal</u> distance between points P1 and P2. (You can override this value by selecting the Text option when you are asked for point P3.)

A real drawing is likely to contain groups of linear Dimensions, often in close physical proximity. These Dimensions can be drawn end-to-end, in a 'chain', or may be 'stacked', one on-top of another. These two possibilities are shown in Figure 6–16.

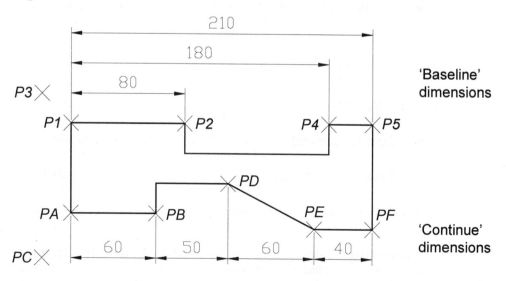

Figure 6–16. The BASELINE and CONTINUE dimensioning sub-commands.

With both methods, the first step is to draw a single linear Dimension in the normal way (points *PA–PC* or *P1–P3* in Figure 6–16). At this point the BASELINE or CONTINUE dimensioning sub-command is entered (or selected from the **Draw** pull-down menu). Further Dimensions may then be created, simply by entering the coordinate of each <u>second</u> extension line origin (points *P4–P5* or *PD–PF* in Figure 6–16).

The DDIM command, which will be considered shortly, controls many aspects of the appearance of Dimensions, and allows different dimension styles to be created and made current. Some of the more basic aspects of Dimensions, such as the numerical precision of the displayed dimension text, or the appearance of the text itself may also be controlled using standard AutoCAD LT commands.

The DDUNITS command was first introduced in Chapter 2 (Figure 2–14 and the associated text). This command controls not only the units used for linear and angular measurement, but also the numerical precision of any displayed values. By altering the settings associated with this dialogue box, you can control the number of decimal places which are used when linear or angular Dimensions are <u>subsequently</u> drawn. (To update the text associated with an <u>existing</u> Dimension, you must first use the DDUNITS command to change the numeric precision and then issue the UPDATE dimensioning sub-command to modify the chosen Dimension.)

Similarly, the textual settings used to draw the dimension text are taken from the text style which is <u>current</u> at the time when the Dimension is created (or updated). As we saw in Chapter 3, the STYLE command is used to create new text styles (also available by choosing the **Text Style...** option from the **Settings** pull-down menu). You can also view or alter the current text style by selecting the appropriate option from the DDEMODES command's main (Entity Creation Modes) dialogue box.

Tutorial 17 **Numeric Precision and Text Styles with Dimensions**

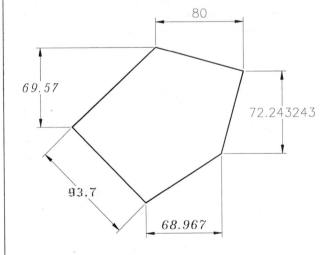

The aim here is to control the number of decimal places displayed by Dimensions, and the text style used.

1. Turn off the snap feature. Use freehand drawing techniques to draw an irregular polygon, similar to that shown.

2. Use the DDUNITS command to control numeric precision and the STYLE command to control the active text style. After selecting appropriate values, create linear Dimensions similar to those shown.

Radial Dimensions

Radial Dimensions allow Circles and Arcs to be dimensioned. Using these sub-commands, you can dimension a radius or a diameter, and optionally add a centre mark or a pair of centre lines. Some of the possibilities are shown in Figure 6–17.

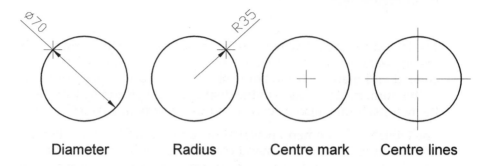

Diameter   Radius   Centre mark   Centre lines

Figure 6–17. The available range of radial Dimensions.

When diameter or radius type Dimensions are created, it is only necessary to indicate a single point on the circumference of the Circle or Arc. This coordinate serves the dual purpose of selecting the object to be dimensioned, and also indicates the position of the dimension line and text label. (You also have the option of moving the text further away from the dimensioned feature by indicating a *leader* length.)

Whether or not a centre mark or a pair of centre lines is added automatically to the radius or diameter Dimension, depends on whether the dimension line is drawn inside or outside of the dimensioned feature. If the dimension line is drawn <u>inside</u> (which is the default – as shown in Figure 6–17), then centre marks or centre lines are <u>not</u> drawn. The position of dimension arrows and text may be controlled using the DIMTIX and DIMTOFL system variables, but it is easier to control these settings using the DDIM command, due to its range of user-friendly dialogue boxes! (To be precise, you would start the DDIM command and then click on the **Dimension Line...** button. The **Force Interior Lines** checkbox would then be enabled or disabled, as required. Look ahead to Figure 6–22 to see this dialogue box.)

You can add centre marks and centre lines <u>manually</u> by using the CENTER dimensioning sub-command. A quick way to select the CENTER sub-command is to pick **Draw**, **Radial Dimensions** and **Center Mark** in that order from the pull-down menu system. The type of feature which is produced (centre mark or centre lines) depends on the current value of the DIMCEN system variable. You can alter this variable from the Command line, but it is easier to use the DDIM command. The appropriate dialogue box may be found by pressing the **Extension Lines...** button, after starting the DDIM command. This is illustrated in Figure 6–18.

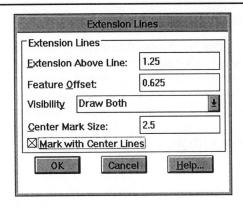

Figure 6–18. Controlling centre lines and marks using the DDIM command.

Angular Dimensions

As you would expect, this type of Dimension is used to indicate an included angle, such as that between two Lines. A typical example is shown in Figure 6–19, together with the selection points used during its creation.

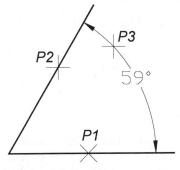

Figure 6–19. A typical angular Dimension.

The command sequence is straightforward, as shown below.

Command: **DIM1**	- Draws a single Dimension.
Dim: **ANGULAR**	- Select an angular dimension type.
Select arc, circle, line, or RETURN:	- Select first line (*P1*).
Second line:	- Select second line (*P2*).
Dimension line location (Text/Angle):	- Indicate point *P3*.
Dimension text <59>:	- Press ↵ to accept.

Adding Annotations with Leaders

A *leader* is simply an arrowed line (or a series of linked lines), with an associated textual message. This feature is typically used to add annotations to a drawing, where the arrowed line indicates the feature of interest, and also provides a link to the annotation. Leaders are also useful where dimensional information cannot be placed in its default location, due to the possibility of it obscuring important detail, or of creating a cluttered drawing. A typical leader is shown in Figure 6–20, together with the coordinates used during its creation.

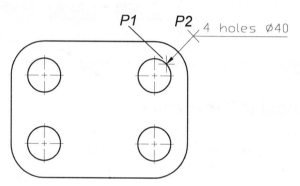

Figure 6–20. A typical leader, used to add an annotation to a drawing.

This is this simplest form of leader, with a single arrowed line pointing to the message. You can indicate as many coordinates as you wish when defining the leader line. AutoCAD LT prompts for the textual message after you press the ↵ key. (Notice here that the '%%c' escape sequence has been used to obtain a 'diameter' symbol.)

Unlike other types of Dimension, leaders are not *associative*, so they are not automatically updated if associated objects are edited. Normal AutoCAD LT commands are used to edit leaders, including the DDEDIT command to edit textual messages.

Ordinate Dimensions

An ordinate Dimension measures the distance from an origin along a single axis (hence a coordinate is the junction between two or more ordinates). By default, the distance measured is from the drawing origin, although, as we will see later, you can optionally define your own origin (called a *User Coordinate System* or *UCS*).

The ORDINATE dimensioning sub-command is used to create ordinate Dimensions, which may also be activated by selecting the **Ordinate Dimensions** option from the **Draw** pull-down menu. (A sub-menu is then displayed, offering 3 variations on the same basic command.)

Once the command has been started, you are asked to select the feature of interest, which is the equivalent of an 'extension line origin' in a linear Dimension. At this stage, you can explicitly define the axis in which measurement is to take place by typing **X** or **Y**, or you can allow AutoCAD LT to decide this for you automatically, based on the position of the ordinate text (the 'Leader endpoint').

A typical command dialogue is shown below.

Command: **DIM1**	- Draws a single Dimension.
Dim: **ORDINATE**	- Select an ordinate dimension type.
Select feature:	- Indicate the feature to be dimensioned.
Leader endpoint (Xdatum/Ydatum):	- Enter **X** or **Y** or indicate the desired text position.
Dimension text <220>:	- Press ↵ to accept.

Figure 6–21 shows a typical application of ordinate dimensioning, where distances are indicated from a datum point, with reference to the *X* and *Y* axes.

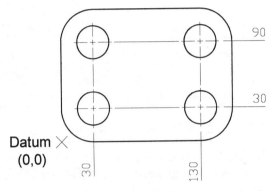

Figure 6–21. An example of ordinate dimensioning.

Optionally, a rectangular box may be placed around the dimension text, which is known as a *basic* Dimension or a *boxed* Dimension. Whether a boxed Dimension is produced depends on the value of the DIMGAP system variable (which is associated with the current dimension style) but the simplest method is to set or clear the **Basic Dimension** checkbox using the DDIM command, as shown below.

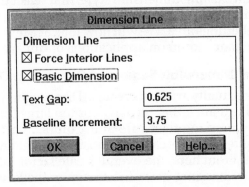

Figure 6–22. The DDIM command's Dimension Line dialogue box.

Working with Dimension Styles

AutoCAD LT uses the DDIM command to create and manipulate dimension styles. As we have already seen, a dimension style controls the appearance of dimensions which are drawn using that style, based on the values of certain internal system variables. These system variables appear to the user as *settings* in a series of dialogue boxes, all of which are accessed from a central dialogue box, as shown in Figure 6–23.

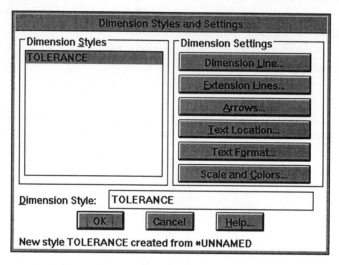

Figure 6–23. The DDIM command's main dialogue box.

To start the DDIM command, select the **Dimension Style...** option from the **Settings** pull-down menu, or type **DDIM** (or **DM**) at the Command prompt.

The name of the current dimension style is shown highlighted in the **Dimension Styles** list box, which is called *UNNAMED to begin with. You can create a new style (inheriting all settings from the current dimension style), simply by typing the new name in the **Dimension Style** edit box and then clicking on the **OK** button. A message will then appear along the lower edge of the dialogue box, giving the name of the new style, and the style from which it has been created.

To modify an existing dimension style, first select the style by clicking on it in the **Dimension Styles** list box, and then click on the appropriate button(s) in the Dimension Settings area. We will now look at a few examples which demonstrate some of the more common applications of dimension styles.

Altering the Dimension Scale and Dimension Colours

If you have actually tried to create a Dimension, you may have found that the arrows and text are either too small or too large for the drawing. You can easily alter this by pressing the **Scale and Colors...** button in the DDIM command's main dialogue box. This causes a subsidiary dialogue box to appear, as shown in Figure 6–24. From here, the overall 'scale factor' of the dimension style may be modified, by changing the value shown in the **Feature Scaling** edit box.

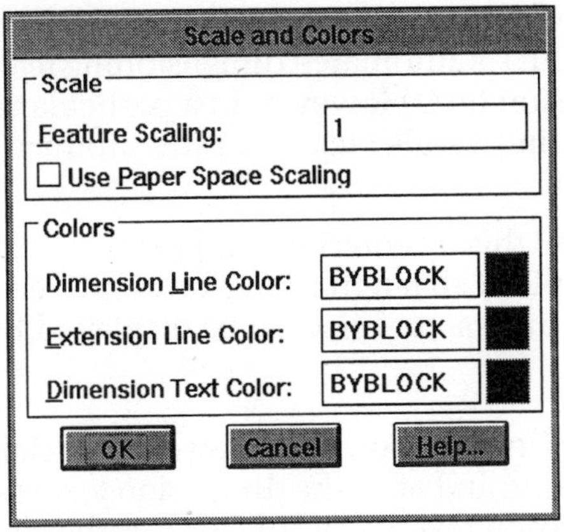

Figure 6–24. The DDIM command's Scale and Colors dialogue box.

From this same dialogue box, it is also possible to modify the colours used to actually draw the Dimension. By default, the logical colour BYBLOCK is used, which causes the Dimension to be drawn in the current drawing colour, but you can explicitly define the colour to be used for dimension lines, extension lines and dimension text. Notice in Figure 6–24 that each of the edit boxes has a colour display button, immediately to its right. Clicking on this button displays the Select Color dialogue box, which was first encountered in Figure 3–17.

Controlling the Text Format of Dimensions

The Text Format dialogue box, which is shown in Figure 6–25, is used to control AutoCAD LT's automatic dimension text generation feature. From here, several useful dimension styles may be configured, as we will now see.

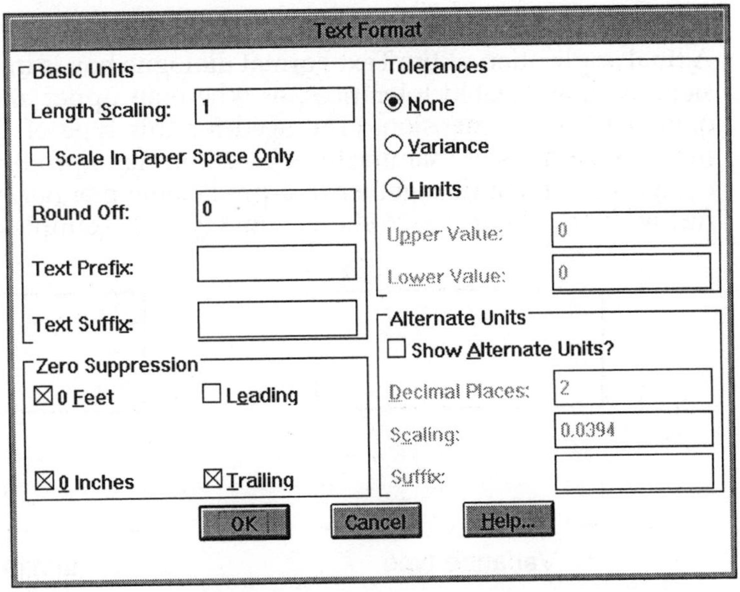

Figure 6–25. The DDIM command's Text Format dialogue box.

Firstly, recall that the standard practice is to draw all objects actual size, so that AutoCAD LT's automated dimensioning features may be used for the generation of dimension text. However, in a particular application, you may want to enter lengths using a scale factor, but still produce dimensions which show all lengths at full size.

You can do this by entering an appropriate value in the **Length Scaling** edit box. For example, if all lengths have been entered at ¼ scale, then a length scale factor of 4 will cause actual sizes to be displayed by linear Dimensions (4 × ¼ = 1).

The Basic Units section also allows you to define a *prefix* and *suffix*, which will be added before and after the dimension text respectively. If for example, you want the dimension text to say '100 mm', rather than simply '100', then this would be achieved by entering 'mm' in the **Text Suffix** edit box.

A related application might require the display of *alternate* units. This may be a requirement where a drawing is to be used internationally, or in a country where the system of units is in transition. A typical example, might require that the drawing should be dimensioned in feet and inches, but with lengths also shown in millimetres (i.e. 8'–4" [2540 mm]). To display lengths in feet and inches, we would firstly click the **Architectural** radio button in the DDUNITS command's Units Control dialogue box. This will set 1 drawing unit to be equivalent to 1 inch, and causes the coordinate display to use a 'feet and inches' format. The next step is to start the DDIM command, and open the Text Format dialogue box. Enable the **Show Alternate Units?** checkbox in the Alternate Units area, and then set the **Scaling** edit box to 25.4. Finally, set the **Suffix** edit box to 'mm'. This will cause the above style of dimension text to be generated whenever linear Dimensions are created using this dimension style.

A final application of the Text Format dialogue box is in the creation of Dimensions with associated tolerances, or where an upper and lower limit must be quoted with a Dimension. (The need for this type of Dimension arises from modern methods of manufacture, based on mass production techniques. Such components must fit together in a predictable manner, without requiring any further work.) Figure 6–26 shows some typical examples.

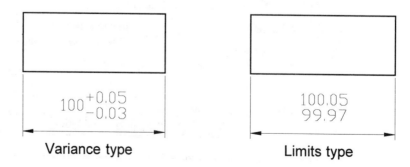

Variance type   Limits type

Figure 6–26. Examples of toleranced Dimensions.

The Tolerance area of the Text Format dialogue box is used to create this type of Dimension. The first step is to indicate the type of toleranced Dimension required, by clicking on either the **Variance** or **Limits** radio button. The amount of variation allowed above and below the nominal Dimension may then be entered in the **Upper Value** and **Lower Value** edit boxes. In a variance type Dimension, these two values appear as tolerances following the nominal value. In a limits type Dimension, these two settings are added and subtracted from the nominal value respectively, thus producing an upper limit and a lower limit.

Drawing Exercise 16   Adding Dimensions to an Engineering Drawing

This exercise requires you to create and use several different dimension styles, each suited to a particular type of Dimension.

1. Use normal AutoCAD LT drawing commands to create the drawing shown below, but without the Dimensions or centre lines.

2. Use the DDIM command to create 5 new dimension styles called AUXILIARY, BASIC, CENTER, LIMIT and TOLERANCE.

3. Using these styles, and the DIM command, dimension the drawing as shown below.

Notes: 1: The BASIC style should be used for all standard Dimensions (linear and angular). 2: Use the CONTINUE dimensioning sub-command to create the 'chained' Dimensions. 3: The AUXILIARY style should use an appropriate text prefix and suffix, so that dimension text is enclosed in brackets. 4: Use the CENTER dimensioning sub-command to create the centre lines. 5: The CENTER dimension style should produce centre lines, rather than a centre mark and this style should be current when the centre lines are created.

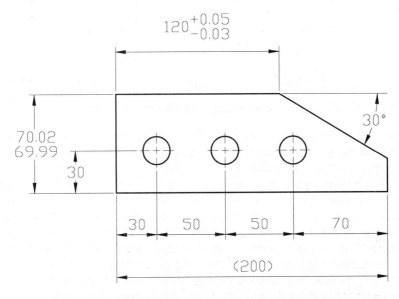

Creating Custom Dimension Arrows

The normal dimensioning practice is to use solid-filled arrows at the extremities of the dimension line. You can change this behaviour, if you wish, by making appropriate changes in the Arrows dialogue box, which is accessed from the DDIM command's main dialogue box.

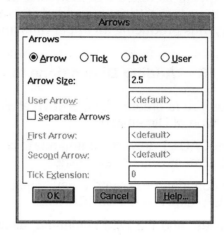

Figure 6–27. The DDIM command's Arrows dialogue box.

Looking at Figure 6–27, we can see that the current dimension style uses arrows with a default length of 2.5 drawing units. (This value is also multiplied by the **Feature Scaling** setting, which is accessed from the Scale and Colors subsidiary dialogue box.) To change the type of 'arrow' used, simply click on the appropriate radio button in the Arrows section. Some of the possibilities are shown in Figure 6–28.

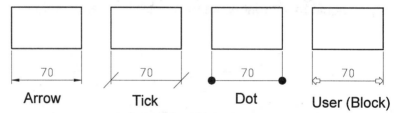

Figure 6–28. Custom forms of dimension 'Arrow'.

Arrows, ticks and dots are simple to use, although the user-defined dimension arrow does require further explanation. As you have probably guessed, this is simply a Block definition which has been defined by the user. For best results, this should have an overall size of 1 unit by 1 unit, so that the **Arrow Size** setting controls the actual size of the Block used in the Dimension. Once the **User** radio button has been selected, the name of the Block may then be entered in the **User Arrow** edit box. Notice that a mirror image of the Block is drawn at the opposite end of the dimension line, so a single Block definition is adequate for most applications. If you do need two different Blocks, then this can be achieved by clicking on the **Separate Arrows** checkbox and then entering the required Block names in the **First Arrow** and **Second Arrow** edit boxes.

Isometric Drawing

There are two methods of sketching 3-dimensional views which are in common use. These are the *isometric* and *oblique* projections, both of which are illustrated in Figure 6–29.

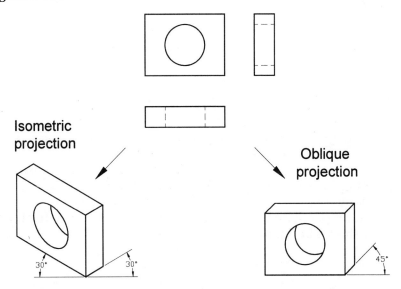

Figure 6–29. Isometric and oblique projection methods.

A sketch of this sort can convey meaning to a reader much more readily than an engineering drawing (particularly if the viewer has not been trained in the interpretation of such drawings). Of these two types of projection, the isometric approach is the most widely used, and this will now be considered.

Notice from Figure 6–29 that all lines in this particular isometric drawing are either vertical, or at 30° to the horizontal. AutoCAD LT allows you to activate a special isometric grid which greatly simplifies the creation of such drawings. The Isometric Snap/Grid section of the DDRMODES command's dialogue box is used for this purpose. (Recall that the control of basic drawing aids such as the snap and grid settings were introduced in Chapter 2; see Figure 2–15 and the associated text for more details.) To enable an isometric grid, the appropriate checkbox should be enabled, as shown in Figure 6–30.

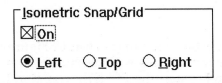

Figure 6–30. Using the DDRMODES command to control the isometric grid.

Notice from Figure 6–30 that AutoCAD LT recognises 3 different isometric planes, only one of which may be active at any time. The best way to understand the significance of these drawing planes is to visualize an isometric projection of a cube, as shown in Figure 6–31.

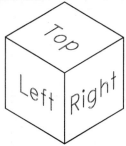

Figure 6–31. The left, right and top isometric drawing planes.

You can select a particular isometric plane by clicking its radio button in the Drawing Aids dialogue box. (A faster method is to press [Ctrl] + [E] at the Command line, which cycles though the three available planes in a repeating sequence.) Depending on which plane is active, you should see a display similar to one of those shown in Figure 6–32.

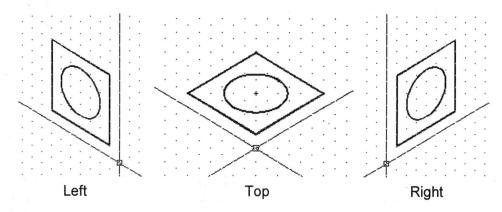

Left   Top   Right

Figure 6–32. The grid and cross-hairs during isometric drawing.

Thus the normal method is to enable the isometric grid and to display a visible grid on screen. The snap feature may then be used to restrain all cursor input to the visible grid. Enabling ortho mode will force any drawing commands to align to the cross-hairs, whose arrangement varies depending on the active isometric plane.

Another interesting feature (as seen in Figure 6–32) is the creation of ellipses, which align automatically with the current isometric plane. To create this type of 'isometric circle', start the ELLIPSE command, with an isometric grid <u>already</u> active. Notice that the command now offers an Isocircle option, which is not normally available. Once selected, this option is similar in use to the CIRCLE command, requesting first a centre point and then a point on the circumference.

Using the ELLIPSE command's Isocircle option it is quite simple to construct circular isometric objects, even if some of these must be partially erased. In such situations, the normal method is to draw the ellipse as usual and then use the TRIM command to remove any unwanted portions. This approach is illustrated in Figure 6–33.

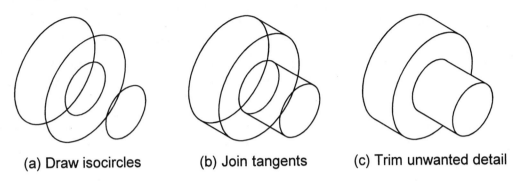

(a) Draw isocircles   (b) Join tangents   (c) Trim unwanted detail

Figure 6–33. Using the ELLIPSE and TRIM commands in isometric drawing.

Drawing Exercise 17   **Basic Isometric Drawing**

Use the techniques introduced in this section to produce isometric drawings of the following objects. All sizes are at your discretion.

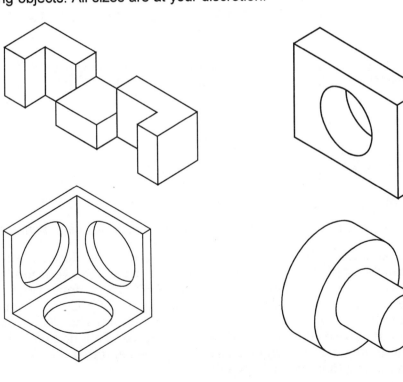

Working with User Coordinate Systems

Until now, we have worked with AutoCAD LT's default coordinate system, which is called the *world coordinate system*, or *WCS*. In this system, the *X* axis is aligned horizontally, with positive movement being to the right. Similarly, the *Y* axis is oriented vertically, with its positive direction pointing upwards. (Recall that the Cartesian coordinate system was first introduced in Chapter 3. Refer to Figure 3–2 and the associated text for more details.)

It is also possible to create your own custom coordinate systems, which are known as *user coordinate systems* (*UCSs*). The careful use of this feature can greatly simplify the entry of awkward lengths and angles, because you are free to choose your own origin, and the alignment of the *X*, *Y* and *Z* axes. There is no limit to the number of named UCSs which can be defined in a drawing. However, only one coordinate system can be active at any time.

Before looking at the methods used to manipulate user coordinate systems, it is a good idea to configure AutoCAD LT to display a coordinate system icon on screen. This will give a visible indication of the position of the drawing origin (0,0), and the alignment of the *X* and *Y* axes. To do this, select the **UCS Icon** option from the **A̲ssist** pull-down menu, or type **UCSICON** (or **UI**) at the Command prompt. The following range of options is then offered at the Command line.

ON/OFF/All/Noorigin/ORigin<OFF>:   - Type **ON** to enable the UCS icon.

First, select the ON option, which cause a UCS icon to appear at the lower left corner of the graphics area. This should be similar to icon (b) in Figure 6–34.

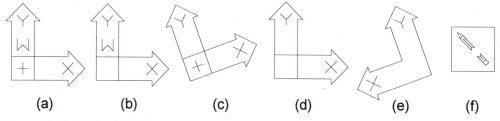

   (a)   (b)   (c)   (d)   (e)   (f)

Figure 6–34. The UCS icon, as it may appear in various circumstances.

At this point the UCS icon is visible, but it will always be placed in the lower left corner of the display. To configure the UCS so that it will move around the screen whenever the UCS is redefined, restart the UCSICON command and choose the ORigin option. (So, to summarize you should use the UCSICON command twice, selecting the ON option and then the ORigin option.) The UCS icon will now attempt to move so that it is over the UCS origin and aligned with the *X* and *Y* axes, assuming that the origin is visible on screen and that the UCS icon can be placed there without being 'clipped'.

Looking at the displayed UCS icon, you should notice that a 'W' appears on the icon, indicating that the current UCS is the <u>same</u> as the WCS. Assuming that you have used the default prototype drawing, the drawing origin should correspond with the lower left corner of the graphics area. The UCS icon cannot be placed over this point without being clipped, so instead it is placed in its default position. If the UCS icon was directly over the origin, then a small 'cross' would be placed on the icon, as in Figure 6–34(a) and (c). (So in Figure 6–34(d), the current UCS is <u>different</u> from the WCS, and the UCS icon is <u>not</u> at the UCS origin.)

The orientation of the X and Y axes can also be determined from the UCS icon, as shown in Figures 6–34(c), (e) and (f). Bear in mind that the UCS can be rotated around any of the three axes, in any sequence, so there are many possible variations here. Figure 6–34(c) shows a simple rotation around in the XY plane (around the Z axis), while Figure 6–34(e) shows a more complex example, where the UCS icon is viewed from 'underneath' (thinking in three dimensions). Lastly, the 'broken pencil' icon of Figure 6–34(f) means that the UCS is aligned almost at 90° to the screen (within 1°), with the result that drawing operations may not produce the required result.

Now that we understand the significance of the UCS icon, the next step is to actually <u>redefine</u> the current UCS. To do this, select the **Set <u>U</u>CS** option from the **Assist** pull-down menu or type **UCS** at the Command prompt. Assuming that you have used the pull-down menu system, a sub-menu should be displayed, as shown in Figure 6–35 (similar options are available from the Command line).

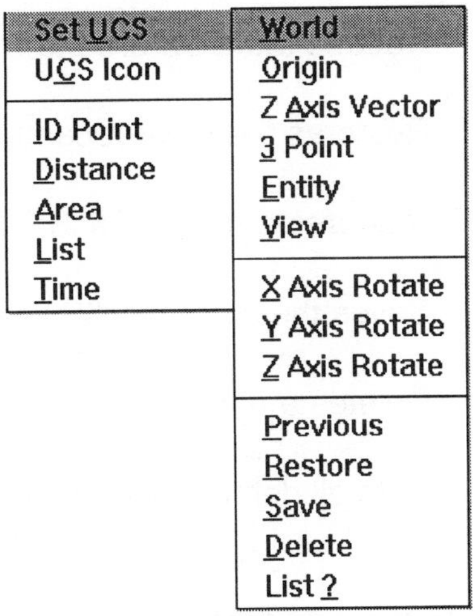

Set <u>U</u>CS	<u>W</u>orld
U<u>C</u>S Icon	<u>O</u>rigin
	Z <u>A</u>xis Vector
<u>I</u>D Point	<u>3</u> Point
<u>D</u>istance	<u>E</u>ntity
<u>A</u>rea	<u>V</u>iew
<u>L</u>ist	
<u>T</u>ime	<u>X</u> Axis Rotate
	<u>Y</u> Axis Rotate
	<u>Z</u> Axis Rotate
	<u>P</u>revious
	<u>R</u>estore
	<u>S</u>ave
	<u>D</u>elete
	List <u>?</u>

Figure 6–35. Menu options available when using the UCS command.

The most basic of operations is to move the UCS origin, which uses the **Origin** option. Simply use the mouse to indicate the new origin coordinate (which should also move the UCS icon, if you have followed the previously described steps). You can also rotate the UCS in the XY plane by choosing the **Z axis rotate** option. (As with the ROTATE command, a positive rotation angle normally represents an anticlockwise rotation.) Table 6–4 lists the significance of each option.

Table 6–4. The options available with the UCS command.

Option	Function performed
World	Sets the current UCS to the world coordinate system (WCS).
Origin	Specifies a new origin for the current UCS.
Z Axis Vector	Rotates the UCS so that the Z axis passes through the specified point.
3-Point	Specifies a new UCS based on 3 points. These are the origin, a point on the positive X axis, and a point anywhere in the positive XY plane.
Entity	Aligns the UCS with a selected entity.
View	Rotates the UCS so that the XY plane is parallel with the current viewing direction.
X Axis Rotate	Rotates the UCS around the X axis (in the YZ plane).
Y Axis Rotate	Rotates the UCS around the Y axis (in the XZ plane).
Z Axis Rotate	Rotates the UCS around the Z axis (in the XY plane).
Previous	Restores the most recently defined UCS.
Restore	Restores a named UCS.
Save	Saves the current UCS with the given name.
Delete	Deletes a named UCS.
List ?	Lists all defined user coordinate systems.

Once a UCS has been made current, the entry of coordinate data will normally be relative to the UCS, rather than to the WCS. Thus the coordinate (0,0) refers to the UCS origin, while the absolute coordinate (100,0) is a point 100 units from the UCS origin, in the direction of the positive X axis of the UCS.

Note: You can override this behaviour. If a UCS is active, a coordinate may be 'forced' to refer to the WCS by preceding it with an asterisk. Thus (100,0) refers to the current UCS, while (*100,0) is relative to the WCS.

The UCS command's Save, Restore, List and Delete options allow you to work with named user coordinate systems. AutoCAD LT also allows you to perform many of these same functions using a dialogue box, which will be preferred by the majority of users. To view and manipulate the user coordinate systems associated with the current drawing, select the **Named UCS...** option from the **Assist** pull-down menu, or type **DDUCS** (or **UC**) at the Command prompt. A dialogue box similar to Figure 6–36 will then be displayed.

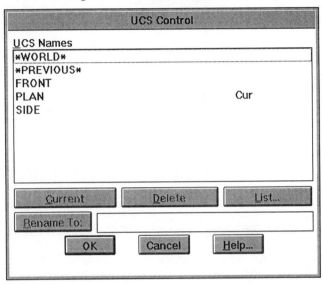

Figure 6–36. The Units Control dialogue box (DDUCS command).

Notice that the names of any previously defined user coordinate systems are listed in the UCS Names list box. To make a particular UCS current, simply highlight it and then click on the **Current** button. The **Delete** and **Rename To** buttons operate in a similar manner, and allow the highlighted UCS to be deleted or renamed respectively. Pressing the **List...** button displays a further dialogue box which gives detailed information about the highlighted UCS. (This is the origin coordinate, together with direction vectors for the X, Y and Z axes.)

When working with 3-dimensional drawings, the UCS must frequently be aligned with a particular drawing plane, or with an existing drawing feature. The UCS command's X, Y and Z options allow the UCS to be rotated through a stated angle around the chosen axis. Alternatively, the 3-Point option may be used to align the UCS in a plane, (based normally on object snap).

Notes: 1: You can use the *right-hand corkscrew rule* to work out the direction of a positive rotation around any axis. Imagine a corkscrew with a right-handed thread to be aligned with the axis of interest. A positive rotation of the corkscrew will move the corkscrew away from the origin (in a positive linear direction).
2: The UCSFOLLOW system variable controls whether a plan view is automatically generated whenever the UCS is changed. This setting is disabled by default.

A dialogue box approach is also available, allowing the manipulation of the orientation of the current UCS. To display the UCS Orientation dialogue box, as shown in Figure 6–37, select the **Preset UCS...** option from the **Assist** pull-down menu, or type **DDUCSP** (or **UP**) at the Command prompt.

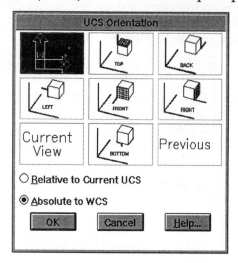

Figure 6–37. Selecting a preset UCS orientation with the DDUCSP command.

It may require some practice before you will be able to manipulate the UCS orientation with confidence using the above dialogue box, however its basic operation is straightforward. The larger 'tripod' in each slide represents the orientation of the world coordinate system (or the current UCS, if the **Relative to Current UCS** radio button has been selected). Bear in mind that the Z axis is shown in red, on screen, although this is not visible in the above figure. The smaller tripod, attached to the cube, shows the alignment of the new UCS, which will result if that button is pressed. (Thus you need to have good 3D visualization skills to use this feature.) The remaining buttons allow the current UCS to be set back to the WCS (top left), parallel to the current view (lower left), or to the most recently defined UCS (lower right).

Drawing Exercise 18   **2D User Coordinate System Manipulation**

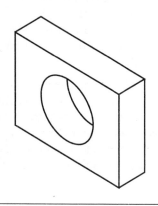

Produce an orthographic drawing of the block shown, using first angle projection (front elevation, side elevation and plan view). Assume that the block is 82 × 64 × 20 units, and that the (centrally positioned) hole has a diameter of 40 units.

For each of the views, create a named UCS, whose origin should correspond to the lower left corner of that view. Ensure that the correct UCS is current when that view is drawn (to simplify the calculation of coordinate data, as far as possible).

Simple 3D Drawing

AutoCAD LT possesses a pretty basic 3-dimensional drawing capability, when compared to the full version of AutoCAD. Nevertheless, with a little ingenuity, the available options may be used to create some surprisingly complex 3D drawings!

Basic 3D Visualization Techniques

Under normal circumstances, the drawing is viewed from a plan view, in which the XY plane is parallel to the screen. Under these circumstances, the positive Z axis points 'out' of the screen (towards you). This is fine for 2D drawing, but may be restrictive with three dimensions. A better viewpoint under these circumstances would provide an 'isometric' view of our 3D drawing, similar to that encountered earlier in this chapter. A range of preset 3D viewpoints are available by selecting the **3D Viewpoint Presets** option from the **View** pull-down menu, as shown in Figure 6–38.

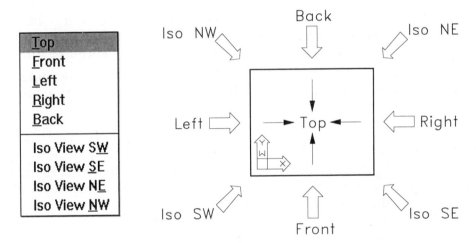

Figure 6–38. Preset 3-dimensional viewpoints, for use with 3D drawing.

The last four options in the above menu produce 'isometric' views of the drawing area, where the viewpoint looks down on the XY plane at an angle of 45°, from a particular compass direction. The remaining five options produce views from directly above (Top), or parallel to the XY plane from one of four possible directions (front, back, left or right).

Note: Before using this feature, it is a good idea to draw a border around your drawing area, and to enable the UCS icon. The border will then fill the screen after the 3D view is selected, while the UCS icon will help you to keep track of the orientation of the X, Y and Z axes.

Note: More advanced 3D viewing options are introduced in the next chapter, including the use of perspective, and the production of solid-filled models.

Using Elevation and Thickness in 3D Drawing

Drawn objects such as Lines, Arcs, Circles, Polylines etc. possess two properties called *elevation* and *thickness*, which are important in the creation of 3D models. To understand the thickness property first, imagine that a 2-dimensional drawing is 'extruded' in the Z direction, as shown in Figure 6–39.

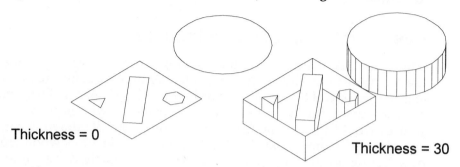

Thickness = 0

Thickness = 30

Figure 6–39. The addition of 'thickness' to normal drawing objects.

Thus in the above example, a Line is transformed into a fence-like structure, while a 'closed' object like a Circle, or a wide Polyline becomes a solid object. (Arcs, Polygons and Ellipses are also transformed into fence-like structures.)

Note: The HIDE command has been used here to remove hidden detail, which would not normally be visible, assuming that the objects are opaque.

You can add thickness to <u>existing</u> objects using the DDCHPROP command. Simply select the object(s) to be modified and then enter an appropriate value in the **Thickness** edit box. A typical application is shown in Figure 6–40. (This was produced from the drawing of Figure 3–10 by changing the thickness to 50 units, and then selecting an 'isometric' viewpoint).

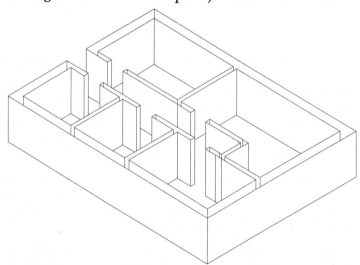

Figure 6–40. Adding thickness to a 2-dimensional floorplan.

The *elevation* of an object is the height of its 'base', when measured in the Z axis. If you imagine the XY plane to be horizontal, then the elevation of an object is its vertical height (measured from the lower edge). For objects which possess non-zero values of thickness and elevation (both of which are measured along the Z axis), then the height of the top face of the object, will be given by the elevation plus the thickness.

The careful use of elevation and thickness in 3D drawing allows one object to be placed on top of another, as shown in Figure 6–41.

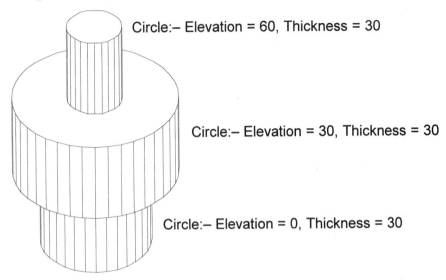

Circle:– Elevation = 60, Thickness = 30

Circle:– Elevation = 30, Thickness = 30

Circle:– Elevation = 0, Thickness = 30

Figure 6–41. Combining thickness and elevation in 3D drawing.

Note: Although the DDCHPROP can be used to alter the thickness of existing objects, it cannot change an object's elevation (neither can the DDMODIFY command). If you need to change the elevation of existing objects then use the CHANGE command, and then select the Properties option from the Command line.

The normal approach when drawing in 3D is to use the DDEMODES (Entity Modes) command to set the default values of elevation and thickness. These values are then inherited automatically by any subsequently drawn objects. (Recall that the DDEMODES command was introduced in Chapter 3. Refer to Figure 3–14 and the associated text for more details.)

You can also combine the use of elevation and thickness, with user coordinate systems (which were introduced in the last section) to produce more complex 3D objects. The elevation and thickness associated with an object are always measured relative to the coordinate system which was in effect when the object was drawn. This will either be the WCS or a custom UCS. By manipulating user coordinate systems, quite complex objects may be created. A simple example, using two different user coordinate systems is shown in Figure 6–42 overleaf.

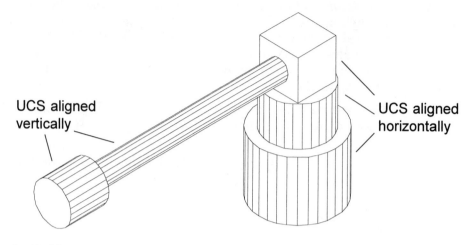

Figure 6–42. The use of elevation, thickness and user coordinate systems.

Drawing Exercise 19   3D Drawing using Elevation and Thickness

Use the techniques introduced in this section to produce and display 3-dimensional drawings of the following objects.

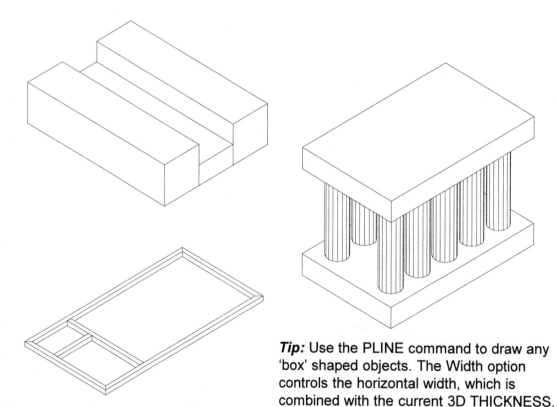

Tip: Use the PLINE command to draw any 'box' shaped objects. The Width option controls the horizontal width, which is combined with the current 3D THICKNESS.

Point Filters and Tracking

At certain times, you may wish to identify a point whose position is related to existing objects, as shown in Figure 6–43.

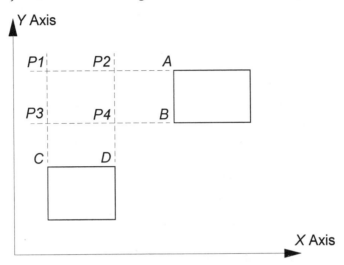

Figure 6–43. Identifying a point, based on existing objects.

For example, points *P1* and *P2* both lie on line *A*, hence sharing the same *Y* coordinate. Similarly, points *P2* and *P4* lie on line *D*, and thus share the same *X* coordinate.

Assuming that the two rectangles already exist, and for some reason you need to identify one of the above intersection points, then one method would be to draw some temporary 'construction' lines, which could later be erased. (You would then use object snap to find the required intersection.)

AutoCAD LT also offers a more elegant solution to this problem, which makes use of *point filters*. Point filters allow you to take part of the coordinate from one existing feature (the X value say), and the remainder from other feature(s). Thus we could find point *P1* (for example) by taking the *Y* coordinate from line *A* and the *X* coordinate from line *C*. This principle can be extended to find points in 3-dimensions by also considering the *Z* coordinate.

Point filters may be used whenever AutoCAD LT requires the entry of coordinate information. Simply type a point filter which specifies what portion of the required coordinate is to be taken from the next entered point. You will then be prompted to specify the remaining value(s). For example, if the X coordinate has been taken (using object snap typically) from one existing feature, then a message will appear in the Command area to the effect that the *Y* and *Z* values must still be given. You can simply indicate another feature, or use further point filters.

Point filters are always preceded by a full stop (.), thus the allowed point filters are **.X, .Y, .Z, .XY, .XZ** and **.YZ**. You can type these point filters at the Command line, or alternatively, you can activate the Cursor menu by pressing Ctrl + ⇧, and then select the **XYZ Filters** option. The two most commonly used point filters are also found as icons in the Toolbox (see margin).

The *tracking* feature is a new introduction in AutoCAD LT Release 2. This feature is typically combined with point filters or object snap to find a particular coordinate. The basic principle is that you can enter a special *tracking* mode and then move a 'track' point around the screen by typing relative or absolute coordinates, selecting object snap points or using point filters. Once the required position has been found, then pressing ⏎ will cause this point to be used by the previously active command. (Thus the active command is temporarily halted once tracking mode is entered.) Tracking mode is entered by clicking the Tracking button in the Toolbox (see margin), or by typing **TRACKING** (or **TK**), whenever the entry of a coordinate is required. Pressing ⏎ exits tracking mode and returns the final coordinate to the previously active command.

Inquiry Commands

AutoCAD LT has a small group of commands whose purpose is to display information concerning the current drawing. These *inquiry* commands allow the drawing database to be interrogated, returning information such as:

❑   coordinates;

❑   distances and angles;

❑   areas and perimeters;

❑   colours, linetypes and layers of selected objects.

In AutoCAD LT Release 2, these commands have been 'promoted', so that they may now be accessed by clicking the appropriate icon in the Toolbox, as shown in Figure 6–44. (Release 2's Toolbox has an additional row of command buttons compared with Release 1.)

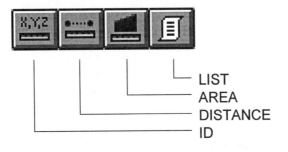

LIST   - drawing database information
AREA   - area of Circles and Polylines
DISTANCE   - distances and angles
ID   - X, Y and Z coordinates

Figure 6–44. Inquiry command icons, as provided by the Toolbox.

Most of these commands are straightforward to use. Simply start the appropriate command and then select the object or feature of interest. (Object snap is often used with these commands to accurately identify a particular coordinate.)

Note: The related TIME command provides useful information about the current drawing, such as the <u>total editing time</u>, which may be used for costing purposes.

The AREA command is perhaps the most complex of these commands, due to its ability to calculate the area of complex regions containing internal 'islands'. This is possible, because the command has two basic modes of operation, allowing subsequent areas to be added or subtracted from a running total. The initial command dialogue is shown below.

Command: **AREA**

<First point>/Entity/Add/Subtract   - Select the option required.

The Entity option allows the area of Circles or closed Polylines to be calculated, while the default is to indicate a series of coordinates forming a closed polygon. Selecting the Add or Subtract option enters additive or subtractive operating modes respectively. By switching from one mode to the other, the area of composite regions may be determined.

Tutorial 18   **Calculating Areas of Complex Regions**

The aim of this exercise is to create a (2-dimensional) drawing of a window frame, and then use the AREA command to calculate the area of each pane of glass, and of the wooden frame.

1. Draw three separate closed Polylines, enclosing areas *a*, *b* and *c*, as shown below. (All sizes are at your discretion – use the snap feature to ensure accurate alignment between Polyline vertices.)

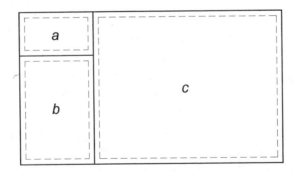

2. Use the OFFSET command to produce a further three Polylines, with each one internal to one of the existing Polylines, and offset by the same distance (shown as dotted lines above).

3. Using the AREA command, find the area of each pane of glass (each of the internal Polylines). Then, by switching between the Add and Subtract operating modes, find the area of the wooden frame.

Drawing Efficiency

Once the basics of using a CAD system have been mastered, you may soon find yourself working on extremely complex drawing projects. Under these circumstances, the operating performance of the computer's hardware and the efficiency of the software may become as important as your own drawing ability. (If you find yourself making a cup of coffee while waiting for a printout, or for the completion of some other calculated operation, then you have reached this point!)

Of course, you should always purchase the best computer that your budget will permit, but the careful use of certain AutoCAD LT commands will allow you to get the most from your existing hardware.

REDRAW and REGEN Commands

If the screen display becomes cluttered, then you can redraw the information in the graphics area by using the REDRAW command. The quickest way to do this is to click on the appropriate option in the Toolbox (see margin), although the command may also be started by selecting the **Redraw** option from the **View** pull-down menu, or by typing **REDRAW** (or **R**) at the Command prompt.

AutoCAD LT actually maintains a list of display vectors, which is used when the display must be refreshed quickly (as used by the REDRAW command). Under some circumstances, these display vectors may become out of date, thus requiring that the display is recalculated from the original drawing database. This process is known as drawing *regeneration* and some commands will cause this regeneration process to take place automatically. (Clearly, it is quicker simply to redraw the screen, rather than recalculate the display vectors each time.) If you suspect that the displayed information is inaccurate then the drawing may be regenerated manually by using the REGEN command.

QTEXT and FILL Commands

Drawing regeneration and plotting operations may become slow due to the use of complex text styles and wide Polylines in large drawings. (This is particularly true with pen plotting, where the pen must draw each line vector individually.)

If a drawing is at an intermediate stage and absolute accuracy is not important, then AutoCAD LT will allow Text to be replaced temporarily by an outline box and can also disable the filling of Solids and wide Polylines. These two options may be controlled from the DDRMODES command's dialogue box, using the **Quick Text** and **Solid Fill** checkboxes, or from the Command prompt by using the QTEXT and FILL commands respectively. (Recall that the DDRMODES was first introduced in Chapter 2. Refer to Figure 2–15 and the associated text for more details.)

Note: Another aid to drawing efficiency was introduced in an earlier part of this chapter. Recall that you can *freeze* unwanted layers in order to speed up the drawing regeneration process, and *thaw* them at a later stage.

7 Display Control

Basic Display Control

A basic feature of *vector*-based drawing editors (like AutoCAD LT), as opposed to *pixel*-based graphics editors (like the Paintbrush for Windows program), is that a small area can be repeatedly enlarged without any loss of detail. AutoCAD allows you to perform basic display control using the PAN and ZOOM commands, or alternatively using the Aerial View window.

The PAN command is the simplest of the display control commands, allowing the display to be effectively scrolled sideways, without changing the apparent size of any displayed drawing objects. To start the PAN command, click the appropriate button in the Toolbox (see margin), select the **Pan** option from the **View** pull-down menu, or type **PAN** (or **P**) at the Command prompt. The command dialogue is similar to that used by the MOVE command, requesting a displacement, followed by a second point. The difference between these two coordinates gives a displacement vector which controls the updating of the graphics display. (Try to imagine that it is the display window which moves, rather than the drawings objects.)

The ZOOM command allows displayed objects to appear larger or smaller, which is analogous to moving closer to, or further away from, the drawing. The ability to 'zoom in' is useful where intricate detail must be examined or added, while 'zooming out' allows larger areas to be visualized.

To start the ZOOM command, click on the appropriate button in the Toolbar (see margin), select the **Zoom** option from the **View** pull-down menu, or type **ZOOM** (or **Z**) at the Command prompt. A typical command dialogue is shown below.

Command: **ZOOM**

All/Center/Extents/Previous/Window/<Scale(X/XP)>: **0.5X**

If you want to zoom in, so that a small area of the current display will fill the screen, then the simplest approach is to indicate two points forming the opposite corners of a window. (You can also explicitly select the Window option, before indicating these points.) The All option may then be used to zoom out so that the entire drawing is visible. Another technique is to zoom in as before, and then use the Previous option to return to the previous view. (AutoCAD LT remembers the 10 most recent views.) Table 7–1 gives a list of the available options for use with the ZOOM command, and their significance.

Table 7–1. The options available with the ZOOM command.

Option	Meaning
All	Zooms to the drawing limits (as set by the LIMITS command) or to the drawing extents (whichever is the larger).
Center	Centres the view on the indicated coordinate, and optionally allows the vertical height of the viewport to be given (in drawing units or as a scale factor relative to the current view).
Extents	Zooms so that the drawing area actually used to draw objects just fills the screen.
Previous	Restores the most recent view (AutoCAD LT stores up to 10 previous views).
Window	Zooms in so that the identified window just fills the screen (while maintaining the screen aspect ratio).
scale	Scales the view relative to the drawing limits, with the centre point being taken from the current view. (A value of 1 displays an area equivalent to the entire drawing limits.)
scaleX	As the previous option, but the scale factor is based on the current view, rather than on the drawing limits. (A value of 0.9X would zoom out very slightly based on the current view.)
scaleXP	As the previous option, but scales the view relative to paper space units (useful for accurately scaling model space objects in a viewport which are to be plotted with paper space active).

An alternative to the PAN and ZOOM commands (which both work from the Command prompt) is to use the Aerial View window. To display this window, click the appropriate button in the Toolbar (see margin), select the **Aerial View** option from the **Settings** pull-down menu, or type **DSVIEWER** (or **DS**) at the Command prompt. A window similar to that shown in Figure 7–1 will then be displayed.

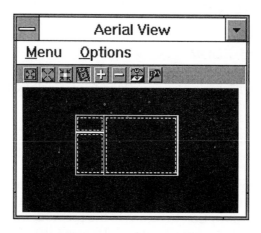

Figure 7–1. The Aerial View window.

Once you recognize the significance of the various command icons, and you become accustomed to the rather unusual functions performed by the left and right mouse buttons, then the Aerial View window can prove quite effective. However, some readers may find it rather confusing at first. Practice is definitely recommended here!

Consider the functions performed by the command icons, as shown in Figure 7-2.

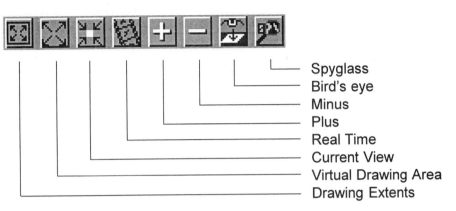

Figure 7-2. The Aerial View window's command icons.

From the left, the first three buttons control the display in the Aerial View window. These allow the display to be set to the drawing extents, the maximum area possible (without regenerating the drawing), or to the current view (in the graphics area) respectively. The Real Time button controls whether or not the graphics display is updated in 'real time' (as changes are made), or on completion of the command. The 'plus' and 'minus' buttons allow the display in the Aerial View window to be increased or decreased in size incrementally. Finally the Bird's Eye and Spyglass icons allow you to pan or zoom dynamically, and only one of these may be active at any time. With the Bird's Eye icon active, you select the required view in the Aerial View window, while the Spyglass icon allows you to perform dynamic zoom and pan operations directly in the main graphics area.

At any time, the Aerial View window shows the region corresponding to the current view (in the graphics area) using reverse video. Thus you can easily see the size and position of the current view, relative to the overall drawing area.

Considering the use of the mouse, as a general principle, you click the right button to switch between pan and zoom modes. A rectangle is displayed showing the size of the view window which will be displayed on completion of the operation. In pan mode, the window is positioned by movement of the mouse, while in zoom mode, sideways movement of the mouse alters the size of this window. Once the desired window size and position has been obtained, then clicking the left button completes the command and updates the graphics display.

Once a particular view has been generated (by whatever means), you may wish to <u>name</u> this view, so that it can be restored easily. The VIEW command allows you to work with named views, as we will now see.

To start the VIEW command, select the **View** option from the **View** pull-down menu, or type **VIEW** (or **V**) at the Command prompt. The following command options are then displayed.

?/Delete/Restore/Save/Window: - Select an option.

The Save option allows the current view to be saved as a named view, so that it can be restored later (using the Restore option). If you are unsure of the names of existing named views, then the ? option may be used for this purpose. Any unwanted views may be erased with the Delete option. Finally, the Window option allows a windowed area of the current view to be saved as a named view, which is generally faster than zooming in, prior to starting the VIEW command.

Working with Viewports

The commands which were considered in the previous section allowed the information displayed in the active view to be controlled quite easily. However, a more flexible arrangement might allow several different views of the same 'model' to be displayed simultaneously, by a series of separate windows or *viewports*. Thus the graphics area might be divided up into several 'tiled' viewports (with edges of viewports touching – just like bathroom tiles), or in a less restrictive manner, with viewports arranged freely in the graphics area. These two possibilities are illustrated by Figure 7–3.

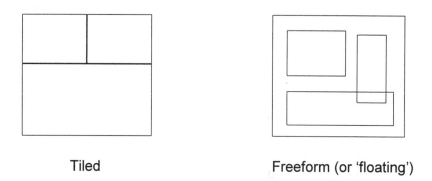

Tiled   Freeform (or 'floating')

Figure 7–3. The use of tiled or freeform viewport configurations.

We will consider the creation of *tiled* viewports first, which requires that the TILEMODE setting should have a value of 1. To examine the current TILEMODE value, use the mouse to click on the **View** pull-down menu. A 'tick' should be visible to the left of the **Tile Mode** option, indicating that the TILEMODE setting is enabled. If this is not the case, then select the **Tile Mode** option once, which will 'toggle' its value from 0 to 1.

The VPORTS command may now be used to control the use of multiple tiled viewports in the graphics area.

To start the VPORTS command, select the **Viewports** option from the **View** pull-down menu, or type **VPORTS** (or **VW**) at the Command prompt. Assuming that the pull-down menu approach has been used, a cascading menu will then appear, as shown in Figure 7–4 (similar options are available from the Command line).

Single
2 Viewports
3 Viewports
4 Viewports
Join
Save
Restore
Delete
List ?

Figure 7–4. The options available with the VPORTS command.

The upper section of the above menu controls the creation and deletion of viewports, while the lower section deals with named viewport configurations.

You can split the active viewport into two, three or four subsidiary viewports by selecting the appropriate option from the above menu. Considerable flexibility is offered in the arrangement of these subsidiary viewports, which may be aligned, horizontally, vertically, or in groups of three with a larger viewport linked to two smaller ones. (Triple viewport combinations, such as that shown in Figure 7–3 (to the left) can be classified based on the position of a larger viewport, which may be above, below, left or right of the two smaller viewports.)

Only one of the viewports is allowed to be 'active' at any time, and this is indicated by a slightly thicker border drawn around the active viewport. You can make a particular viewport active by clicking anywhere <u>inside</u> the viewport with the mouse. Notice that the normal drawing crosshairs are only displayed when the cursor is over the active viewport. At other times a standard mouse pointer is shown. All drawing and display control commands operate normally in the active viewport and changes to the drawing are reflected in all viewports.

The Single option returns to a single viewport configuration, while the Join option allows two adjacent viewports to be linked to form a single larger viewport.

The VPORTS command may also be used to save or restore entire viewport configurations. (This is similar in operation to the VIEW command, which may be used to save or restore the settings associated with a single viewport.) Thus the Save, Restore, Delete and List options all perform analogous functions, allowing named arrangements of viewports to be controlled. (All named viewport configurations are saved as part of the current drawing.)

One major limitation associated with tiled viewports becomes obvious if you try to plot such a multiple viewport drawing. In this case, it is only the <u>active</u> viewport which is plotted. This problem is overcome using non-tiled viewports.

The MVIEW command is used to create and control non-tiled viewports, but before using this command it is necessary to set the TILEMODE setting to 0. To do this, activate the **View** pull-down menu and ensure that the **Tile Mode** option is unchecked (as explained previously).

To start the MVIEW command, select the **Viewports** option from the **View** pull-down menu, or type **MVIEW** (or **MV**) at the Command prompt. (Notice that this is the <u>same</u> menu option that was used to activate the VPORTS command! The menu system is actually 'intelligent' and activates the correct command, based on the value of the TILEMODE setting.) Assuming that the pull-down menu approach has been used, then a cascading menu will appear, as shown in Figure 7–5 (with similar options being offered by the Command line version).

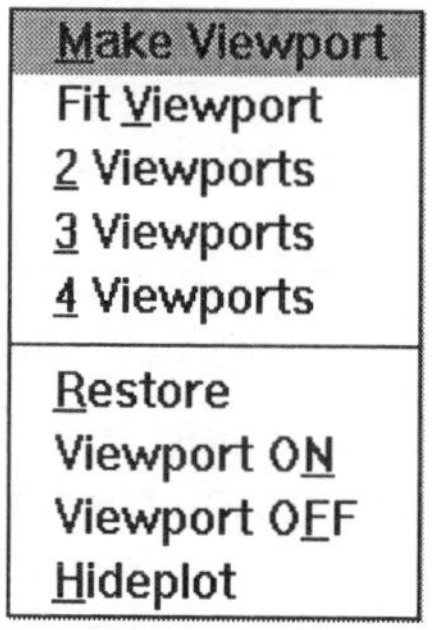

```
┌─────────────────────┐
│ Make Viewport       │
│ Fit Viewport        │
│ 2 Viewports         │
│ 3 Viewports         │
│ 4 Viewports         │
├─────────────────────┤
│ Restore             │
│ Viewport ON         │
│ Viewport OFF        │
│ Hideplot            │
└─────────────────────┘
```

Figure 7–5. Using the MVIEW command to control viewports.

The simplest way to create a new viewport is to indicate two diagonally opposite points anywhere in the graphics area (although you can also explicitly select the **Make Viewport** option from the above menu). A viewport is then created, which will display any previously drawn objects. You can repeat the command as often as required, creating viewports at any desired location. Unlike the tiled viewports previously considered, these viewports may be arranged freely, and are even allowed to overlap. A surprising feature is that you can use normal editing commands such as ERASE, MOVE or COPY to delete, arrange or create new viewports. You can even edit existing viewports by using the grips feature.

The **Fit Viewport** option creates a new viewport which just fills the graphics area, while the following three options allow arrangements of two, three, or four (tiled) viewports to be created inside a windowed area. These options are very similar to those offered by the VPORTS command, and it is even possible to restore viewport configurations saved with the VPORTS command, by selecting the **Restore** option.

Existing viewports may be enabled or disabled by selecting the appropriate options from the above menu. When disabled, a viewport is cleared, which may be useful if the time taken for drawing regeneration is excessive. Lastly, the **Hideplot** option allows you to control the removal of hidden lines in individual viewports during plotting operations (more on 3D plotting later).

The freeform arrangement of viewports in the graphics area is analogous to planning the layout of individual sketches on a piece of paper. In fact this is exactly what you are doing! With the TILEMODE setting cleared (0), AutoCAD LT recognises two different operating modes, which are referred to as *model space* and *paper space*. Paper space is active when the paper space button is selected in the Toolbar (see margin). Clicking on this button repeatedly, switches from one operating mode to the other.

Paper space is used when viewports are created or arranged, which, as we have already seen, is just like arranging the layout of information on a sheet of paper. In addition to arranging the viewport configuration, you can also use normal AutoCAD LT drawing commands to produce annotations in paper space, such as borders or titles.

In contrast, model space is used when the actual drawing or model is created. This is similar in operation to the use of tiled viewports where only a single viewport is allowed to be active at any time. The active viewport has a thickened border and all drawing and editing operations take place through this active viewport. As with tiled viewports, the crosshairs are only visible <u>inside</u> the active viewport (which may be changed by clicking on a new viewport at any time).

Note: Unlike tiled viewports, if a plot is produced with paper space active, then the <u>entire</u> drawing is plotted, including all model space viewports and any objects drawn in paper space. This is a big improvement, compared with the plot capabilities available with tiled viewports.

The ability to plot multiple viewport views onto a single piece of paper does raise some complex issues. For example, if one viewport shows a magnified view of a component, then linetype spacings will naturally appear larger or 'coarser' in the enlarged view. Linetypes drawn in paper space will also be scaled differently to those in model space. In some applications, it may be desirable to scale linetypes uniformly across different viewports and between paper space and model space. The PSLTSCALE setting controls whether dot dash sequences in linetypes are based on paper space, or on model space drawing units. If these are based on paper space (PSLTSCALE = 1), then all linetypes will be identically scaled in different viewports. (You may need to use the REGEN command to see the effect of changing the PSLTSCALE setting.) Similarly the DIMSCALE and DIMLFAC settings control the behaviour of Dimensions in model space and paper space. See the *AutoCAD LT User's Guide* for more details.

Note: The LIMITS command may be used to set the drawing limits in model space <u>and</u> in paper space. It is best to think of paper space units as representing the units used to measure the size of the paper (millimetres for example), while model space units refer to the units used in the actual design. You can also set different grid and snap spacings in model space and paper space.

3D Display Control

Simple 3-dimensional drawing and display control techniques were introduced in the previous chapter. Recall from Figure 6–38 and the associated text, that the **View** pull-down menu offers a number of 3D viewpoint presets, which are quite easy to use.

These preset options are actually produced by the VPOINT command, which as its name implies, is used to select the point in 3-dimensional space from where the model is to be viewed, and the viewing direction or 'line of sight'. To start the VPOINT command, select the **3D Viewpoint** option from the **View** pull-down menu, or type **VPOINT** (or **VP**) at the Command prompt. The viewpoint may then be specified by entering a 3D vector, a pair of angles, or by dynamically rotating a set of *3D axes* and an associated *compass* display.

Imagine the process of taking a photograph. The camera must first be positioned at a particular coordinate in 3-dimensional space, which is referred to as the *viewpoint* by the VPOINT command. This information by itself is insufficient, because the camera must also be pointed towards the subject, or *target*. By default, the target is the coordinate (0, 0, 0), which is relative to the active coordinate system, but this can be altered by the user. (The value used is actually stored by the TARGET system variable.) This is illustrated by Figure 7–6.

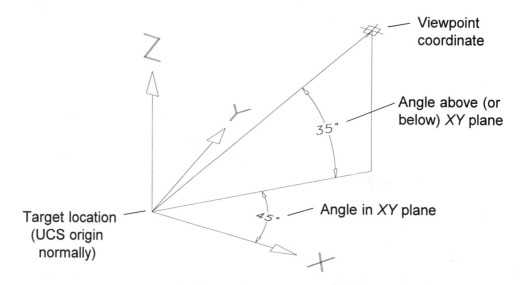

Figure 7–6. Specifying the viewpoint position with the VPOINT command.

In the vector-based approach, the viewpoint coordinate is normally specified as a *unit vector*, so for example a viewpoint directly above the *XY* plane would be entered as (0,0,1). The magnitude of the vector (which may be thought of as the distance between the camera and target) has no significance here. A second method is to specify the viewing direction by giving the angle <u>in</u> the *XY* plane (horizontally), and the angle <u>from</u> the *XY* plane (vertically). Finally, you can dynamically rotate a representation of the *XYZ* axes and an associated compass, to fix the viewpoint, as shown in Figure 7–7.

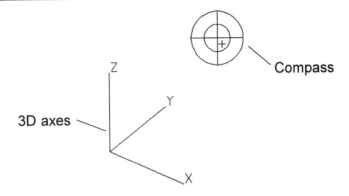

Figure 7–7. The VPOINT command's 3D axes and compass display.

When using the 3D axes display, it is useful to visualize the plane of the screen as lying in the *XY* plane. The compass display is really a flattened sphere, with the angular distance between each adjacent line being 90°.

When the new view is actually displayed, notice that the drawing is scaled so that it <u>fills</u> the active viewport (this is equivalent to zooming to the drawing *extents*). This behaviour is desirable under normal circumstances, but it can be confusing if you try to select a 3D viewpoint before anything has been drawn! A good habit to get into is to draw a rectangular border (at least), <u>before</u> switching to a 3D viewpoint.

Once a 3-dimensional viewpoint has been obtained by using the VPOINT command, you may be wondering how to return to your original plan view. The ZOOM PREVIOUS command may be used of course, but there is also a dedicated AutoCAD LT command (PLAN) which is used to produce plan views. To start the PLAN command, select the **3D Plan View** option from the **View** pull-down menu, or type **PLAN** (or **PV**) at the Command prompt. You then have the option of moving to a plan view in the current UCS, in a previously named UCS, or based on the world coordinate system (WCS).

Three-dimensional views may sometimes be visually confusing due to the apparently transparent nature of the 'wire frame' image. The display may also be ambiguous if more than one interpretation of the displayed image is possible, as shown in Figure 7–8.

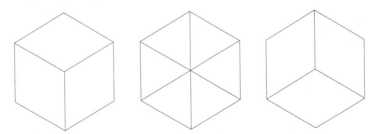

Figure 7–8. Two different interpretations of a 3D wire frame image.

The HIDE command, which was also introduced in the previous chapter, may be used to remove any lines which would not normally be visible from the current viewpoint. To start the HIDE command, select the **Hide** option from the **View** pull-down menu, or type **HIDE** (or **HI**) at the Command prompt.

Bear in mind that this command is provided purely to assist you with the visualization of the model <u>on screen</u>. Other methods are used to remove hidden detail from plotted drawings, as we will soon see. The removal of hidden lines may also be quite slow with complex drawings, so use this command sparingly.

Another shortcoming associated with the displays produced by the VPOINT command, even after hidden line removal, is that a parallel projection method is used. This means that objects further away from the observer appear just as large as those which are nearer. A perspective projection would give a much better result, and this is possible by using the DVIEW (or Dynamic View) command.

The DVIEW command may be activated by selecting the **3D Dynamic View** option from the **View** pull-down menu, or by typing **DVIEW** (or **DV**) at the Command prompt. There are some similarities to the VPOINT command, except that the DVIEW command dynamically modifies the view of a selected group of objects, rather than using an axis and compass. You are initially asked to select the objects on which the command will operate.

Note: If you press ⊡ at the 'Select objects:' prompt, without first selecting any objects, then a 3D model of a house is displayed. This is intended to assist you in keeping track of any changes made to the display. Generally speaking, it is more informative to select your own objects, rather than use the one supplied by default (although the house is useful for practice purposes).

Having selected any objects, the following options will then become available.

CAmera/TArget/Distance/POints/PAn/Zoom/TWist/CLip/Hide/Off/Undo/<eXit>:

The DVIEW command uses a 'camera' and 'target' analogy to select the viewpoint and target locations respectively. The CAmera option allows the selected objects to be rotated dynamically, with horizontal mouse movement spinning the selected objects around a vertical axis. Moving the mouse up or down tips the selected objects towards or away from the viewer, allowing you to view the objects from above or below. Once the ideal viewpoint (camera position) has been found then click ⌁ to select this view. The target position is always at the centre of the viewport, so you may sometimes need to change its position. This can be achieved using the TArget option, or you may select the POints option and define the CAmera and TArget locations in a single operation.

Notice that DVIEW offers a Hide option which will temporarily remove hidden lines, as well as an Undo option. This eliminates the need to leave the DVIEW command to access these basic functions.

A 3D perspective view may be activated by selecting the Distance option. A 'slider' control is then displayed which allows you to dynamically alter the distance of the selected objects from the observer, as shown in Figure 7–9.

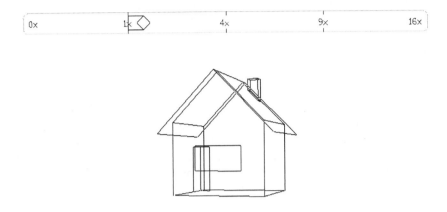

Figure 7–9. Using the DVIEW command's Distance option.

The slider is graduated in multiples of the original distance, so moving the slider to the right makes objects appear further away. (One peculiarity associated with the Distance option is that you may need to repeat this option several times, selecting the maximum distance on each occasion, to be able to see the entire image.)

At first sight, the Zoom and Distance options seem to perform an identical function. In fact, the Zoom option carries the camera-target analogy even further, because (with perspective enabled) it operates by altering the focal length of a virtual 'camera'. The default is 50 mm, which gives a normally-sized view with realistic perspective. Shorter lens lengths tend to exaggerate perspective, while making objects appear further away (like a 'fish-eye' lens). Conversely, a longer focal length makes objects appear closer, but reduces the degree of perspective. Thus you can use the Zoom option to set the degree of perspective required, and then use the Distance option to control the apparent size of the image. If the image appears off centre in the graphics area, then this may be corrected by using the PAn option. Figure 7–10 illustrates the effect of camera focal length on 3D perspective.

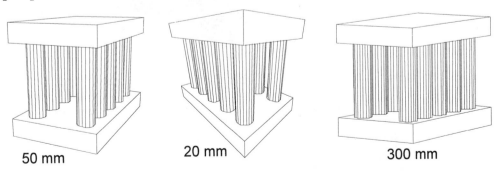

Figure 7–10. Modifying the camera's focal length with the DVIEW command.

Many AutoCAD LT commands will not operate with a perspective projection active. For this reason it is normally better to complete the construction of the 3D model, before getting too involved with display control. If necessary, you can disable the perspective projection by selecting the DVIEW command's Off option. (A separate viewport may also be used for the perspective view.)

Note: If the UCS icon is visible (as controlled by the UCSICON command), and a perspective projection has been selected, then the UCS icon will appear as a 3D perspective view of a cube.

In some 3D visualization applications, it may not be possible to view a particular feature, due to the presence of an obstruction in the observer's line of sight. In other cases, you may want to remove distant objects which form an unwanted distraction to the main subject. The CLip option allows objects to be removed at the front or back of the image by the careful positioning of *front* and *back* clipping planes respectively. Once again, this process is performed dynamically, by using a slider control similar to that shown in Figure 7–9. To disable any active clipping planes, select the CLip and Off options in sequence.

A final step towards visual realism would be to shade the faces of a 3-dimensional model, as shown in Figure 7–11.

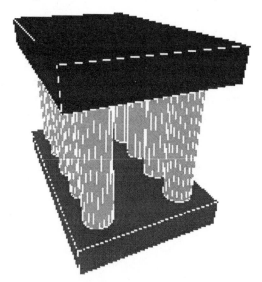

Figure 7–11. Using the SHADE command to produce a solid-filled image.

This effect is produced using the SHADE command, which may be started by selecting the **S**hade option from the **V**iew pull-down menu, or by typing **SHADE** (or **SH**) at the Command prompt. If the command is started from the menu system, then a series of further options are displayed in a subsidiary menu, as shown in Figure 7–12.

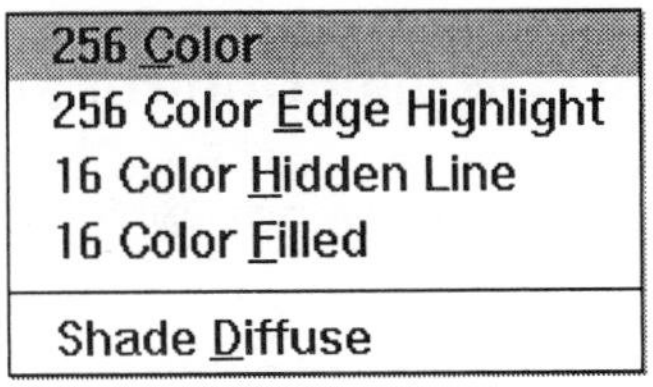

```
256 Color
256 Color Edge Highlight
16 Color Hidden Line
16 Color Filled

Shade Diffuse
```

Figure 7–12. The options available with the SHADE command.

The SHADE command can give some very colourful results, but you should first assign suitable colours to the objects in your drawing. You can do this explicitly by assigning a colour to an object, or by associating colours to particular layers.

The quality of the final shaded image will depend on the capabilities of your computer. So-called *Super VGA* displays can display at least 256 colours, while VGA-based systems (found on some older computers) are limited to 16 colours at any time.

Super VGA (256 colour) displays are capable of producing diffuse shaded images, where the brightness of a particular face depends on the original colour of the object, and also on the angle the face makes to the *light source*. This light source is assumed to be behind the observer, which produces an effect similar to illuminating an object with a hand-held torch. The **Shade Diffuse** option controls the percentage of diffuse reflected light to ambient light, which is set to 70% diffuse (hence 30% ambient) by default. Increasing this value, prior to shading an image, will add more contrast to the final image.

Plotting 3D Drawings

The PLOT command and its associated dialogue box were first encountered in Chapter 2 (refer to Figure 2–20 and the associated text for more details). There are small differences between the plotting of 3-dimensional drawings, depending on whether the plot is produced from model space, or from paper space.

If you plot a 3-dimensional drawing with model space active, (even if you remove hidden detail with the HIDE command), you will find that hidden lines will <u>still</u> be visible in the final printout. To remove hidden detail with the PLOT command, ensure that the **Hide Lines** checkbox in the Additional Parameters area is enabled before plotting.

When plotting from paper space (with one or more model space viewports on screen), the PLOT command's **Hide Lines** checkbox has no effect on the removal of hidden detail. Instead, you should use the MVIEW command's Hideplot option to control the removal of hidden detail in individual model space viewports. Once the Hideplot option has been chosen, you are asked whether the removal of hidden lines should be enabled or disabled, after which you must select the viewports which are to be affected by this change. You can use the PLOT command's **Preview...** option to confirm that hidden lines are being removed in the intended viewports, prior to producing the actual printout.

Tutorial 19   **3D Display Control and Plotting**

Take any one of the 3-dimensional drawings, which were produced in Drawing Exercise 19.

1.   From the **View** pull-down menu, disable the **Tile Mode** setting.

2.   Use the MVIEW command to create 3 different views of your model, each in a separate viewport. Experiment with the layout of these viewports to provide a visually pleasing result (working in paper space).

3.   Switch to model space. In the first viewport, use the VPOINT command to produce a parallel projection view of the model. In the second viewport, use the PLAN command to produce a plan view. In the third viewport, use the DVIEW command to produce a perspective view of the model.

4.   Switch to paper space. Use the DTEXT command to add a descriptive title below each of the viewports.

5.   Use the MVIEW command's Hideplot option to enable the removal of hidden detail in the first and third viewports (but not in the plan view).

6.   With paper space active, use the PLOT command to produce a printout of the entire drawing.

---

8   Customizing AutoCAD LT

Introduction

One of AutoCAD LT's most powerful features is its 'open architecture', which permits many aspects of the software to be modified by the user. Features of interest here include:

❑   linetypes and hatch patterns;

❑   slides and scripts files;

❑   extraction of Block-related Attributes (parts lists);

❑   user defined command abbreviations;

❑   customizing the Toolbox and Toolbar;

❑   custom menu systems.

Most of the applications considered in this chapter require that the user should be proficient in the use of an ASCII-based text editor. A suitable program is the Notepad (Windows) application, which you may find in the Accessories folder. (A DOS-based alternative is the EDIT.EXE program, which is found in the DOS directory on most systems.)

Linetypes and Hatch Patterns

AutoCAD LT stores its default linetype definitions in the files ACLT.LIN or ACLTISO.LIN. Which file is used depends on the settings in force when a new drawing project is started, and linetypes are subsequently loaded (Metric or Imperial units for example). All linetype files have a file extension of '.LIN'.

Note: The linetype definitions in ACLTISO.LIN are intended for Metric drawings, and are hence 'coarser' than those in ACLT.LIN by a factor of 25.4.

You can create your own linetype definitions, either by adding them to an existing linetype file, or by creating your own text file from scratch. It is possible to create your own linetype definitions <u>without</u> using a text editor, by using the LINETYPE command's Create option. You are first asked to select the linetype definition filename. If this exists, then your linetype definition will be appended to the file; otherwise a new file is created.

You are then asked to enter an informative message which will describe the linetype to others. Finally, the actual linetype definition is entered at the 'A,' prompt. The linetype is defined as a repeating sequence of lines and spaces. A positive number specifies the length of a drawn line, while a negative number gives the length of a space. Each entry is separated from the next by a comma, and sufficient detail must be given to define one complete sequence of the linetype.

A typical example would be the HIDDEN linetype, which is used to indicate hidden detail in engineering drawings. This is defined as a line of length 0.25 drawing units, followed by a space of 0.125 units. The linetype is generated by repeating this sequence of lines and spaces as the line is drawn. A typical definition, as it might appear in a linetype definition file, is shown below.

```
*HIDDEN, __  __  __  __  __  __  __  __  __  __  __  __  __  __
A,.25,-.125
```

Note: You can use a dot in a linetype definition, by entering a line length of zero.

Hatch pattern definitions have some similarities to linetypes, although they are more complex. Default hatch pattern definitions are stored in the files ACLT.PAT or ACLTISO.PAT. (As with linetypes, which file is used depends on the active measurement system, which is controlled by the PREFERENCES command.)

There are two methods which may be used to create a new hatch pattern. The first is to edit the default hatch pattern file (ACLT.PAT for example), and then append your own definition to this file. The second method is to create your own hatch pattern file. If you create a new hatch pattern file, then the filename should have an extension of '.PAT'. Unlike linetypes, you are only allowed to store a single hatch pattern definition in the new file, and the name of the hatch pattern must be the same as the filename. For example, a hatch pattern called CUBES would be stored in a file called CUBES.PAT.

The first line of a hatch pattern definition is the same as that used by a linetype definition. This is an asterisk, followed immediately by the name of the hatch pattern. This is optionally followed by a comment which is intended to describe the hatch pattern to other users. An example is shown below.

```
*CUBES, You can optionally put a comment line here
```

The remainder of the hatch pattern file specifies the pattern of lines and spaces which form the pattern. Simple patterns may be defined in a single line, although complex definitions may be constructed using a carefully interlinked series of lines and spaces. Each line description has the form

```
angle, x origin, y origin, x repeat, y repeat,linetype...
```

When designing a new hatch pattern, it is a good idea to make a sketch using graph paper. This will help considerably when it comes to the entry of the hatch pattern definition. Consider the hatch pattern CUBES, which is shown in Figure 8–1.

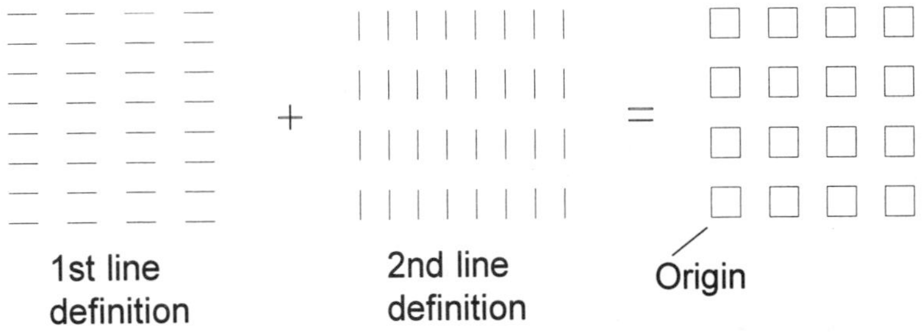

| 1st line definition | 2nd line definition | Origin |

Figure 8–1. The user-defined hatch pattern CUBES.PAT.

As you can see, a pattern of squares may be formed by overlapping a repeating sequence of horizontal and vertical lines. Each line is identical, consisting of a line followed by a space of equal length. If we decide the length of any side of the cube is to be 0.5 units, then the horizontal line is described by the following definition.

```
0,    0, 0,    0, 0.5,    0.5, -0.5
```

The first number (0) is the angle of the line, which is horizontal. This is followed by the start coordinate of the line, relative to an assumed origin (0, 0). To cause the linetype to be repeated vertically upwards, the next two values give a repeat distance of (0, 0.5). The remaining values give the linetype definition, which in this case is (0.5, –0.5).

Note: The linetype definition considered here is very simple (2 values only). More complex sequences may be needed by some patterns.

The vertical line definition is identical, except that the line is drawn at an angle of 90°, as shown below.

```
90,    0, 0,    0, 0.5,    0.5, -0.5
```

Note: The repeat distance is measured in a direction which is relative to the angle of the line. Thus for a line drawn at 90°, the coordinate (0, 0.5) moves to the left.

Thus the complete hatch pattern definition is:

```
*CUBES,  A pattern of squares
0,    0, 0,    0, 0.5,    0.5, -0.5
90,    0, 0,    0, 0.5,    0.5, -0.5
```

Once our user defined hatch pattern has been created, AutoCAD LT must be correctly configured to actually <u>use</u> this new pattern. To do this, firstly start the PREFERENCES command and set the **Meas_urement** option to English, and then begin a new drawing (using the NEW command). This will set the drawing limits to a reasonable size, compared to the scale of the CUBES hatch pattern. Now draw a closed polygon and then start the BHATCH command. From the displayed dialogue box, set the **Pattern Type** option to Custom, and then enter the name of your hatch pattern (CUBES) in the **_C_ustom Pattern** edit box. You can now hatch your closed polygon to test the hatch pattern definition.

Note: The custom hatch pattern should be stored in the main AutoCAD LT directory (C:\ACLTWIN if you followed the default installation options).

Slides and Script Files

A *slide* may be thought of as an electronic 'photograph' of the AutoCAD LT graphics area. Slides are created using the MSLIDE command (make slide) and may later be viewed by the VSLIDE command (view slide).

In a typical application, you might want to create some slides of certain views of a drawing, to show to some clients. This may be quicker (and less error prone) than manually loading each drawing and then trying to find an ideal viewpoint. (With complex drawings, there could also be significant delays during drawing regeneration, or during the removal of hidden detail from 3-dimensional designs.)

Slides also have their uses in the development of custom menu systems. It is possible to activate special *icon menus*, where the user selects an option from an array of graphical symbols. Each of these symbols is actually drawn from a slide, so the ability to create slides is one of the first steps in the development of custom menus. (Select the **_T_ext Style...** option from the **_S_ettings** pull-down menu to see a typical icon menu.)

It is also possible to create an automated 'slide show' where slides are displayed at regular intervals of time, optionally in a continuously repeating sequence. This may be achieved by placing the necessary AutoCAD LT commands into a *script file*. When a script file is activated, AutoCAD LT reads its command input from an external (ASCII) text file, rather than from the keyboard. Bear in mind that script files can do considerably more than just display slide shows, because you can put virtually any sequence of commands into such a file. The only limitation is that commands must operate entirely from the Command line, with no need for input from the user, and no dialogue boxes. (This restriction is the main reason why command line versions of popular AutoCAD LT commands are still supported.)

Note: You can force some AutoCAD LT commands to operate from the Command prompt by setting the CMDDIA system variable to 0.

The first step when creating a slide is to produce or load an AutoCAD LT drawing, containing the required image. You should keep this drawing on disk because the only way to update a slide definition is to modify the original drawing and then recreate the slide. (Slides cannot be edited directly.) Zoom in so that any items of interest fill the graphics area, which will maximize the visual impact when the slide is later displayed. (This is particularly true if the slide will be reduced in size, as with icon menus.)

Slide files have a file extension of '.SLD'. To create a new slide, use the pull-down menu system and select **File**, **Import/Export** and **Make Slide** in that order, or type **MSLIDE** (or **ML**) at the Command prompt. The Create Slide File dialogue box will then appear, allowing you to select the filename and directory in the normal way.

The VSLIDE command is used to view slides, which may be started by selecting **File**, **Import/Export** and **View Slide** in that order from the pull-down menu, or by typing **VSLIDE** (or **VS**) at the Command prompt. Once again, a standard dialogue box is used to select the slide file.

Note: Do not make the mistake of trying to edit a displayed slide. It is actually the loaded drawing (if any) which is edited. To erase a slide, simply redraw the screen.

Running a Slide Show

Once a series of slides have been created, you may wish to automate their display by using AutoCAD LT's *script file* facility.

A script file is simply an ASCII text file, having a file extension of '.SCR'. This script may be activated using the SCRIPT command, which may be started by selecting the **Run Script** option from the **File** pull-down menu, or by typing **SCRIPT** (or **SR**) at the Command prompt.

A typical script file is shown below. This loads the slides PICT1, PICT2 and PICT3 in a repeating sequence, with a 10 second delay between each slide.

```
VSLIDE PICT1
DELAY 10000
VSLIDE PICT2
DELAY 10000
VSLIDE PICT3
DELAY 10000
RSCRIPT
```

The DELAY command is used here to provide a time delay before the next slide is loaded from disk. The actual time delay used is measured in milliseconds, so a value of 10000 is equivalent to 10 seconds. An RSCRIPT command is placed at the end of the script file, which causes the script file to start again from the beginning (and so run continuously). The GRAPHSCR and TEXTSCR commands may also be found in script files which switch between text and graphics screens.

If the time taken to load the slides from disk is excessive, then the next slide may be 'preloaded' while the current one is being viewed. To do this, use the VSLIDE command and precede the slide name with an asterisk. This will load the new slide into memory while the previous slide is being displayed. Then issue a VSLIDE command without any parameters, which will display the previously loaded slide. A suitably modified version of the previous script file is shown below.

```
VSLIDE PICT1
VSLIDE *PICT2
DELAY 10000
VSLIDE
VSLIDE *PICT3
DELAY 10000
VSLIDE
DELAY 10000
RSCRIPT
```

Attribute Extraction and Parts Lists

The creation of Blocks and their associated Attributes was discussed in Chapter 6. Recall that Attributes are used to hold textual information associated with Block definitions.

Clearly, it would be useful to be able to extract this type of information from a drawing, perhaps to form a *parts list* or a *bill of materials*. A text file containing such information could be printed out and might be used for costing or ordering purposes. With an assembly drawing for example, it may be a requirement that a list of the component parts should appear in the drawing itself. This could be achieved by first extracting a parts lists from the drawing as explained above, and then 'pasting' this information back into the drawing.

Before Attributes are extracted from a drawing, you must create a *template file*, which specifies exactly what information is to be removed from the loaded drawing, and its format. Each line in this template file contains the name of an Attribute, or the name of a Block-related parameter. In either case, this is followed on the same line by a *format string* which controls the display format used when the information is written to an external file. A simple template file is shown below.

```
BL:NAME      C008000
BL:X         N009002
BL:Y         N009002
DESCRIPTION  C020000
PRICE        N009002
MATERIAL     C015000
```

Considering this format string, the extracted information is either numeric or character based. This is reflected in the first character of the format string (N or C respectively). In character-based data, the next three digits specify the maximum width of the extracted data or *field*. (The last three digits are always zero.) For numeric data, the first three digits give the total width of the field, while the last three digits give the number of places after the decimal point. Thus a format string N009002 indicates data of the form '123456.78'. Table 8-1 lists some of the more common field definitions. (A complete list is given in the *AutoCAD LT User's Guide*.)

Table 8–1. Commonly used field types, as used in template files.

Field	Type of data
Attribute_name	Attribute value.
BL:NAME	Block name.
BL:X, BL:Y, BL:Z	Block insertion point.
BL:XSCALE, BL:YSCALE, BL:ZSCALE	Block scale factors.

Note: The template file should be an ASCII text file, with a file extension of '.TXT'. AutoCAD LT can be sensitive to the presence of superfluous characters in the template file, so make sure that there are no unwanted spaces or blank lines in the file. You should also use spaces rather than tabs to align columns.

The DDATTEXT command is used to extract Block-related information from a drawing, including Attributes and information about the individual Block insertions themselves. To start the DDATTEXT command, select **File**, **Import/Export** and **Attributes Out** in that order from the pull-down menu, or type **DDATTEXT** (or **DAX**) at the Command prompt. The dialogue box of Figure 8–2 will then be displayed.

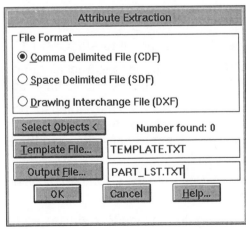

Figure 8–2. The Extract Attributes (DDATTEXT command) dialogue box.

The extracted data can be written to the text file in one of three different formats. *Space delimited* format is ideal for printed tables, because the different columns will be aligned, if a monospaced text font is used. *Comma delimited* format is particularly useful where the extracted data is intended to be loaded into an external database. Finally, the *drawing interchange (DXF)* format is useful where the data is to be exported to another CAD system.

Once the DDATTEXT command has been started, you should select the required file format, and then click on the **Select Objects** button to select the relevant Block insertions. The name of the template file, and the output file name must also be given before clicking **OK**.

Note: You can use the Notepad program to load the output file and examine its content. This information may be loaded into your current drawing by first copying the information to the Windows clipboard and then pasting the data into AutoCAD LT. To copy the output file to the clipboard from within Notepad, highlight the text and then select the **Copy** command from the **Edit** menu. From within AutoCAD LT, start the DTEXT command, and at the 'Text:' prompt, select the **Paste Command** option from the **Edit** menu.

Tutorial 20   Extracting Attributes to Create a Parts List

This exercise uses the office layout drawing of Drawing Exercise 14, in which Blocks representing computers and printers were inserted into a fictitious office floorplan. The aim here is to extract the Attribute data from this drawing, and then to insert this data back into the drawing as a parts list.

1.   Use the Notepad text editor to create a template file having a format similar to that shown below.

```
BL:X          N009002
BL:Y          N009002
TYPE          C010000
SPEC          C015000
SERIAL_NO     C010000
```

2.   Load the office layout drawing into AutoCAD LT.

3.   Use the DDATTEXT command to extract all Attribute data from the drawing to a text file PARTS.TXT. The text file should be in space delimited format.

4.   Load the file PARTS.TXT into the Notepad program and obtain a printout. Confirm that this file contains all Attribute data from the drawing. Copy the entire file to the Windows Clipboard before leaving the Notepad program.

5.   Return to the office layout drawing. Start the DTEXT command and, at the 'Text:' prompt, paste the data from the Clipboard by using the **Paste Command** option from the **Edit** menu.

6.   Use normal drawing commands to add titles and a border for your table.

Creating Abbreviations for AutoCAD LT Commands

Most AutoCAD LT commands have an abbreviation or *command alias* which allows the command to be started quickly from the keyboard. Some of the more commonly used abbreviations were given in Table 2–1, while an exhaustive list is available in the Appendix.

You can examine or alter these command aliases by editing the text file ACLT.PGP, which is normally found in the C:\ACLTWIN directory.

The format of the file is quite straightforward. A typical entry has the form

```
Command_alias,          *Command_Name_in_full
```

Note: Any line preceded by a semicolon is treated as a comment by AutoCAD LT.

Drawing Exercise 20   Adding Command Aliases to the ACLT.PGP File

At the time of writing, some of the newly introduced AutoCAD LT commands do not have command aliases. This exercise requires you to edit the ACLT.PGP and enter suitable abbreviations for these commands.

1.   Make a backup copy of the ACLT.PGP file, so that it can be restored later (should you make a serious mistake when editing the file).

2.   Load the ACLT.PGP file into the Notepad text editor. Study the format of the file carefully.

3.   Add the following entries to the file (at the correct locations), and then save the file before exiting the Notepad program.

```
BH,     *BHATCH
DD,     *DIVIDE
ME,     *MEASURE
```

4.   Start AutoCAD LT and confirm that the keyboard shortcuts **BH**, **DD** and **ME** activate the BHATCH, DIVIDE and MEASURE commands respectively.

Customizing the Toolbox and Toolbar

The Toolbar and Toolbox areas allow commonly used AutoCAD LT commands to be accessed, simply by clicking on an icon with the mouse. This may be faster then selecting the equivalent option from the pull-down menu, or typing the appropriate name at the Command prompt. (Although such savings are small, they will accumulate over time.) It is quite easy to customize the existing buttons, or to add new icons to the Toolbar and Toolbox areas, as we will now see.

If you examine the right-most section of the Toolbar, you may notice some buttons which are 'blank'. (This depends on the size of the Toolbar buttons, relative to the active screen resolution. See Figure 2–5 for a typical example.) Clicking ✍ on these buttons has no effect, because they are currently unprogrammed.

The process of customizing existing buttons or adding new commands to the Toolbar is remarkably straightforward. Simply move the mouse over the button of interest and click ✍. A dialogue box similar to Figure 8–3 will then appear.

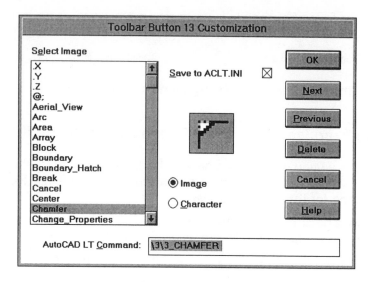

Figure 8–3. Customizing button 13 in the Toolbar area.

The **Image** and **Character** radio buttons control whether a bitmap image, or an alphanumeric character appears on the button's surface. Assuming that the image option is selected, then the **Select Image** list box is used to select the bitmap which is actually used. Finally, the **AutoCAD LT Command** edit box contains the actual command string which is issued when the button is 'pressed' by the user (more on command strings in a moment).

Clicking **OK** will save the currently selected options, and update the previously selected button. This would make sense if an existing button was being edited, such as one of the unused buttons in the Toolbar. If the **Save to ACLT.INI** checkbox is enabled, then these changes will be permanent, otherwise they will only be effective for the current session.

The **Next** and **Previous** buttons allow you to move left or right across the Toolbar, while the button which is currently being edited always appears depressed in the Toolbar. A Toolbar button may be erased by clicking on the **Delete** button (the button becomes blank), while pressing **Cancel** will prevent any mistaken changes from being saved.

A similar dialogue box is displayed when one of the Toolbox buttons is edited (by clicking ✍ on the Toolbox button of interest). There are small differences in the command buttons, and a new area which controls the <u>width</u> of the Toolbox.

Looking at the Toolbox itself, this consists of 48 buttons (30 in Release 1), which may be arranged in a floating window, or may be 'docked' to the left or right margins. The maximum capacity of the Toolbox is 60 buttons (40 in Release 1), so there is room for a further 12 user defined buttons (10 in Release 1).

The horizontal width of the Toolbox may be altered by changing the appropriate value in the Toolbox Width section. As you would expect, the value in the **Floating** edit box controls the width of the Toolbox, when it appears as a mobile window (12 buttons by default in Release 2). Similarly, the value in the **Locked** edit box specifies the width of the Toolbox when it is docked to the left or right margins (2 buttons normally).

You can edit existing Toolbox buttons in the same way as with the Toolbar. The only difference is the presence of **Insert** and **Delete** buttons, in place of the previously mentioned **Next** and **Previous**. Clicking **Insert** creates a new button at the current position, and causes any subsequent buttons to shuffle down. Similarly, pressing **Delete** erases the currently selected button and moves any subsequent buttons up by one place.

Note: The easiest way to add new buttons to the end of the Toolbox is to select the lower right button and then click **Insert** once for each new button that is required. This will create several identical copies of the last button, which may then be edited individually to provide the required functions.

Considering the command string, this may be any sequence of AutoCAD LT commands, with a maximum length of 255 characters. There are also some special purpose characters which you may wish to add to the command string, as shown in Table 8–2.

Table 8–2. Character strings used in the Toolbox and Toolbar.

Character string	Function performed
\2	Toggle snap mode on/off
\3	Cancel (Use \3\3 to cancel <u>All</u> commands)
\4	Toggle coordinates on/off
\5	Next Isometric drawing plane
\7	Toggle grid on/off
\n	Enter
\\	Single backslash, as used in pathnames
;	Suppresses addition of Spacebar to the command string
Spacebar	Command separator
_Command	Command name (The leading underscore ensures correct operation with foreign language versions of AutoCAD LT.)

Customizing the Menu System

Introduction

Along with most other aspects of AutoCAD LT, the pull-down menu system may also be customized. You can use these techniques to completely redesign the menu system, if you wish. At a rather less ambitious level, you may simply want to add one or two options of your own to the existing menu system.

This section assumes that the reader's ambitions fall into the latter category! The emphasis here is therefore on gaining a <u>basic</u> understanding of the structure of the existing menu system, with a view to making a few simple alterations of your own. (Those readers who require a complete coverage of menu system design, including the DIESEL programming language, are referred to the *AutoCAD LT User's Guide* for more details.)

Note: As a major example of menu customization, the present section will focus on the addition of a *3D Construction* section to the existing Draw pull-down menu area. (The menu system discussed here is included on the diskette which accompanies this book.)

Overall Structure

The standard menu system is contained in an ASCII text file ACLT.MNU, which is normally stored in the main AutoCAD LT program directory (C:\ACLTWIN by default). In AutoCAD LT Release 2, the name and location of this menu file are set using the PREFERENCE command's **Menu File** edit box. (Thus you can switch to a custom menu system, simply by editing this entry so that it contains the name of the alternate menu file.) This arrangement is different from that used by Release 1, where two standard menu systems were provided in the files ACLT.MNU and ACLT2.MNU. These provided 'short' and 'full' menu systems respectively, and a provision was made to switch between them.

When a new menu system is loaded, AutoCAD LT compiles the menu system into a binary format, which may be more easily interpreted by the software. This compiled file has the extension '.MNX', rather than '.MNU'. If the text version of the menu file is updated (by editing it using Notepad for example), then the menu will be <u>automatically</u> recompiled, on the next occasion the menu is loaded into AutoCAD LT.

The menu system is divided into several distinct sections, each of which deals with a different type of menu. In AutoCAD LT, these are the:

❑ auxiliary menus   - programmed mouse button functions;

❑ Cursor menu   - a menu which appears at the cursor position;

❑ pull-down menus   - a series of pull-down menu areas;

❑ icon menus   - graphical selection windows.

The menu file itself is divided into several major sections, each of which corresponds to one of these areas. For example.

`***AUX1`	- 'Normal' mouse buttons.
`***AUX2`	- Shift + mouse buttons.
`***AUX3`	- Ctrl + mouse buttons.
`***AUX4`	- Ctrl + Shift mouse buttons.
`***POP0`	- Cursor menu (appears at cursor position).
`***POP1`	- First pull-down menu.
`***POP2`	- Second pull-down menu.
	- (through to ***POP16 maximum.)
`***ICON`	- Icon menu section begins here.
`**SUB_SECTION1`	- Named icon menu.
`**SUB_SECTION2`	- Named icon menu.
	- (through to last named icon menu.)

Following each of these section headings is the actual detail of the menu system, which we will now consider.

Auxiliary Menus

Clicking ⌐⊕ with the mouse is interpreted as a 'pick' function, which is typically used for functions such as coordinate entry, or object selection. If you use a two button mouse, then the first line of each AUXn section may be used to control the function performed when the ⌐⊕ button is pressed, in combination with an appropriate keypress. As an example, consider the following extract from a custom menu system.

`***AUX1`	- 'Normal' mouse buttons.
`;`	- Clicking ⌐⊕ enters ⏎ (a command separator).
`***AUX2`	- Shift + mouse buttons.
`$P0=POP0  $P=*`	- Clicking Shift + ⌐⊕ activates the cursor menu.

Table 8–3 lists some of the special characters, which may be used in the auxiliary (and other) menu areas.

Table 8–3. Some commonly used characters strings in button menus.

Character	Operation performed
^B	Snap on/off.
^C	Cancel command (use ^C^C to cancel <u>all</u> commands).
^D	Coordinate display on/off.
^E	Select next isometric drawing plane.
^G	Grid on/off.
^O	Ortho on/off.
^V	Select next viewport.
;	Carriage return (↵).

Pull-down and Cursor Menus

The basic format of a pull-down menu area is quite straightforward, as shown in Figure 8–4.

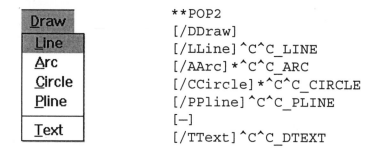

Figure 8–4. A simple pull-down menu and its equivalent textual definition.

After the menu section name, the next line defines a title which appears above the list of menu options. This is followed by the menu options themselves, each on a separate line. Notice that the text which appears on the menu corresponds to the information inside the brackets, and that the first two characters optionally define a keyboard shortcut (these appear underlined on the menu). The special code '[--]' is used to insert a divider into the menu, thus allowing related groups of commands to be grouped together.

To the right of the parentheses is the command string (or menu *macro*) which will be executed if the appropriate menu option is selected by the user. The command string '^C^C' is used to cancel any previously active commands, prior to carrying out the remainder of the menu macro. Command names and other reserved keywords should ideally be preceded by an underscore, as this ensures correct operation with foreign language versions of AutoCAD LT.

Note: In the above example, the ARC and CIRCLE commands use '*^C^C', rather than '^C^C'. This causes the command to repeat automatically (unless cancelled) which may be convenient if several Arcs or Circles are to be drawn.

As a further aid to the grouping of related items, you can optionally create cascading menus, such as that shown in Figure 8–5.

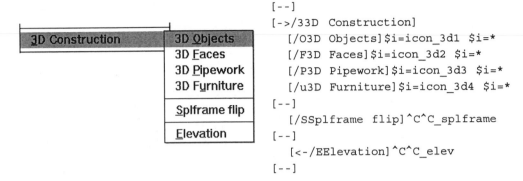

```
[--]
[->/33D Construction]
    [/O3D Objects]$i=icon_3d1 $i=*
    [/F3D Faces]$i=icon_3d2 $i=*
    [/P3D Pipework]$i=icon_3d3 $i=*
    [/u3D Furniture]$i=icon_3d4 $i=*
[--]
    [/SSplframe flip]^C^C_splframe
[--]
    [<-/EElevation]^C^C_elev
[--]
```

Figure 8–5. A cascading menu.

Thus, the character sequence '->' marks the start of a cascading menu, while '<-' returns to the parent menu. (You can also use '<-<-' to close two cascading menus in a single operation.)

The structure of the Cursor menu is very similar to that of a pull-down menu, except that it is normally activated by one of the mouse buttons, rather than by selecting an option from the menu bar. Even though the cursor menu does not display a title, you must still enter a notional title in the first line of the ***POP0 section. (The cursor menu may also use cascading menus, as shown above.)

Icon Menus

If the **3D Objects** option is selected from the above menu system then an icon menu will appear, as shown in Figure 8–6.

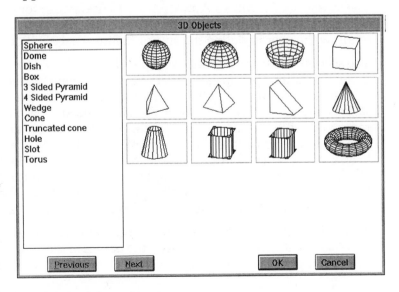

Figure 8–6. The 3D Objects icon menu.

When the 3D Objects option is selected, the menu macro '$i=icon_3d1 $i=*' first sets the icon menu to refer to the menu section **ICON_3D1 (which is after the main ***ICON section heading), and then displays this icon menu. The actual icon menu definition is shown below.

```
***icon
**icon_3d1
[3D Objects]
[3d(sphere,Sphere)]^C^C_insert sphere \xyz
[3d(dome,Dome)]^C^C_insert dome \xyz
[3d(dish,Dish)]^C^C_insert dish \xyz
[3d(box,Box)]^C^C_insert box \xyz
[3d(pyramid3,3 Sided Pyramid)]^C^C_insert pyramid3 \xyz
[3d(pyramid4,4 Sided Pyramid)]^C^C_insert pyramid4 \xyz
[3d(wedge,Wedge)]^C^C_insert wedge \xyz
[3d(cone,Cone)]^C^C_insert cone \xyz
[3d(cone50,Truncated cone)]^C^C_insert cone50 \xyz
[3d(hole,Hole)]^C^C_insert hole \xyz
[3d(slot,Slot)]^C^C_insert slot \xyz
[3d(torus,Torus)]^C^C_insert torus \xyz
```

Notice that the first line after the section heading specifies the title used by the icon menu (3D Objects), and that each subsequent option refers to one of the graphical symbols (reading across and then down). The structure of following lines are similar to that used by pull-down menus, with a bracketed section, followed by the command sequence which will be carried out if that particular option is chosen.

When an option is selected, a 3-dimensional Block is inserted into the drawing. The string '\XYZ' causes AutoCAD LT to first pause for user input ('\' – which selects the insertion point) and then choose the INSERT command's XYZ option to allow the user to define the size of the inserted 3D Block in the drawing.)

The section inside the parentheses specifies the name of a slide file which will be displayed at the appropriate point in the icon menu. Rather than use individual slide files, you can optionally use the SLIDELIB utility program to create a single *slide library* file containing all of the slides used in your custom menu. (This reduces the number of individual files which must be supplied with a custom application.) Thus in the above example a single slide library called 3D.SLB has been created, which contains the slides SPHERE.SLD, DOME.SLD, DISH.SLD etc. The slide SPHERE, for example, may then be referred to in the menu as '3D(SPHERE)'. (An optional second parameter is allowed here which defines the title text shown at the left side of the icon menu – refer back to Figure 8–6.)

To use the SLIDELIB program you must create all of your slides in the normal way and then create a text file containing the names of these slides (one slide per line). Then start the SLIDELIB program from DOS with a command of the form:

C:\ACLTWIN\> **SLIDELIB library <listfile**

Appendix   Command Reference

Introduction

This appendix contains an alphabetically ordered summary of all commands supported by AutoCAD LT. The information presented here provides a complete command reference, bringing together information from a wide variety of different sources. A typical command entry contains the following information.

Command Name

This is the name of the command, given in full. Typing this name at the Command prompt, followed by a *command separator* ([Spacebar], [↵] or ᐟᑫᔤ) will start the command.

Where the command name is preceded by an apostrophe ('ABOUT for example), the command may be issued while another command is in progress. On completion of the *transparent* command, the previously active command will resume automatically. To activate a command transparently, precede the command name with an apostrophe.

If the command name entry does not begin with an apostrophe, then you must cancel any previously active command, before beginning the new command. To do this, press [Ctrl] + [C], or press the *Cancel* icon in the Toolbar, before proceeding (see margin).

Abbreviation

The file ACLT.PGP contains a list of abbreviations for most commonly used commands. Entering the abbreviation at the Command prompt, followed by a command separator has the same effect as typing the full command name. (Some users find it quicker to type an abbreviated command name, when compared to other available methods. Others prefer to use the pull-down menu system or the Toolbox and Toolbar regions.)

Menu Pick Sequence

Most commands may be accessed from the pull-down menu system (if you know where to look). For example, the CIRCLE command may be accessed by selecting the **Circle** option from the **Draw** pull-down menu. A particular option can also be selected by entering its *keyboard short-cut*, which is shown underlined. Thus to select the above option using the keyboard, enter [Alt], followed by [D] and finally [C].

Release Number and Status of Each Command

A software package such as AutoCAD LT does not remain static. New commands are periodically added to the instruction set, while existing commands are improved, and others are 'retired'. (At the time of writing there have been two major versions of the software, these being referred to as *Release 1* and *Release 2*.)

Given its 'open architecture', many users customize AutoCAD LT by designing there own menu systems, or use script files to automate command sequences. It is therefore important to be aware of the status of each command, to ensure portability across different versions of the software.

Most of the available commands were introduced in AutoCAD LT Release 1, although some (such as DIVIDE and MEASURE) were not available until Release 2. An entry of 'R1' or 'R2' in the margin gives the date of introduction of the command.

Some commands (such as CIRCLE) have been enhanced by the addition of new command options. This is indicated by the presence of a ☺ symbol in the margin. Other commands have been partially or completely removed, as indicated by the ☹ symbol. In either case, an explanatory note is given in the main text.

Command Icon

Most popular commands have a command icon, either in the Toolbar or the Toolbox area. The appearance of this icon is given in the margin, to the left of the command description. (To avoid confusion, only those icons which are available as standard are given.)

Once again, there have been some changes between Releases 1 and 2. Some command icons have been redesigned (DDEDIT for example) in order to make their function more obvious. In these cases, both versions are shown, provided that both versions were available as standard. (There have also been minor changes in the appearance of the Toolbar and Toolbox, which are not discussed here.)

Command Description

This section explains the function performed by the command and explains the available range of options. Miscellaneous issues related to the command are then discussed in a series of numbered notes. Finally, a cross reference gives the names of any related commands. (This can be especially useful when searching for a command, whose exact name is unknown.)

Note: There is some overlap between commands and system variables (or *settings*) in AutoCAD LT. For example, you can type the name of a setting at the Command prompt, followed by a command separator to either display or modify the variable's value. (This is an alternative to using the GETVAR and SETVAR commands.) To qualify for a separate entry in this section, the command must do more than simply display or modify an internal variable.

3DPOLY   **(No abbreviation)   (No menu pick sequence)**

R 1   Creates a 3D Polyline. The 3DPOLY command has the advantage, when compared to PLINE (2D polyline), that Z coordinates may be specified during command entry. Available options are **U** – Undo last segment, **C** – join first and last points (Close Polyline) and ⏎ – exit command. ***Notes:*** 1: Restrictions when compared to PLINE include the removal of the *width* and *arc* features. 2: Once a 3D Polyline has been defined, a B-spline curve may be fitted using the PEDIT command. ***See also:*** DLINE, LINE, PLINE and PEDIT commands.

'ABOUT   **AB**   <u>H</u>elp > <u>A</u>bout AutoCAD LT

R 1   Displays a dialogue box showing the AutoCAD LT serial number, release date and the name of the authorized user. The content of the ACLT.MSG file is also displayed in a scrollable text window. ***Notes:*** 1: The content of the AutoCAD LT message file may be altered using a text editor, (such as Notepad in the Accessories folder). 2: Typing an apostrophe before the command name causes the ABOUT command to be issued *transparently*.

'APERTURE   **AP**   **(No menu pick sequence)**

R 1   Specifies the size of the target box used when one or more object snap modes are active. ***Note:*** Typing an apostrophe before the command name causes the APERTURE command to be issued *transparently*. (This allows the size of the object snap target box to be changed <u>during</u> an editing command.) Most users will prefer using the DDOSNAP command, which also allows running object snap modes to be set transparently with a dialogue box. ***See also:*** DDOSNAP and OSNAP commands. APERTURE setting.

ARC   **A**   <u>D</u>raw > <u>A</u>rc

R 1   Draws a circular Arc. By default, a three-point Arc is drawn, but other definition points may be specified by the user. Available options are **A** – included Angle, **C** – Centre of Arc and **E** – Endpoint coordinate. ***Notes:*** 1: By default, entering a positive value for the included angle causes the Arc to be drawn in an anticlockwise direction (so negative values produce a clockwise result). 2: Pressing ⏎ in response to the 'Start point' prompt causes the start coordinate and start direction to be inherited from the most recently drawn Arc or Line. (This is particularly useful when an Arc must be blended with an existing object – so ensure that the reference Line or Arc was the <u>last</u> object drawn.) ***See also:*** CIRCLE and FILLET commands.

AREA   AA   <u>A</u>ssist > <u>A</u>rea

R 1

☺

Calculates the area and perimeter (or circumference) of a closed Polyline, Circle, Polygon or other enclosed region. Available options are **A** – Add mode, **S** – Subtract mode, **E** – select Entity and ✋ – pick defining points of an enclosed region (press ↵ to finish). By toggling between *add* and *subtract* modes, it is possible to compute the area of complex regions having internal 'islands'. ***Notes:*** 1: The BOUNDARY command may be used to create a Polyline around the perimeter of an enclosed region, thus simplifying the calculation of enclosed areas. 2: The PEDIT command may also be used to convert a region bounded by Lines and Arcs into a single Polyline. 3: In Release 2, the AREA command may also be started from the Toolbox. ***See also:*** BOUNDARY, DISTANCE, ID and LIST commands. AREA setting.

ARRAY   AR   <u>C</u>onstruct > <u>A</u>rray

R 1

Makes multiple copies of selected objects. Available options are **P** – polar or circular array and **R** – rectangular array. The ARRAY command is useful when a single object must be copied in a regular circular or rectangular pattern. (In other situations, the COPY and ROTATE commands may be used.) ***Note:*** A rectangular array may be produced at an angle by altering the 'Snap Angle' option in the 'Drawing Aids' dialogue box (DDRMODES command) before creating the array. ***See also:*** COPY and DDRMODES commands.

ATTDEF   AD   (No menu pick sequence)

R 1

Defines an Attribute, which is used to hold textual information associated with a Block definition. ***Note:*** The DDATTDEF command allows attributes to be defined using a dialogue box, which is preferred by most users. Command line entry – as provided by the ATTDEF command – may be required by some *script files*. ***See also:*** ATTEDIT, ATTEXT, DDATTDEF, DDATTE, DDATTEXT, DDEDIT and DDMODIFY commands.

'ATTDISP   AT   (No menu pick sequence)

R 1

Controls the visibility of Attributes associated with Blocks in a drawing. Available options are **ON** – all Attributes visible, **OFF** – all Attributes invisible and **N** – attribute visibility defined by the visible/invisible setting associated with each individual Attribute (Normal mode). ***Note:*** Typing an apostrophe before the command name causes the ATTDISP command to be issued *transparently*. ***See also:*** ATTDEF and DDATTDEF commands. ATTDIA, ATTMODE and ATTREQ settings.

ATTEDIT **AE** **(No menu pick sequence)**

R 1 Allows Attribute definitions to be edited – either globally or one at a time. This command offers a range of powerful features for global editing of Attributes based on wild-card string searches and string manipulation commands. ***Note:*** The DDEDIT command allows single Attributes to be edited using a dialogue box, which will be preferred by most users. The command line Attribute editing provided by the ATTEDIT command may be required where an Attribute's height or text style must be altered, where repetitive editing actions must be performed, and by some script files. ***See also:*** DDATTE, DDEDIT and DDMODIFY commands.

ATTEXT **AX** **(No menu pick sequence)**

R 1 Allows Block-related data including Attributes to be extracted from a drawing to produce a parts list, bill of materials, database-compatible file or DXF file. ***Note:*** The DDATTEXT command allows attributes to be extracted using a dialogue box, which is generally preferred. Command line entry – as provided by the ATTEXT command – may be required by some script files. ***See also:*** DDATTEXT command.

'BASE **BA** **<u>S</u>ettings > Dra<u>w</u>ing > <u>B</u>ase**

R 1 Defines the origin used when the current drawing is inserted as a Block into another drawing. Specifying the base point of a drawing explicitly before saving the file can be useful if the required insertion point does not correspond with the drawing origin. ***Notes:*** 1: If an entire drawing is inserted into another drawing as a Block, only those objects which were created in model space will be imported. 2: Typing an apostrophe before the command name causes the BASE command to be issued *transparently*. ***See also:*** BLOCK, BMAKE and WBLOCK commands.

BHATCH **(No Abbreviation)** **<u>D</u>raw ><u>B</u>oundary <u>H</u>atch**

R 2 Allows a closed region to be hatched with the specified hatch pattern. New features, when compared to HATCH, include the ability to automatically detect the boundary of a closed region, and the introduction of *associative* hatching. With associative hatching, if the shape of the boundary is modified by an edit command, then the hatching is automatically updated to reflect the changes in the boundary. (This is similar to the behaviour of associative Dimensions, where the dimension text changes when the related object(s) in the drawing are modified.) The BHATCH command is the preferred method of hatching for users of AutoCAD LT Release 2. ***Notes:*** 1: The BHATCH command normally uses a dialogue box, but may be forced to use the command line by setting the CMDDIA setting to 0, prior to starting the command. (This may be useful when invoking BHATCH from a script file or a menu macro.) 2: Pre-defined hatch patterns are available in the files ACLT.PAT and ACLTISO.PAT.

To select the appropriate hatch pattern file for your drawing, use the PREFER-ENCES command to set the desired system of units to either English or metric respectively. (This alters the default prototype drawing, hatch pattern and linetype definition files.) 3: A user-defined hatch pattern uses the current drawing linetype. The distance between Lines is given in the **Spacing:** edit box, while the angle is selected using the **Angle:** edit box. Selecting the **Double:** check box, causes a second set of lines to be drawn at 90° to the first. 4: A custom hatch pattern is stored in a hatch pattern file, which must have a file extension of '.PAT'. The name of the hatch pattern in the **Custom Pattern:** edit box must be the same as the name of the hatch pattern file, omitting the file extension. 5: If the **Explode:** checkbox is enabled, then the hatching is drawn as separate Lines, rather than as a single Block. (You can also use the EXPLODE command if you decide to edit individual Lines in an existing hatched area.) 6: The **Pick Points:** button allows the boundary to be identified by picking one or more internal points, while the **Select Objects:** button allows the boundary objects to be specified manually. (The BOUNDARY command may also be used to form a Polyline around a closed region, which may then be selected as a single object by the BHATCH command.) 7: The 'Remove Islands:' button causes any internal 'islands' (unhatched areas) to be removed from the boundary, prior to hatching. 8: To prevent existing Text from being hatched through, select the Text as one of the boundary objects, prior to hatching. 9: If you want to create a hatched area which is similar to one that already exists, then use the **Inherit Properties:** option. 10: When experimenting with the selection of hatch patterns and scale factors, the **Preview Hatch** option may be used as often as required, prior to finally *applying* the hatch pattern to the selected boundary. *See also:* BOUNDARY, HATCH and HATCHEDIT commands.

'BLIPMODE   BM   (No menu pick sequence)

R 1   Determines whether temporary marker blips are created during drawing operations. Available options are **ON** – enable blips and **OFF** – disable blips. The DDRMODES command is generally preferable, as it allows a wide range of drawing defaults to be controlled using a single dialogue box. Some script files may require the command line setting of blip generation, which is provided by the BLIPMODE command. *Note:* Typing an apostrophe before the command name causes the BLIPMODE command to be issued *transparently*. *See also:* DDRMODES command.

BLOCK   B   (No menu pick sequence)

R 1   Creates a Block definition from a group of objects, which is stored as part of the current drawing. *Notes:* 1: The BMAKE command allows Blocks to be defined using a dialogue box, which is preferred by most users. 2: The command line entry used by the BLOCK command may be useful in some script files. *See also:* BASE, BMAKE, WBLOCK and XREF commands.

BMAKE   (No abbreviation)   <u>C</u>onstruct > <u>M</u>ake Block

R 1   Creates a Block definition from a group of objects, which is stored as part of the current drawing. All important features (including the block name, base point and object selection) are defined using a single dialogue box. ***Note:*** If the **Retain Entities:** checkbox is enabled, then the original objects are <u>not</u> erased when the Block is defined. (Or you can use the OOPS command to retrieve objects which have just been deleted during Block creation, without erasing the Block itself.) ***See also:*** BASE, BLOCK, WBLOCK and XREF commands.

BOUNDARY   (No abbreviation)   <u>D</u>raw > Boundary

R 2   Draws separate Polylines which follow the perimeter of a selected region and of any internal 'islands' (if the 'island detection' feature is enabled). ***Notes:*** 1: The CMDDIA system variable controls whether BOUNDARY uses a dialogue box, or the command line (0 = command line, 1 = dialogue box). 2: The BOUNDARY command is actually part of the BHATCH command, so there is no need to use this command, if you intend to proceed to use BHATCH. 3: The AREA command is easier to use when the separate regions are formed as single Polylines. Thus the BOUNDARY command may be used to create Polylines of the outer boundary, and any internal islands, prior to starting the AREA command. ***See also:*** AREA, BHATCH and HATCH commands.

BREAK   BR   <u>M</u>odify > <u>B</u>reak

R 1   Allows part of a Line, Polyline, Circle or Arc to be erased between two defining points. Under normal circumstances, selecting the object with the pickbox also specifies the <u>first</u> defining point. If this is not the intention then type **F** to indicate that the first defining point follows. ***Note:*** When using the BREAK command on Arcs and Circles, remember to indicate the two defining points in the same direction as the object was drawn (anticlockwise by default). ***See also:*** TRIM and EXTEND commands.

CHAMFER   CF   <u>C</u>onstruct > C<u>h</u>amfer

R 1   Produces a chamfer at the intersection of two Lines. The Lines will be either extended or truncated, as required. Available options are **D** – set chamfer first and second Distances, **P** – chamfer an entire Polyline and ⌂ – select object(s). ***Note:*** Chamfering two lines, having previously set the two chamfer distances to zero, is a quick method of correcting untidy Line junctions. ***See also:*** FILLET command.

CHANGE   CH   <u>M</u>odify > <u>C</u>hange Point

R 1   Allows common properties of selected objects to be altered. Available options are **P** – Properties (**C** – Color, **E** – Elev, **LA** – LAyer, **LT** – LType, **T** – Thickness) and '<Change point>'. **Notes:** 1: The 'Change point:' option may be used to tidy junctions where the endpoints of selected objects do not meet, as intended. 2: General object properties, such as linetype or colour may also be modified using the DDCHPROP command. 3: The CHANGE command may be used to modifying Text properties such as height, or rotation angle, although the DDMODIFY command is generally preferred. 4: The DDEDIT command is easier to use than CHANGE, where an existing Text string is to be modified. **See also:** DDCHPROP, DDEDIT and DDMODIFY commands.

CHPROP   CR   (No menu pick sequence)

R 1   Allows basic properties to be modified from the command line. Available options are **C** – Color, **LA** – LAyer, **LT** – LType and **T** – thickness. The DDCHPROP command – which uses a dialogue box – is preferred by most users. CHPROP may be useful in some script files or menu macros. **See also:** CHANGE, DDCHPROP and DDMODIFY commands.

CIRCLE   C   <u>D</u>raw > <u>C</u>ircle

R 1

Draws a Circle. By default the centre and radius are specified, but the circle may also be defined using a 3-point arc, or as being tangential to two existing objects, with a given radius. Available options are **C** – Center, **R** – Radius, **D** – Diameter, **3P** – 3 points and **TTR** – Tangent, Tangent and Radius. **Notes:** 1: The CIRCLE command has been upgraded in AutoCAD LT Release 2 by the inclusion of a *diameter* option. This is an alternative to the *radius* option which was offered by Release 1. (These options become available once the centre coordinate has been specified.) 2: The tangent, tangent and radius option is useful where a Circle must be blended between two existing Lines or Arcs, particularly where the centre coordinate is unknown. The FILLET command is preferred where a tangential Arc is required, rather than a Circle. **See also:** ARC, DONUT, FILLET and POLYGON commands.

'COLOR   CO   (No menu pick sequence)

R 1   Specifies the colour to be used when <u>subsequent</u> objects are drawn. **Notes:** 1: To change the colour of <u>existing</u> objects, use the DDCHPROP command. 2: The DDEMODES (entity modes) command allows common object properties, such as colour, layer, linetype, text style, elevation and thickness to be specified using a single dialogue box, which will be preferred by most users. 3: It is also possible to allocate different colours to groups of objects by placing each group on a different layer. To avoid confusion, avoid mixing these two methods in a single drawing. 4: Typing an apostrophe before the command name causes the COLOR command to be issued *transparently*. **See also:** DDCHPROP, DDEMODES, DDLMODES and DDMODIFY commands.

COPY **CP** <u>C</u>onstruct > <u>C</u>opy

R 1

Produces one or more copies of selected objects. The **M** option allows multiple copies to be produced by specifying a series of destination coordinates. (Press ↵ to finish copying.) ***Notes:*** 1: The COPY command leaves the original object(s) unaltered, while MOVE deletes the original selection set. 2: Drawing file size may be minimized by using Blocks, rather than making copies of identical groups of objects. (This is because a Block is stored only <u>once</u> in the drawing, together with information about each insertion of the Block into the drawing.) 3: You can also use the *grips* feature to copy objects. ***See also:*** ARRAY and MOVE commands.

COPYCLIP **CC** <u>E</u>dit > Copy <u>V</u>ectors

R 1

Copies selected objects to the Clipboard in both AutoCAD LT and *Windows metafile format* (*WMF*). The content of the clipboard may subsequently be 'pasted' into another program which is capable of interpreting AutoCAD LT or WMF data (desktop publishing or word processing software for example). ***Notes:*** 1: If the application does not support AutoCAD LT or WMF (vector-based) data, then try the COPYIMAGE command, which uses a 'bitmap' data format. 2: Other, more powerful commands exist for exchanging data between applications. These make use of Window's *object linking and embedding* (*OLE*) feature. ***See also:*** COPYEMBED, COPYIMAGE, COPYLINK and PASTECLIP commands.

COPYEMBED **CE** <u>E</u>dit > Copy <u>E</u>mbed

R 1

Copies selected objects to the Clipboard to be 'embedded' in another drawing. When the objects are pasted into the destination document, a copy of the actual objects is stored <u>with</u> the document, which means that the original AutoCAD LT drawing is no longer required. Double-clicking on the drawing in the destination document causes AutoCAD LT to be automatically started with the appropriate objects loaded, thus allowing modifications to be made. Once the modifications have been completed, choose the 'Update' option from the File menu and then choose 'Exit'. ***Note:*** An alternative is to use the COPYLINK command to create a 'link' between an AutoCAD LT drawing and a destination document. ***See also:*** COPYCLIP, COPYIMAGE, COPYLINK and PASTECLIP commands.

COPYIMAGE **CI** <u>E</u>dit > Copy <u>I</u>mage

R 1

Copies selected objects to the Clipboard in 'bitmap' format (as a 2-dimensional array of *pixels*). The content of the clipboard may subsequently be 'pasted' into another program which is capable of interpreting data in bitmap format (a paintbrush program for example). ***Notes:*** 1: The Windows metafile format (WMF) supported by the COPYCLIP command is generally preferred over bitmap data as it allows images to be 'stretched' without loss of resolution. 2: Other, more powerful commands exist for exchanging data between applications. These make use of the *object linking and embedding* (*OLE*) features provided by the Windows environment. ***See also:*** COPYEMBED, COPYCLIP, COPYLINK and PASTECLIP commands.

COPYLINK   CL   Edit > Copy Link

R 1   Creates a 'link' between an AutoCAD LT drawing and a destination document. The drawing may be updated either by editing the underline original AutoCAD LT drawing, or by double-clicking on the drawing in the destination document. **Note:** Before using the COPYLINK command to copy drawing information to the Clipboard several preparatory steps should be performed. 1: ensure that the drawing is currently in model space (as paper space is not supported by the *object linking and embedding (OLE)* mechanism). 2: Use the VIEW command to create a named View. (A View called 'OLE2' is automatically created if you omit this step.) 3: Save the drawing. **See also:** COPYCLIP, COPYIMAGE, COPYLINK and PASTECLIP commands.

DBTRANS   (No abbreviation)   (No menu pick sequence)

R 1   A file conversion utility which may be required when certain AutoCAD drawings are loaded into AutoCAD LT. The DBTRANS command converts 8-bit text fonts into a form which is compatible with the Windows environment.

DDATTDEF   DAD   Construct > Define Attribute

R 1   Defines an Attribute, which is used to hold textual information associated with a Block definition. Available options include **I** – visible/Invisible mode toggle, **C** – Constant/variable mode toggle, **V** – Verify on/off mode toggle, **P** – Preset on/off mode toggle. For each Attribute, a *tag*, *prompt* and default *value* must be specified. The tag may be thought of as the *name* of the Attribute (which is used during Attribute extraction). The prompt and default values are displayed when the Attributes associated with a Block are edited. **Note:** The related ATTDEF command allows attributes to be defined using the command line, which may be required by certain *script files*. **See also:** ATTDEF, ATTEDIT, ATTEXT, DDATTDEF, DDATTE, DDATTEXT, DDEDIT and DDMODIFY commands.

DDATTE   DE   Modify > Edit Attribute

R 1   Allows the Attributes associated with an inserted Block to be edited. A dialogue box is displayed showing a series of *prompts*, together with the current *value* associated with each Attribute. **Notes:** 1: This dialogue box will be displayed automatically during Block insertion if the ATTREQ (attribute request) setting has been set to 1. (Set ATTREQ to 0 during Block insertion, if you prefer to edit Attributes at a later stage.) 2: The ATTDIA setting determines whether attribute requesting (during Block insertion) uses the command line or a dialogue box (0 = use command line, 1 = use dialogue box). 3: The ATTDISP command controls the visibility of Attributes in a drawing. (See the ATTDISP command entry for more details.) **See also:** ATTDISP, ATTDEF, ATTEXT, DDATTDEF and DDATTEXT commands. ATTDIA, ATTMODE and ATTREQ settings.

DDATTEXT **DAX** <u>F</u>ile > <u>I</u>mport/Export > <u>A</u>ttributes Out

R 1 Allows Block-related data including Attributes to be extracted from a drawing to produce a parts list, bill of materials, database-compatible file or DXF file. Available file types include *space delimited format (SDF)*, *comma delimited format (CDF)* and *drawing interchange format (DXF)*. Before extracting data, a *template file* should be created, which specifies the types of data and the required output data format in each case. An ASCII output file is produced which may be printed, edited or imported into other software such as a database, spreadsheet or Basic program. This command allows attributes to be extracted using a dialogue box, which is generally preferred, although the ATTEXT command is also available. ***Notes:*** 1: See the main text for details of template file structure. 2: You can paste a parts list into an AutoCAD LT drawing. To do this, load the file containing the extracted Attribute data into a Windows text editor, such as Notepad. Copy the information to the clipboard before switching to AutoCAD LT. Finally start the DTEXT command and, at the 'Text:' prompt, select the **Paste** option from the **E**dit menu. ***See also:*** ATTEXT command.

DDCHPROP **DC** <u>M</u>odify > Change Properties

R 1 Displays a dialogue box allowing basic object properties to be altered. The colour, layer name, linetype and thickness of an object can all be modified using the DDCHPROP command. ***Notes:*** 1: The DDCHPROP command may be used to alter properties of <u>several</u> objects in a single operation. DDMODIFY allows more advanced properties to be modified, but only for a <u>single</u> selected object. 2: The special term BYLAYER causes the colour or linetype of an object to be inherited from the layer on which it is drawn. 3: Objects with a colour or linetype setting of BYBLOCK will inherit the currently active colour or linetype when they are inserted as a Block into another drawing. 4: The CHANGE command allows properties to be altered from the command line, which may be required in some script files. 5: To modify the actual text string associated with Text, use either DDEDIT or DDMODIFY. ***See also:*** CHANGE, DDEDIT and DDMODIFY commands.

DDEDIT **ED / TE** <u>M</u>odify > E<u>d</u>it Text

New icon

Old icon

R 1

The DDEDIT command may be used to edit Text or Attribute definitions using a dialogue box. With Text, the dialogue box has a single line containing the text string to be modified. The Attribute editing facility allows an Attribute definition to be edited, <u>before</u> the Attribute has been associated with a Block. When an Attribute is selected for editing, the dialogue box allows the *tag*, *prompt* and default *value* of the Attribute to be modified. ***Notes:*** 1: If detailed Text or Attribute properties such as height or rotation angle must be altered then use the DDMODIFY command. 2: See Table 4–2 for details of text editing keystrokes. 3: The ATTEDIT command allows Attributes to be edited from the command line, which may be required by some script files. ***See also:*** ATTEDIT, CHANGE and DDMODIFY commands.

DDEMODES   EM   <u>S</u>ettings > <u>E</u>ntity Modes

R 1

Sets properties which will be used when objects are <u>subsequently</u> drawn. The DDEMODES command allows the currently active colour, layer, linetype, text style, elevation and thickness to be set from a single dialogue box. **Notes:** 1: The colour of the DDEMODES button in the Toolbar changes to reflect that of the currently active drawing colour. 2: The special term BYLAYER causes the colour or linetype of an object to be inherited from the layer on which it is drawn. 3: Objects with a colour or linetype setting of BYBLOCK will inherit the currently active colour or linetype when they are inserted as a Block into another drawing. 4: To change common properties of <u>existing</u> objects, use the DDCHPROP command. 5: To change more advanced properties of a single object, use the DDMODIFY command. **See also:** COLOR, DDCHPROP, DDMODIFY, ELEV, LAYER, LINETYPE, STYLE and commands.

'DDGRIPS   GR   <u>S</u>ettings > <u>G</u>rips Style

R 1

Allows the *grips* facility to be enabled or disabled and provides detailed configuration options for the use of grips within the current drawing. The dialogue box permits the size and colour of selected and unselected grips to be chosen, and controls whether individual grips within Blocks are displayed. **Notes:** 1: Grips may be used to stretch, move, copy, rotate, scale or mirror objects. See Chapter 4 for details of editing objects using grips. 2: The DDGRIPS command may be started transparently by typing an apostrophe in front of the command name. **See also:** COPY, MOVE, ROTATE, SCALE and STRETCH commands.

DDIM   DM   <u>S</u>ettings > Di<u>m</u>ension Style

R 1

Controls the creation of dimension styles from a main dialogue box, from where a series of subsidiary dialogue boxes may be accessed. Each button on the main dialogue box allows a particular feature of the currently selected dimension style to be examined or modified. Available options are **Dimension <u>L</u>ine**, **<u>E</u>xtension Lines**, **<u>A</u>rrows**, **<u>T</u>ext Location**, **Text F<u>o</u>rmat** and **<u>C</u>olors**. Dimension styles allow a range of standard Dimension types to be developed for use in a drawing. This encourages the standardization of dimensioning and means that all Dimensions of a particular style may be altered in a single operation, simply by modifying the style definition. **Notes:** 1: To create a new dimension style, based on an existing style, first select the parent style and then type the name of the new style in the **Dimension Style** edit box (and press ⏎). The new style inherits all settings from the parent style. 2: To import existing Dimension styles into a new drawing, use the existing drawing as a *prototype* when creating the new drawing (NEW command). 3: To create a new Dimension, select a suitable option from the **<u>D</u>raw** pull-down menu, or use either the DIM or DIM1 command. 4: To edit an existing Dimension, select the **Edit Dimension** option from the **<u>M</u>odify** pull-down menu, or use either the DIM or DIM1 command. **See also:** DIM and DIM1 commands.

DDINSERT   I   <u>D</u>raw > Insert Bloc<u>k</u>

R 1   Inserts a copy of a previously defined Block (or an entire drawing file) into the current drawing. The use of Blocks allows drawings to be constructed from a series of simpler objects. Blocks encourage standardization due to the use of libraries of standard parts. (Drawing file sizes also tend to be reduced.) Options such as the insertion point, X, Y and Z scales, rotation angle and whether the Block should be *exploded* during insertion may be selected from the displayed dialogue box, or during the insertion process. The **File** button allows an existing drawing file to be selected for insertion, while the **Block** button permits Blocks already defined within the current drawing to be chosen. ***Notes:*** 1: There is little difference between a Block which has been created with the WBLOCK command and a drawing file which has been saved in the normal way. Both can be inserted using the DDINSERT command. However, with complete drawing files, only those objects which were created in *model space* will be inserted into the new drawing. 2: Once a drawing file has been inserted, it becomes a named Block within the current drawing. Subsequent insertions may be made by selecting the **Block** button. 3: A Block which is inserted with different X, Y and Z scales <u>cannot</u> be exploded. If this is the intention then insert the Block with the **Explode** button selected and then use the SCALE command to alter the size of selected objects. 4: A useful convention is to create Blocks which are 1 unit by 1 unit in size. The X, Y and Z scale options may then be used to specify the <u>absolute</u> size of the inserted Block in the drawing. 5: The properties associated with a previously inserted Block may be edited using either the DDCHPROP or DDMODIFY commands. 6: Attributes associated with a Block may be edited using the DDATTE command. 7: Attributes may be extracted to create a parts list using the DDATTEXT command. 8: The ATTDIA, and ATTREQ settings, together with the ATTDISP command, control the use and appearance of Attributes associated with Blocks. Whether or not Attributes values are requested during Block insertion is controlled by the ATTREQ setting (1 = request Attribute values during Block insertion, 0 = accept default values – or edit Attributes later using DDATTE). The ATTDIA setting determines whether Attribute requesting uses a dialogue box, or the command line (0 = command line, 1 = dialogue box). The ATTDISP command controls the visibility of Attributes in a drawing. (See the ATTDISP entry for more details.) 9: Blocks may be inserted from the command line using the INSERT command, which may be required with some script files. ***See also:*** ATTDISP, DDATTE, DDATTEXT, DDCHPROP, DDMODIFY and INSERT commands. ATTDIA, ATTMODE and ATTREQ settings.

'DDLMODES   LD   <u>S</u>ettings > <u>L</u>ayer Control

New icon

Old icon

R 1

Permits new layers to be created and allows properties of existing layers to be modified using a dialogue box. Layers provide a useful method for structuring drawing information. By placing related information on a particular layer, the colour, linetype and visibility of that information can easily be controlled. **Notes:** 1: To create a new layer, type the layer name in the edit box and then click the **Ne<u>w</u>** button. 2: To change the *current* layer, pick the layer name from the list box and click the **<u>C</u>urrent** button. (Objects created with drawing commands such as LINE, ARC etc. are placed on the current layer, but see note 8 for an exception.) 3: To change the colour of one or more layers, select the required layer name(s) from the list box and click the **Set Color...** button. 4: To change the linetype of an existing layer (or group of layers), select the required layer name(s) from the list box and click the **Set <u>L</u>type...** button. (You may have to *load* linetypes using the LINETYPE command before choosing this option.) 5: To make one or more layers invisible, select the required layer name(s) from the list box and click the **Of<u>f</u>** button. (The **<u>O</u>n** button has the reverse effect.) 6: *Freezing* (and later *thawing*) unwanted layers can speed up drawing regeneration because information on the frozen layers is ignored during the regeneration process. 7: To *lock* an existing layer (or group of layers), select the required layer name(s) from the list box and click the **Loc<u>k</u>** button. (The **<u>U</u>nlock** button has the reverse effect.) Locking a layer prevents objects previously drawn on that layer from being unintentionally altered. (You can still create new objects on a locked layer – either by making the layer *current* and using a drawing command, or by inserting a Block.) 8: Objects drawn on a particular layer will be placed on the <u>same</u> layer when they are inserted as a Block into another drawing. If that layer does not exist in the new drawing, it is created. An exception to this is layer 0. Objects drawn on layer 0 are placed on the <u>current</u> layer when they are inserted into a new drawing. 9: It is possible to freeze and thaw layers on the current viewport only, using the buttons in the 'Cur VP' area. Similarly, the freeze/thaw status of layers on newly created viewports can be controlled from the 'New VP' section. 10: Typing an apostrophe before the command name causes the DDLMODES command to be issued *transparently*. **See Also:** LAYER, LINETYPE and VPLAYER commands.

DDMODIFY   (No abbreviation)   <u>M</u>odify ><u>Modif</u>y Entity

R 2

Allows properties associated with single objects to be modified. Having selected the object to be modified, a dialogue box appears, whose exact appearance depends on the type of object selected. **Notes:** 1: Use the DDCHPROP command to alter basic properties (such as colour or linetype) associated with one or more objects in a single operation. Use DDMODIFY to alter specialist properties for a <u>single</u> selected object. 2: The CHANGE command is an alternative to the DDMODIFY command, particularly where command line entry is a requirement. 3: The version of DDMODIFY supplied with AutoCAD LT Release 2 is slightly simpler than that available with the full version of AutoCAD. In particular, the range of objects which can be edited has been restricted. **See also:** CHANGE, DDCHPROP and DDRENAME commands.

'DDOSNAP   OS   <u>A</u>ssist > <u>O</u>bject Snap

R 1 Displays a dialogue box which allows *running* (or permanently enabled) object snap modes to be enabled or disabled. The size of the object snap target box (the *aperture*) may also be set using this dialogue box. Object snap is particularly useful when drawing or editing operations must refer to existing drawing geometry. Available object snap modes are **<u>E</u>ndpoint** – Line or Arc endpoint, **<u>M</u>idpoint** – Line or Arc midpoint, **<u>C</u>enter** – centre of an Arc or Circle, **<u>N</u>ode** – existing Point, **<u>Q</u>uadrant** – 0, 90, 180 or 270° point of an existing Arc or Circle, **Int<u>e</u>rsection** – intersection of two Lines, Arcs or Circles (in any combination), **In<u>s</u>ertion** – Block insertion point, **<u>P</u>erpendicular** – at 90° to the selected Line, Arc or Circle, **<u>T</u>angent** – tangential to an Arc or Circle , **Nea<u>r</u>est** – nearest point to the graphics cursor on an existing Line, Arc or Circle and **Q<u>u</u>ick** – first identified object snap point within the target box area. *Notes:* 1: Object snap is particularly useful when creating Dimensions, as it allows extension lines to be accurately attached to existing points on the drawing. 2: Typing an apostrophe before the command name causes the DDOSNAP command to be issued *transparently*. *See also:* APERTURE and OSNAP commands.

'DDPTYPE   (No abbreviation)   <u>S</u>ettings > P<u>o</u>int Style

R 1 Displays a dialogue box which allows the size and appearance of Point entities to be controlled. (20 different Point shapes are available.) *Notes:* 1: To change the appearance of previously drawn Points, use the DDPTYPE command to select the new style and then use the REGEN command. 2: Typing an apostrophe before the command name causes the DDPTYPE command to be issued *transparently*. *See Also:* POINT command.

DDRENAME   DR   <u>M</u>odify > Re<u>n</u>ame

R 1 Allows certain types of item to be renamed using a dialogue box. Features capable of being renamed (within a drawing) include Blocks, Dimension styles, layers, linetypes, Text styles, user coordinate systems, views and viewport configurations. *Notes:* 1: To rename an item, select the required type from the **Named Objects** list box, and the item name from the **Items** list box. Type the new name in the **Rename To** edit box and then click the **Rename To** button. 2: Wild card operators such as '?' (match a single character) and '*' (match any character string) may be used in the **Old Name** and **Rename To** edit boxes, thus allowing several matching items to be renamed in a single operation. (See the *AutoCAD LT Release 2 User's Guide* for a full list of wild card operators.) 3: Certain items, such as layer 0 and the CONTINUOUS linetype cannot be renamed. *See also:* RENAME command.

'DDRMODES   DA   <u>S</u>ettings > <u>D</u>rawing Aids

R 1

Sets a range of drawing aids using a single dialogue box. Features which may be controlled are **<u>O</u>rtho**, **Solid <u>F</u>ill, <u>Q</u>uick Text**, **<u>B</u>lips**, **<u>H</u>ighlight**, **<u>S</u>nap**, **<u>G</u>rid** and **<u>I</u>sometric Snap/Grid**. *Notes:* 1: Use *ortho* mode during line drawing to restrict freehand drawing to be either horizontal or vertical. (See note 3 for an exception to this rule.) Angles (when drawing Arcs for example) are also forced to 90° increments. 2: *Snap* mode forces the crosshairs to snap to an invisible rectangular grid, which is convenient when sizes to be entered are a multiple of a basic snap setting. 3: Altering the angle of the snap grid also alters the angle used by ortho mode (which is horizontal and vertical by default). 4: *Quick text* mode causes Text to be drawn as an outline box, which is intended to speed up drawing regeneration and plotting operations. (Turn quick text off before producing the final printout.) 5: The *blips* setting controls the generation of temporary marker blips during drawing operations. If the screen appears 'cluttered' then disable this setting. 6: The *highlight* option determines whether selected objects appear highlighted during editing operations. 7: A rectangular array of dots may be displayed using the *grid* option. The grid spacing is normally set to be the same as the snap increment – but this is not compulsory! 8: An *isometric grid* may be displayed by selecting the **On** button in the Isometric Snap/Grid section. Ortho mode should also be enabled to force lines to be drawn parallel to the isometric grid. 9: The active isometric plane may be set from this dialogue box, but most users will find pressing [Ctrl] + [E] during drawing operations to be faster. 10: For transparent operation, type an apostrophe before the command name. *See also:* ORTHO, QTEXT, BLIPMODE, SNAP, GRID and ISOPLANE commands.

'DDSELECT   SL   <u>S</u>ettings > Sele<u>c</u>tion Style

R 1

Controls the methods used to select objects during editing commands. It also allows the size of the object select *pickbox* to be altered and controls the order in which objects (entities) are processed by certain commands. Available options include **<u>N</u>oun/Verb Selection**, **<u>U</u>se Shift to Add**, **<u>P</u>ress and Drag** and **<u>I</u>mplied Windowing**. By default, *noun/verb selection* and *implied windowing* are both enabled. (You can restore this setting by pressing the **<u>D</u>efault Selection Mode** button.) *Notes:* 1: When noun/verb selection is enabled, objects may optionally be *pre-selected*. (You can choose the objects <u>first</u> and then enter the appropriate command.) Some edit commands will not allow pre-selection of objects. Examples include the BREAK, EXTEND, TRIM, CHAMFER, FILLET, OFFSET and PEDIT commands. 2: The **<u>U</u>se shift to Add** setting (which is disabled by default) allows objects to be added to the selection set by holding down the [Shift] key while picking objects. With this mode disabled, each object picked is added to (or subtracted from) the current selection set. 3: When **Implied Windowing** is enabled, objects may be picked in the normal way, by screen pointing. If the indicated point does not correspond to an existing object, it is assumed to be the first point of a *window* or *crossing* selection (which is made by picking two diagonally opposite points). If the first point is at the <u>left</u> side, a *window* selection is made, where objects must be entirely within the box to be selected. If the first point is at the <u>right</u>, a *crossing* selection is made in which objects need only be partly within the box to be selected.

(A *window* selection box is drawn using solid lines, while a *crossing* box is drawn using dotted lines.) 4: Various selection options may be entered at the 'Select objects:' prompt, which may be used to modify the default object selection method. These include **L** – Last created (and visible) object, **All** – All objects (other than those on frozen layers), **F** – Fence drawn through selected objects, **P** – Previous selection set (a very useful option where successive edit commands must operate on the same group of objects), **A** – Add following objects to the selection set, **R** – Remove following objects from the selection set, **WP** – *Window* Polygon selection where a series of points is used to form a window selection region (press ↵ to close the polygon) and **CP** – *Crossing* Polygon selection in which a series of points is used to form a crossing region (press ↵ to close the polygon). 5: Typing an apostrophe before the command name causes the DDSELECT command to be issued *transparently*. *See also:* SELECT command.

DDUCS	**UC**	**<u>A</u>ssist > <u>N</u>amed UCS**

R 1   Displays a dialogue box allowing named user coordinate systems to be selected (made current), renamed, deleted or examined (listed). User coordinate systems are particularly useful when producing 3D drawings, as they tend to simplify coordinate entry. The currently active UCS is indicated in the list box by the abbreviation 'Cur' to the right of the UCS name. If the UCS has been previously modified, then the '*PREVIOUS*' selection may be chosen repeatedly to 'step backwards' through UCS modifications. If the current UCS has not been named it is referred to as '*NO NAME*'. *Notes:* 1: To make a named UCS *current*, select the UCS name from the list box and press the **<u>C</u>urrent** button. 2: To *delete* a named UCS, select the UCS name from the list box and press the **<u>D</u>elete** button. 3: To list a particular UCS, select the UCS name from the list box and press the **<u>L</u>ist** button. This causes a *direction vector* to be displayed for the X, Y and Z axes of the UCS, together with the coordinate of the UCS origin. 4: To rename a UCS select the existing UCS name from the list box, type the new UCS name in the edit box and press the **<u>R</u>ename To** button. 5: If the UCSFOLLOW setting is set to 1 (on), then a plan view is automatically generated when the UCS is modified. The default value for UCSFOLLOW is 0 (off). In drawings with multiple viewports, each viewport may have its own UCSFOLLOW value. *See also:* DDUCSP, UCS, and UCSICON commands. UCSFOLLOW setting.

DDUCSP	**UP**	**<u>A</u>ssist > <u>P</u>reset UCS**

R 1   Provides a range of UCS presets which may be individually selected from a dialogue box. The displayed slides each show the reference coordinate system using a tripod, with a red line indicating the direction of the Z axis. This reference may refer either to the world coordinate system, or to the current UCS. The direction of the 'next' UCS is then shown attached to one of the faces of a cube. Other options allow the UCS to be set to the plane of the screen (the current view), to the world coordinate system, or to the previous UCS setting. *See also:* DDUCS, UCS and UCSICON commands. UCSFOLLOW setting.

'DDUNITS   DU   <u>S</u>ettings > <u>U</u>nits Style

R 1   Allows the measurement system used for coordinates, distances and angles to be defined. The numeric precision of units and angles may also be controlled from this dialogue box. Available options for linear units are **S<u>c</u>ientific**, **De<u>c</u>imal**, **<u>E</u>ngineering**, **<u>A</u>rchitectural** and **<u>F</u>ractional**. Available options for angular measurements are **De<u>c</u>imal Degrees**, **Deg/<u>M</u>in/Sec**, **<u>G</u>rads**, **<u>R</u>adians** and **Sur<u>v</u>eyor**. **Notes:** 1: As a general rule drawings should be entered 'actual size' with 1 drawing unit corresponding to 1 unit of length of the object. The PLOT command's print scaling facility may be used later to fit the drawing onto paper of the chosen size, or to produce an accurately scaled printout. 2: The engineering and architectural modes are exceptions to the previous rule because they assume that 1 drawing unit represents 1 inch. 3: It is possible to control the suppression of leading or trailing zeroes in dimensions. To do this choose the **Text F<u>o</u>rmat** option from the dialogue box which is displayed by the DDIM command. The Zero Suppression section of the displayed dialogue box may then be used to obtain the required setting. 4: The DDUNITS dialogue box controls the numeric precision used when dimension text is displayed. To alter the number of decimal places displayed by an existing Dimension, first use the DDUNITS command to set the required numeric precision and then choose the UPDATE dimension sub-command (**<u>M</u>odify** > **Ed<u>i</u>t Dimension** > **<u>U</u>pdate Dimension**). 5: To alter the precision used by new Dimensions, first set the required precision using the DDUNITS command and then create the Dimension. 6: Typing an apostrophe before the command name causes the DDUNITS command to be issued *transparently*. **See also:** UNITS command.

'DELAY   **(No abbreviation)**   **(No menu pick sequence)**

R 1   Delays the execution of following commands for the specified number of milliseconds. (For example, the command 'DELAY 2000' will cause a 2 second delay.) This facility is normally used in script files, where a series of AutoCAD LT commands is issued from a previously created ASCII text file (which happens under the control of the SCRIPT command). **Notes:** 1: Actual time delays generated may vary slightly from one machine to another, due to differences in processor type and computer performance. 2: Typing an apostrophe before the command name causes the DELAY command to be issued *transparently*. (This could be used in a script file to cause a pause <u>during</u> command operation.) **See also:** GRAPHSCR, RESUME, RSCRIPT, SCRIPT and TEXTSCR commands.

DIM   D   **(No menu pick sequence)**

R 1   Enters dimensioning mode, from where a range of dimension sub-commands may be accessed. Dimensioning mode is indicated by the 'Dim:' prompt, which replaces the more usual 'Command:'. The major difference between the DIM and DIM1 commands is that the DIM1 command creates a single Dimension and then exits to the Command prompt. In contrast, to exit from the DIM command, it is necessary to type EXIT (or press Ctrl + C) when 'Dim:' is displayed. Use the DIM command when several Dimensions must be created in sequence, or use DIM1 to create a single Dimension.

Available sub-commands are ALIGNED, ANGULAR, BASELINE, CENTER, CONTINUE, DIAMETER, EXIT, HOMETEXT, HORIZONTAL, LEADER, OBLIQUE, ORDINATE, RADIUS, REDRAW, ROTATED, STATUS, STYLE, TEDIT, TROTATE, VERTICAL, UNDO and UPDATE. Some of these sub-commands are used to create new Dimensions, while others allow features of existing Dimensions to be modified. The remainder provide replacements for common AutoCAD LT utility commands (UNDO for example), which allow the appropriate facility to be accessed without the need to return to the Command prompt. ***Notes:*** 1: In some circumstances it may be necessary to press ⌊Ctrl⌋ + ⌊C⌋ twice to exit fully from a dimensioning sub-command. 2: The general appearance of a Dimension is controlled by the active dimension style, which is set using the DDIM command. 3: As a general rule, use object snap to force Dimensions to refer accurately to the appropriate drawing features. 4: Linear Dimensions (which measure distances) may be created using the HORIZONTAL, VERTICAL, ALIGNED or ROTATED sub-commands. The HORIZONTAL and VERTICAL options are used to measure horizontal or vertical distances respectively. ALIGNED Dimensions, as the name suggests, measure distances parallel to the indicated extension line endpoints. The ROTATED sub-command causes the dimension line to be rotated through the indicated angle. (A dimension line drawn horizontally underneath the measured length is used as a reference, when calculating the angle of rotation.) 5: Multiple linear Dimensions may be created by using the BASELINE or CONTINUE dimension sub-commands. The CONTINUE option allows Dimensions to be linked end to end in a 'chain', while the BASELINE command causes Dimensions to be 'stacked', one above another, with each Dimension measuring the distance from a common datum line. To use either option, first create a single linear Dimension, and then choose either the BASELINE or CONTINUE option. Further Dimensions may then be created by indicating the second extension line origin of each subsequently drawn linear Dimension. 6: The ORDINATE sub-command is used to display the *X* or *Y* coordinate of an indicated drawing feature. Once the ORDINATE option has been chosen, indicate the required drawing feature, and then the position of the leader endpoint. (In automatic mode, the relative position of the leader and the feature determines whether an X or Y ordinate is drawn.) When calculating the default value of the Dimension, the origin of the current UCS is used as the datum, so it is useful to first move the UCS to the required reference point, before creating an ordinate Dimension. 7: When creating radial dimensions choose either the RADIUS or DIAMETER sub-command to give the appropriate Dimension type. (Note that the point chosen to indicate the Arc or Circle is also used as one of the endpoints of the Dimension line.) The **Extension Lines** dialogue box which is accessed using the DDIM command, determines whether centre lines or centre marks are automatically drawn when the RADIUS, or DIAMETER sub-commands are used. (Set the Centre mark size to zero to disable centre marks.) 8: The CENTER sub-command may be used to cause centre lines or centre marks to be drawn for an existing Circle or Arc. Once again it is the **Extension Lines** dialogue box of the DDIM command which controls the appearance of any centre marks or lines drawn. 9: The ANGULAR sub-command draws an angular Dimension between two lines (which must both exist prior to drawing the Dimension). 10: The LEADER sub-command is used to draw an arrow, with an optional textual message.

Having selected the option, first indicate the arrow startpoint, and then each junction coordinate in the leader line (press ⏎ to finish). Finally, enter a message at the 'Dimension text:' prompt. 11: The STYLE sub-command allows another dimension style to be made current. (Dimension styles may be created and modified using the DDIM command.) 12: The STATUS sub-command displays the current values of all system variables (settings) associated with the current dimension style. 13: The TEDIT (text edit), HOMETEXT (home text) and TROTATE (text rotate) sub commands modify the position and rotation angle of the textual portion of a Dimension. Use TEDIT and TROTATE to move and rotate the text and HOMETEXT to revert to the default position. 14: The OBLIQUE sub-command causes the extension lines of an existing Dimension to be redrawn at the specified angle (the default angle is 90º). 15: The UPDATE sub-command causes an existing Dimension to be redrawn in the current dimension style. Any changes in the current text style or measurement conventions following the creation of the Dimension, will also be reflected in the updated Dimension. Thus for example, to change the number of decimal places in linear Dimensions, use the DDUNITS command, followed by DIM UPDATE to correct any existing Dimensions. 16: See the main text for examples of dimension styles, including limits, tolerances and alternate units Dimensions. *See also:* DDIM and DIM1 commands. DIMALT – DIMZIN settings.

DIM1   D1   <u>D</u>raw > (5 options), <u>M</u>odify > Ed<u>i</u>t Dimension

R 1 Creates or edits a single Dimension and then returns to the Command prompt automatically. See the DIM command entry for details of available options. *See also:* DDIM and DIM commands. DIMALT – DIMZIN settings.

'DIST   DI   <u>A</u>ssist > <u>D</u>istance

R 1 Measures the distance and angle between two indicated points. *Notes:* 1: To measure the distance between two existing drawing features, remember to use object snap. 2: To find the coordinate of a particular point, use the ID command. 3: Typing an apostrophe before the command name causes the DIST command to be issued transparently. *See also:* AREA, ID and LIST commands.

DIVIDE   (No abbreviation)   Construct > Divide

R 2 Places Point entities or named Blocks at regular intervals along the perimeter of an object, thus dividing the object into a specified number of segments. With named Blocks, the DIVIDE command may be used as an alternative to the ARRAY command. Points are normally used as an intermediate step in the construction of more complex objects, with the Node object snap operating mode (see the DDOSNAP command). *Notes:* 1: Having selected the object to divide (a Line, Arc, Polyline, Circle or Ellipse for example), you are then asked to enter the required number of segments, or give a Block name, followed by the number of segments. 2: With Blocks, you can optionally align each Block as it is placed. *See also:* ARRAY, DDOSNAP, DDPTYPE and MEASURE commands.

DLINE   DL   <u>D</u>raw > Dou<u>b</u>le Line

R 1

Draws a series of parallel Lines. Available options are **A** – Arc, **B** – Break, **CA** – CAps, **CE** – Center, **CL** – CLose, **D** – Dragline, **E** – Endpoint, **L** – Line, **O** – Offset, **S** – Snap, **U** – Undo and **W** – Width (not all of which are available at the same time). The DLINE command is particularly useful for drawing walls or other similar features which have inner and outer edges. *Notes:* 1: When beginning the DLINE command, the normal method is simply to indicate a start point. You can also use the Offset option to specify the startpoint as a distance and direction from an indicated point. 2: The Arc and Line options switch between drawing Lines and Arcs. (The Center and Endpoint options refer to the next Arc segment and are specific to this drawing mode.) 3: The Width option specifies the distance between the Lines or Arcs. 4: By default, indicated points are taken to be midway between the two Lines or Arcs. The Dragline option allows this behaviour to be modified, offering options of **L** – Left, **R** – Right or **C** – Center. 5: The Close option causes the first and last points to be linked by the appropriate type of double line segment. 6: The Undo option erases the most recently drawn segment. 7: If snap mode is enabled, the DLINE command ends automatically when an endpoint is found to be in close proximity to an existing Line or double line segment. 8: The Break option controls whether or not a break is automatically created where the current double line segment meets an existing Line or double line segment (see also note 8). 9: When you finish drawing a double line, the CAps option controls whether the ends are left open or 'capped'. 10: Use the OFFSET command if you want to create parallel Lines, Polylines, Arcs, or concentric Circles – based on <u>existing</u> objects. *See also:* 3DPOLY, LINE, OFFSET and PLINE commands.

DONUT   DO   <u>D</u>raw > <u>D</u>onut

R 1

Creates a circular, hollow object. The command begins by requesting the inner and outer diameters of the doughnut, followed by a series of centre coordinates. *Notes:* 1: AutoCAD LT will also accept the alternate spelling DOUGHNUT. 2: You can also use the PLINE command (and the Arc option) to draw a circular Polyline of the required width. The PEDIT command may be used to alter the width of an existing Polyline. *See also:* CIRCLE, PEDIT and PLINE commands.

DSVIEWER DS   <u>S</u>ettings > <u>A</u>erial View

R 1

☺

Allows dynamic pan and zoom operations to be carried out using the Aerial View window. This is an alternative to the PAN and ZOOM commands, which are also available. With complex drawings, where frequent changes are made to the display, the Aerial View window may prove to be particularly useful. In other cases, it may be more important to be able to see the entire graphics area. The Aerial View's Toolbar contains eight icons. From left to right these are the Drawing extents, Virtual drawing area, Current view, Real time, Plus, Minus, Bird's eye and Spyglass icons. *Notes:* 1: The functional operation of the DSVIEWER command has been improved in AutoCAD LT Release 2. In particular, the Aerial View Toolbar is a new feature. 2: The first three buttons control the information displayed in the Aerial View window.

The drawing *extents* is the smallest rectangle which just encloses all of the objects in the drawing. The virtual drawing area is the largest region which can be displayed without the need to regenerate the drawing (see the REGEN command for more details). As the name suggests, the Current view button sets the Aerial View window to be the same as the graphics area. By comparing the Aerial View and graphics windows, it can be seen that the information actually displayed in the graphics area is shown using reverse video in the Aerial View window. 3: The Real time button controls whether dynamic zoom and pan operations cause the graphics area to be updated as changes occur (in *real time*). 4: The Plus and Minus buttons allow incremental changes of scale in the Aerial View window. 5: The Bird's eye and Spyglass buttons are used to perform pan and zoom operations, with the Bird's eye button being selected by default. The difference between these two modes is that with the Bird's eye feature, you point to the Aerial View window to specify the new display, but with the Spyglass, you point to the graphics area. 6: To switch between panning and zooming, click ⟨⊕. When zoom mode is active, moving the mouse to the left or right causes the size of the view box to be reduced or increased respectively. When panning, moving the mouse causes the view box to be moved in the indicated direction. Click ⟨⊕ to exit and update the graphics display. 7: Another technique for panning is to click ⟨⊕ in the Aerial View window. If the indicated point is outside of the reverse video region, the display is panned so that the given point is at the centre of the graphics area. If the point is inside of the reverse video region, then dynamic pan mode is selected, as explained above. 8: The DSVIEWER command works in *model space* only, showing the content of a single viewport at any time. **See also:** DVIEW, PAN, PLAN, VPOINT and ZOOM commands.

DTEXT   T / DT   <u>D</u>raw > <u>T</u>ext

R 1

Draws one or more lines of Text, using the selected text style, size and rotation angle. The text is drawn 'dynamically', so it appears in the graphics area, as it is typed. Available options are **J** – Justification and **S** – Style. *Justification* refers to the arrangement of the Text, which may be *left*, *centre*, *right* or *middle* justified. The Text may also be *aligned* or *fitted* between two points. (See Figure 3–16 for details of these justification options.) The Style option allows a named *text style* to be selected, including such features as the *font*, *width factor* and *obliquing angle*. **Note:** See Table 3–5 for text control sequences. **See also:** DDCHPROP, DDEDIT, DDMODIFY, DDRENAME, TEXT and STYLE commands.

DVIEW   DV   <u>V</u>iew > 3D D<u>y</u>namic View

R 1

Allows 3D drawings to be viewed dynamically from any angle, with optional hidden line removal and perspective projection. Available options include **CA** – CAmera, **TA** – TArget, **D** – Distance, **PO** – POints, **PA** – PAn, **Z** – Zoom, **TW** – TWist, **CL** – CLip, **H** – Hide, **O** – Off, **U** – Undo and **X** – eXit. **Notes:** 1: The command begins with the selection of objects (to be dynamically viewed). If this stage is bypassed, then the Block DVIEWBLOCK is used. (This is a simple model of a house by default, but you can create your own 1 × 1 Block if you wish.) The command uses the analogy of a camera (observer) and target (subject) to specify the viewpoint and viewing direction. The Camera and Target positions may be given separately by selecting the options with the same names, or together by using the POints option. 2: The PAn option allows the selected objects to be panned without the need to exit the command, while the TWist option rotates the objects around the line of sight, through a specified angle. The Distance option allows the selected objects to be moved away from or towards the observer and also enters the perspective viewing mode. (It may be necessary to repeat this option several times to move objects to a sufficient distance.) Select the Off option to return to a parallel projection. 3: The detailed operation of the Zoom option depends on whether parallel or perspective viewing mode is active. In parallel projection, the Zoom option alters a *scale factor*, with values greater than unity making the selected objects appear to be closer to the observer. With the perspective viewing mode active, the camera analogy is used once again. The Zoom option then alters the 'lens length' of the camera, with the default value being 50 mm. Shorter lengths increase the degree of perspective and produce a wider field of view (like a 'fish-eye' lens). Longer lens length gives a flatter perspective and a larger image, simulating the effect of a telephoto lens. To obtain the desired image size and degree of perspective, use the Zoom option to set the lens length, followed by the Distance option to alter the distance from the camera. 4: The CLip option offers allows front and back *clipping planes* to be enabled and positioned. Use this feature to remove unwanted detail which is either too close to the camera (front clipping plane), or too far away from the camera (back clipping plane). 5: Having created the required perspective or parallel projection, use the Hide option to remove hidden detail. 6: If the UCS icon is enabled (see the UCSICON command), and a perspective view is active, the normal icon is replaced by a 'cube'. Many AutoCAD LT operations are disabled at this time. *See also*. HIDE, PAN, SHADE, VPOINT and ZOOM commands.

DXFIN	**DN**	<u>F</u>ile > <u>I</u>mport/Export > <u>D</u>XF In

R 1   Loads the *entities* section (only) of a *drawing interchange file* (a file with an extension of '.DXF', rather than the normal '.DWG') into the current drawing. The DXF file format is supported by a wide range of CAD software and is therefore useful where drawing information needs to be transferred from one system to another. **Note:** The OPEN command opens a new drawing which may have a file extension of either '.DWG' or '.DXF', as set by the **List files of type:** list box. Use DXFIN to load objects (entities) into an existing drawing and OPEN to create a new drawing. **See also:** DXFOUT, OPEN and WMFIN commands.

DXFOUT	**DX**	<u>F</u>ile > <u>I</u>mport/Export ><u>D</u>XF Out

R 1   Allows all or part of the current drawing to be saved as a *drawing interchange format* (DXF) file. The DXF file format is widely supported by CAD packages, thus allowing the transfer of data between otherwise incompatible systems. **Note:** Once the command has been started, you may optionally specify the degree of accuracy of output data. The **E** – Entities option also allows specific objects to be written to the DXF file, rather than the entire drawing (which is the default). **See also:** DXFIN, MSLIDE, PLOT, PSOUT, SAVEDIB, and WMFOUT commands.

'ELEV   **EV**   **(No menu pick sequence)**

R 1   Sets the drawing *elevation* (Z height) and *thickness* (Z depth) for subsequently drawn objects. **Notes:** 1: The settings elevation and thickness are used in 3-dimensional drawing, where they allow normally 2-dimensional objects to be extruded in the direction of the Z axis (of the currently active UCS), thus forming truly 3-dimensional objects. For example, a Circle becomes a cylinder and a series of Lines becomes a 'fence'. 2: By suitable modification of these properties during drawing, it becomes possible to place one object on top of another, while drawing. 3: The normal method of setting ELEVATION, THICKNESS, and other drawing properties, is from the DDEMODES dialogue box. 4: Typing an apostrophe before the command name causes the ELEV command to be issued *transparently.* **See also:** DDEMODES command. ELEVATION and THICKNESS settings.

ELLIPSE   **EL**   **Draw > Ellipse**

R 1   Draws a circular ellipse. The normal method is to give two points at opposite ends of the first axis, followed by the distance from the centre line to the other axis endpoint. Alternatively, you can specify a rotation angle which simulates the effect of a circle being rotated through a specified angle in the third dimension. **Notes:** 1: The ellipse is actually drawn as a Polyline consisting of a series of short circular arcs. Thus, it can be edited using the PEDIT command. 2: During isometric drawing, the I – Isocircle option becomes available, which allows isometric circles to be drawn on the left, right or top drawing planes. (Press Ctrl + E to move to the next plane.) **See also:** CIRCLE and DDRMODES commands.

END   **(No abbreviation)**   **(No menu pick sequence)**

R 1   Automatically saves the current drawing and then leaves AutoCAD LT. This is equivalent to typing QSAVE, followed by EXIT. **Note:** If the drawing has not been named, then you are prompted to give a drawing filename at the 'Create Drawing File' dialogue box. **See also:** QUIT, QSAVE, SAVE and SAVEAS commands.

ERASE   **E**   **Modify > Erase**

R 1   Removes the objects contained in the *selection set* from the drawing. **Notes:** 1: If you accidentally erase the wrong objects, then use the OOPS, U or UNDO commands to restore the drawing to its former state. 2: The DDSELECT command allows the object selection method to be altered. Available options include **Noun/verb selection**, **Implied Windowing**, **Press and Drag** and **Use Shift to add**. The size of the object selection *pickbox* is also controlled from this dialogue box. 3: As with most editing commands (MOVE, COPY etc.), a range of object selection methods may be chosen at the 'Select objects:' prompt. These include **C** – Crossing window, **CP** – Crossing Polygon, **F** – Fence, **W** – Window and **WP** – Window Polygon. 4: If the implied windowing feature is enabled, a *window* selection may be made by drawing the object selection window from left to right (so objects must be completely within the object selection window to be selected). Drawing the selection box from right to left, causes a *crossing* window selection to be made (in which objects need only be partly within the specified region to be selected). A window selection box is drawn as a solid line, while a crossing selection uses a dotted line. 5: By default, objects are added to the selection set as they are picked. Objects may be removed by selecting the **R** – Remove objects options (the **A** – Add option returns to additive selection mode). 6: The **ALL** option selects all objects in the drawing (except those on frozen layers). 7: The **P** – Previous option may be used to activate the selection set which was used by the most recent editing command (if any). This is useful where a series of editing commands must operate on the same group of objects. 8: The **L** – Last option selects the most recently created object which is currently visible. 9: The **BOX** option (no abbreviation) is commonly used in menu macros and prompts for two opposite corners of an object selection window. As with note 4, a crossing or window selection is made by giving the two points from right to left, or from left to right respectively. 10: The **SI** – SIngle operating mode causes the ERASE command to accept the first selected object, or group of objects and then erase them in a single operation. This contrasts with the normal operating mode where the 'Select objects:' prompt repeats until you make a null response. 11: The **M** – Multiple operating mode may be used with complex drawings, where it speeds up the selection of objects. When enabled, it allows a series of pick points to be entered, terminated by a command separator. In multiple mode, the drawing is scanned once (only) for objects, rather than after each individual selection. 12: The **AU** – AUto operating mode has the same effect as the Implied windowing feature. When enabled, if the selected point contains an object, then the object is selected in the normal way. If no object is found, then the indicated point is assumed to be the first point of an object selection window. *See also:* DDSELECT, OOPS, REDO, U and UNDO commands. PICKBOX setting.

EXPLODE (No abbreviation) Modify > Explode

R 1

Breaks a complex object into its constituent parts, allowing these to be edited individually. *Notes:* 1: A Polyline becomes a series of individual Lines and Arcs and any width information is lost. 2: Ellipses are broken down into a series of Arcs. 3: Donuts become 2 individual Arcs and the width information is lost. 4: A Block is decomposed into the component objects from which it was formed. Any Attribute data entered using the DDATTE command (or from the Command Line) is lost, although the Attribute itself remains. Nested Blocks become independent, although these in turn may be exploded. 5: Exploding a Block does not affect the Block definition, so further copies of the Block may be inserted into the drawing. 6: The DDINSERT command offers the option to explode a Block as it is inserted into the drawing. 7: You cannot explode a Block which has different *X*, *Y* or *Z* scales. *See also:* DDATTE and DDINSERT commands.

EXTEND   EX   <u>M</u>odify > E<u>x</u>tend

R 1 Extends an existing object (such as a Line or Arc), until it meets a boundary object. This command is useful for tidying junctions between objects. It also finds application where existing objects are extended to form construction lines, as an intermediate step in the creation of other views of the model. **Notes:** 1: The command dialogue consists of two main parts. The first is the selection of boundary objects, which is terminated by a null response. This is followed by the selection of object(s) to be extended. 2: The object is extended from the endpoint which is closest to the indicated point. **See also:** BREAK, CHANGE and TRIM commands.

FILEOPEN   (No abbreviation)   (No menu pick sequence)

R 1 Opens a drawing using the Command line. Most users will prefer to use the OPEN command which uses a dialogue box. See also: OPEN command.

'FILL   FL   (No menu pick sequence)

R 1 Controls whether objects possessing 'width' are filled with colour when displayed on screen, or with ink when printed or plotted. Types of object which are affected include wide Polylines, donuts and Solids. **Notes:** 1: Disabling fill mode during plotting can speed up the production of a plot, particularly with pen plotters. The saving of ink or toner may also be of financial benefit when generating prints for checking purposes only. 2: Drawing regeneration on some types of display may be speeded-up if solid objects are left unfilled. 3: After enabling or disabling the filling of solid objects, you must use the REGEN command (rather than REDRAW) to update <u>existing</u> objects on screen. 4: The DDRMODES command allows the FILLMODE setting to be displayed or altered using the **Solid <u>F</u>ill** checkbox, which will be preferred by most users. 5: Typing an apostrophe before the command name causes the FILL command to be issued *transparently*. **See also**: DDRMODES, PLOT and REGEN commands. FILLMODE setting.

FILLET   F   <u>C</u>onstruct > <u>F</u>illet

R 1 Draws an Arc of the specified radius, forming a connection between two existing objects. The objects may be extended or truncated, as necessary, so that a neat intersection is produced. Available options are **P** – Polyline, **R** – Radius and – select objects. **Notes:** 1: The radius option sets the fillet radius for subsequently drawn fillets and then exits the command. 2: The Polyline option allows each junction of the indicated Polyline to be filleted in a single operation. 3: When selecting each object, ensure that the pick point is as close as possible to the intended location of the endpoints of the fillet. This is particularly true where a fillet may be drawn in more than one direction. 4: The FILLET command requires two Lines, Arcs or Circles. You cannot fillet Polyline arc segments, so objects such as ellipses and doughnuts cannot be selected. 5: If you fillet two Polyline line segments, then these must both be from the same Polyline, and must not be separated by more than one segment.

6: If the two objects are on the same layer then the fillet is drawn on this same layer. If the objects are on different layers then the fillet is drawn on the current layer. *See also:* CHAMFER command.

'GETENV   (No abbreviation)   (No menu pick sequence)

R 1   Reads the values of environment variables stored in the general section of the ACLT.INI file. *Notes:* 1: To change the value of an environment variable (in the ACLT.INI file), use the SETENV command. 2: You can determine the current value of an AutoCAD LT system variable by typing its name at the Command prompt. Those system variables which are not read only may also be altered. 3: The SETVAR command may also be used to change the value of a system variable (or setting). 4: Typing an apostrophe before the command name causes the GETENV command to be issued *transparently*. *See also:* SETENV and SETVAR commands.

'GRAPHSCR   (No abbreviation)   (No menu pick sequence)

R 1   Switches from the text window to the graphics window. The same effect may be achieved by pressing function key [F2]. *Notes:* 1: This may be useful during the operation of a script file, where function keys are unavailable. 2: The TEXTSCR command switches from the graphics screen to the text screen. 3: Typing an apostrophe before the command name causes the GRAPHSCR command to be issued *transparently*. *See also:* TEXTSCR command.

'GRID   G   (No menu pick sequence)

R 1   Controls the visibility and arrangement of an array of visible dots in the graphics area. The use of a grid may assist with the estimation of position and length, and can also be combined with the *snap* feature. Available options are **ON**, **OFF**, **S** – Snap, **A** – Aspect, with the default grid spacing being offered as the default. *Notes:* 1: ON and OFF enable or disable the grid. 2: Snap sets the grid to be the same as the snap grid. If the snap mode is subsequently changed, then the visible grid will change accordingly. 3: The Aspect option allows different X and Y spacings (the *aspect ratio*) to be given to the grid. 4: The DDRMODES command controls a range of general drawing setups from a single dialogue box, including the grid. Most users will prefer to use this dialogue box. 5: The grid may be enabled or disabled at any time by typing [Ctrl] + [G] or function key [F7]. 6: Typing an apostrophe before the command name causes the GRID command to be issued *transparently*. *See also:* DDRMODES, ORTHO and SNAP commands.

HANDLES (No abbreviation) (No menu pick sequence)

R 1 Controls the allocation of unique reference numbers or handles to each object in a drawing. When enabled, each object is allocated a unique reference number (which is a *hexadecimal* or base 16 number). This feature allows individual objects to be referred to by other programs, such as databases or user-defined programs. Available options are **ON** and **DESTROY** (no abbreviations are allowed). ***Notes:*** 1: The ON option enables the allocation of unique handle information to each object in a drawing, which is preserved during the lifetime of the drawing. 2: As its name suggests, the DESTROY option deletes all handle information in the current drawing. This means that any links between particular objects and external applications, such as those created by Attribute extraction (the DDATTEXT command) or by exporting drawing interchange file (DXF) information, are lost. Due to the potential seriousness of this option, you must type a password before handle information is actually deleted. ***See also:*** DDATTEXT, DXFIN and DXFOUT commands. HANDLES setting.

HATCH H <u>D</u>raw > <u>H</u>atch (in Release 1 only)

R 1 Hatches an area with the specified hatch pattern. The BHATCH command (boundary hatch), is the preferred method of hatching for users of AutoCAD LT Release 2. (HATCH is no longer available from the pull-down menu system.) Once the command has been started, you are prompted to select the hatch pattern, scale factor, rotation angle, and then to choose the objects forming the boundary. For correct results, the selected objects should form a *proper*, closed boundary, with objects joined 'end-to-end'. Any gaps or overlaps between objects will cause the hatch pattern to appear outside of the intended boundary. ***Notes:*** 1: Typing '?' when asked for the name of the hatch pattern, allows a list of previously defined hatch pattern names to be displayed. You can limit the range of displayed hatch pattern styles by entering a suitable wild-card ('A*' for example), at the appropriate prompt. 2: Typing 'U' in place of the hatch pattern name allows you to define your own hatch pattern by answering a series of questions. 3: For users of Release 1, there are two basic methods of hatching an improper boundary. The first is to use the BREAK command to separate any 'improper' boundary objects into simpler parts, prior to selecting boundary objects. The second method is to draw a Polyline around the boundary (using object snap normally). The Polyline may then be selected using the **L** – Last option at the 'Select objects:' prompt. ***See also:*** BHATCH and HATCHEDIT commands.

HATCHEDIT (No abbreviation) <u>M</u>odify > Edit <u>H</u>atch

R 2 Allows an existing hatched area to be edited. A modified version of the BHATCH command's dialogue box is displayed, with some of the options being disabled. In general, you can select new hatch patterns, alter properties associated with the current hatch pattern, or modify the hatch style. ***Notes:*** 1: Use the **Pattern T<u>y</u>pe:** drop-down list and the options available in the Pattern Properties region to define the hatch pattern.

2: The <u>I</u>nherit Properties button allows the hatch pattern to be loaded from an existing hatched area. This may be useful where adjacent areas are to be hatched with similar patterns – perhaps only differing in their rotation angles. 3: Clicking the <u>A</u>dvanced... button allows the hatch style to be altered. Available options are Normal, Outer and Ignore. In Normal mode, all internal boundaries are selected. Alternate regions are then hatched. The Outer option selects the outermost region only. Internal detail within any islands is ignored. The Ignore option causes all internal detail to be ignored, thus hatching the entire region. 4: If the **Associati<u>v</u>e:** checkbox is enabled then the hatched area will be automatically recalculated if any of the objects forming the boundary are edited. *See also:* BHATCH and HATCH commands.

'HELP   (No abbreviation)   Help > (First 3 options)

R 1

Displays help information of a general or specific (context sensitive) nature. To obtain general help, select the required option from the **Help** pull-down menu, press function key F1, or click the Help icon in the Toolbar at the Command prompt. To obtain context sensitive help, activate HELP while a particular command is in progress. *See also:* ABOUT command.

HIDE   HI   <u>V</u>iew > <u>H</u>ide

R 1

Performs hidden line removal with 3-dimensional drawings. This can help with the visualization of complex models. **Notes:** 1: The calculation of hidden line information can be time-taking, so use this option sparingly. 2: Hidden line information is lost when the drawing is regenerated (either automatically or using the REGEN command). 3: The VPOINT command allows a 3-dimensional drawing to be viewed from different locations, as does the DVIEW command. Additionally, DVIEW allows perspective projections to be produced, and also offers a hidden line removal option of its own. 4: The PLOT command offers a **Hide <u>L</u>ines** option which controls the removal of hidden lines when a drawing is plotted from model space. (In model space, only the active viewport is plotted.) 5: If a drawing is plotted from paper space, the MVIEW command's HIDEPLOT option controls the removal of hidden lines for individual viewports. (This option overrides the global setting in the PLOT command's dialogue box, when drawings are plotted from paper space.) *See also:* DVIEW, MVIEW, VIEW and VPOINT commands.

'ID   (No abbreviation)   <u>A</u>ssist > <u>I</u>D Point

R 1

Returns the *X*, *Y* and *Z* values of the indicated coordinate. *Notes:* 1: Use object snap to find the coordinate of an existing geometric feature, such as the endpoint of a Line, or the centre of a Circle. 2: In AutoCAD LT Release 2, inquiry commands may now be accessed from the Toolbox. 3: Typing an apostrophe before the command name allows the ID command to be issued *transparently*. *See also:* AREA, DISTANCE and LIST commands.

INSERT   IN   (No menu pick sequence)

R 1   Inserts a previously created Block (or drawing file) into the drawing. Most users will prefer to use the related DDINSERT command, which allows all options to be selected from a dialogue box. Once the command has been started, you are asked to type the Block name, or to type '?' to see a list of Blocks which are defined within the current drawing. The dialogue then proceeds with the selection of insertion point, scale factor and rotation angle: ***Notes:*** 1: After typing '?' to see previously defined Blocks, accept the '*' wild card option to see all Blocks. Note that unnamed (or anonymous) Blocks are not available to the INSERT command. (Unnamed Blocks are features such as Dimensions or hatch patterns, which are stored internally in the same way as a user-defined Block.) 2: If the named Block is not already defined in the drawing, then AutoCAD LT will search for a drawing file with the same name. You can force this by explicitly giving a drive name and pathname (for example C:\ACLTWIN\BLOCKS\WIDGET). 3: To load a Block from disk and give it a name which is <u>different</u> from the filename, use the convention **Block Name = Path Name**, at the 'Block name (or ?):' prompt. 4: To cause a Block to be exploded as it is inserted, precede the Block name with an asterisk (i.e. *WIDGET, rather than WIDGET). 5: At the 'X scale factor <1>/ Corner/XYZ:' prompt, press ↵ to accept the default scale factor, or enter a new value. Where different *X* or *Y* scales are required, these can be entered separately, or the Corner option may be used to give *X* and *Y* scales in a single operation (the two corners of the rectangle are the Block's insertion point and the indicated corner). The XYZ option allows separate *X*, *Y* and *Z* scale factors to be entered when 3-dimensional Blocks are inserted. 6: The EXPLODE command may be used to decompose a Block into its component parts, allowing these to be individually edited. You cannot explode a Block which has different *X*, *Y* or *Z* scale factors. 7: To edit properties associated with an existing Block, use the DDCHPROP command to alter basic properties, such as colour or layer, and the DDMODIFY command to change specialist properties such as *X*, *Y* or *Z* scale factors. 8: The ATTDISP command controls the display of Attributes associated with inserted Blocks, while the ATTDIA and ATTREQ settings control the requesting of Attribute information during Block insertion. See the ATTDISP and DDINSERT entries for further details. ***See also:*** ATTDISP, BLOCK, BMAKE, DDCHPROP, DDINSERT, DDMODIFY and EXPLODE commands. ATTDIA, ATTMODE and ATTREQ settings.

'ISOPLANE   IS   (No menu pick sequence)

R 1   Allows the current isometric plane to be altered, which may be required during isometric drawing. Available options are **L** – Left, **T** – Top, **R** – Right and ↵ – Toggle isometric plane. ***Notes:*** 1: Most users will prefer to set up an isometric drawing plane using the DDRMODES command's dialogue box. 2: The quickest way to cycle through the three isometric drawing planes is to type Ctrl + E while drawing. 3: This command may prove useful in some script files. 4: Typing an apostrophe before the command name allows the ISOPLANE command to be issued *transparently*. ***See also:*** DDRMODES command.

'LAYER　　　　　**LA**　　　　　**(No menu pick sequence)**

R 1　Controls the use of layers within the current drawing. Most users will prefer to use the DDLMODES command to control layers, due to its extensive use of dialogue boxes. (The Toolbar also displays the name of the current layer. The associated drop-down list box provides a rapid mechanism for changing the name of this active layer.) Available options are **?** – List, **M** – Make, **S** – Set, **N** – New, **ON**, **OFF**, **C** – Color, **L** – Ltype, **F** – Freeze, **T** – Thaw, **LO** – LOck and **U** – Unlock. *Notes:* 1: To make a specified layer *current* (so that newly drawn objects will be on this layer), use either the Make or Set option. The layer must already exist for the Set option to work, while the Make option will create the layer, if necessary, before making it current. 2: Type ? to see a list of currently defined layers and their status. 3: The New option creates a new layer, without affecting the current layer. 4: To turn a layer on or off, use the ON or OFF options respectively. (Turning a layer off causes any objects drawn on that layer to become invisible. See also the Freeze and Thaw options.) 5: The Color option changes the colour associated with a particular layer. (To be affected, objects must be drawn on that layer, and using the logical colour BYLAYER.) 6: The LType option controls the linetype associated with a particular layer. To work correctly, the specified linetype must already have been loaded. Objects should also have their linetype property set to BYLAYER, if they are to be drawn with the linetype associated with their layer. 7: Freeze and Thaw are similar in effect to the ON and OFF options already encountered. However, objects on frozen layers are completely ignored during drawing regeneration and hidden line removal. In some circumstances, this can considerably improve performance. 8: The LOck and Unlock options allow information on certain layers to be protected from unintentional erasure or modification. Objects on locked layers can be made visible or invisible and can have their colour or linetype altered. You can draw <u>new</u> objects on a locked layer and insert Blocks, but <u>existing</u> objects on locked layers cannot be modified. 9: The LAYER and DDLMODES commands allow global changes to layers, while the VPLAYER command controls the visibility of layers on an individual viewport basis. *See also:* DDLMODES and VPLAYER commands. CLAYER setting.

'LIMITS　　　　　**LM**　　　　　Settings > Dra<u>w</u>ing > <u>L</u>imits

R 1　Sets the size of the drawing area (in *drawing units*) and enables or disables *limits checking* during drawing operations. It is normal practice to enter drawing information at full size, with any scaling for printing purposes controlled by the PLOT command. Thus the definition of the drawing limits is one of the first steps in the creation of a new drawing. (In AutoCAD LT Release 2, the user is provided with the option of changing the drawing limits during the creation of a new drawing. This option is now available as part of the NEW command, if either the **Q**uick or **C**ustom option is chosen.) *Notes:* 1: The ON and OFF options enable or disable the limits checking feature. When enabled, if the user tries to draw an object, either partly or wholly outside of the defined drawing limits, then an error message is generated. 2: If you use a prototype drawing when creating a new drawing, then all limits settings are inherited from the prototype. 3: Model space and paper space may have different drawing limits, and are separately controlled. *See also:* NEW command. LIMCHECK, LIMMIN and LIMMAX settings.

LINE   L   <u>D</u>raw > <u>L</u>ine

R 1

Draws one or more Lines. Options available at the 'To point:' prompt are **U** – Undo and **C** – Close. The Undo option removes the last segment, allowing it to be redrawn. Assuming that at least two segments have already been drawn, the Close option causes a Line to be drawn from the last point, to the first, effectively creating a closed polygon. ***Notes:*** 1: When starting the LINE command, you can continue from the last point reached by pressing ↵ at the 'From point:' prompt. If the last object drawn was a Line, then its endpoint is taken as the startpoint of the new Line. If the most recently drawn object was an Arc, then the Line's startpoint and <u>direction</u> are inherited from the Arc. 2: To convert one or more (linked) Lines and Arcs into a Polyline, use the PEDIT command, followed by the JOIN option. 3: To change the properties associated with a group of Lines, use the DDCHPROP command. 4: The CHANGE command's 'Change point' option may be used to tidy junctions where endpoints do not meet, as intended. ***See also:*** BREAK, CHANGE, DDCHPROP, EXTEND, LINETYPE, LTSCALE and TRIM commands.

'LINETYPE   LT   <u>S</u>ettings > Li<u>n</u>etype Style

R 1

Controls the creation and selection of Linetypes for use by drawing commands. Available options are **?** – list, **C** – Create, **L** – Load and **S** – Set. ***Notes:*** 1: Linetypes are defined in files having an extension of '.LIN'. The two supplied linetype definition files are ACLT.LIN and ACLTISO.LIN. (Linetype definitions in ACLTISO.LIN are larger by a factor of 25.4, making them suitable for metric drawings.) 2: Select the **?** – list option to list linetypes which are contained in the specified linetype definition file. 3: Use the Set option to specify a new linetype to be used when objects are subsequently drawn. 4: Before you can Set a new linetype, it is first necessary to load the required linetype(s) into the current drawing, using the Load option. First, type the name of the linetype to be loaded (or enter a wildcard such as 'H*' to select several linetypes in a single operation). Finally, select the required linetype definition file from the 'Select Linetype File' dialogue box. 5: To create a new linetype, select the Create option. You are then asked to select the linetype definition file name. If this file already exists, then your definition will be appended (added to the end of the file). Alternatively, a new file is created. The next step is to enter a descriptive message, which describes the new linetype. Finally the actual definition is entered at the 'A,' prompt. The linetype is defined as a repeating series of lines and spaces. A positive number specifies the length of a drawn line, while a negative number gives the length of a space. Each entry is separated by a comma, thus an example of a simple dashed linetype definition would be 'A, 5, –2.5'. 6: The LTSCALE command alters a global linetype scale factor, which makes linetypes appear coarser or finer. 7: To change the linetype of existing objects, use the DDCHPROP command. 8: To switch between the text and graphics windows, press function key F2. 9: Typing an apostrophe before the command name causes the LINETYPE command to be issued *transparently*. ***See also:*** DDCHPROP and LTSCALE commands.

LIST LS <u>A</u>ssist > <u>L</u>ist

R 1

☺

Displays drawing database information about the selected object(s). **Notes:** 1: The exact information displayed depends on the type of object which is selected. It may include any endpoints, centre points, radii, lengths, angles, colours, linetypes, perimeters or areas. Whether the object was created in model space or paper space is also given. 2: If *handles* have been enabled (see the HANDLES command), then this information is also listed. 3: In AutoCAD LT Release 2, the LIST command may also be started from the Toolbox. **See also:** AREA, DIST and ID commands.

LOGFILEOFF (No abbreviation) (No menu pick sequence)

R 1 Cancels the recording of command line information to the file ACLT.LOG. The file may later be printed or edited using a suitable text editor, such as Notepad. **See also:** LOGFILEON command.

LOGFILEON (No abbreviation) (No menu pick sequence)

R 1 Commences the recording of command line information (as displayed in the text window) to the file ACLT.LOG. **Note:** If the file does not exist, it is created. If it exists, then the LOGFILEON command begins a new session, with information being added to the file. Individual sessions are separated in the file by dashed lines. **See also:** LOGFILEOFF command.

'LTSCALE LC <u>S</u>ettings > Li<u>n</u>etype Style > Li<u>n</u>etype Scale

R 1 Sets the scale factor which is used when objects are drawn using linetypes other than CONTINUOUS. **Notes:** 1: When an object is drawn using a particular linetype, the length of each line or space is multiplied by the value defined by the LTSCALE command. Increasing or decreasing the LTSCALE setting causes linetypes to become 'coarser' or 'finer' respectively. 2: The drawing is automatically regenerated, so any changes due to the LTSCALE command are immediately obvious. 3: The PSLTSCALE setting controls whether linetypes are uniformly scaled relative to model space or paper space. If you have several viewports open in paper space and linetype sizes appear different in each viewport (and at different ZOOM magnifications), then set the PSLTSCALE setting to 1 to scale linetypes uniformly relative to paper space. 4: Typing an apostrophe before the command name causes the LTSCALE command to be issued *transparently*. **See also:** LINETYPE command. LTSCALE and PSLTSCALE settings.

MEASURE   (No abbreviation)   <u>C</u>onstruct > Mea<u>s</u>ure

R 2   Places Point entities or named Blocks at measured intervals along the perimeter of an object. With named Blocks, the MEASURE command may be used as an alternative to the ARRAY command. Points are normally used as an intermediate step in the construction of more complex objects, in conjunction with the Node object snap operating mode (see the DDOSNAP command). ***Notes:*** 1: Having selected the object to 'measure' (a Line, Arc, Polyline, Circle or Ellipse for example), you are then asked to enter the distance between objects, or give a Block name, followed by the separation between objects. 2: With Blocks, you can optionally align each Block as it is placed. ***See also:*** ARRAY, DDOSNAP, DIVIDE and DDPTYPE commands.

MINSERT   MN   (No menu pick sequence)

R 1   Creates a rectangular array using a pre-defined Block definition. This command is not available in AutoCAD LT Release 2. ***Notes:*** 1: The command dialogue is initially identical to that of the INSERT command. Once the insertion point, scale factor(s) and rotation angle have been given, you are then prompted to enter the number of rows (horizontal) and columns (vertical), followed by the distance between each row and column. (You can also enter these distances by giving two opposite corners of a rectangle with the mouse – a 'unit cell'.) 2: Users of Release 2 can achieve the same effect by inserting a single Block and then using the ARRAY command. ***See also:*** ARRAY, DDINSERT and INSERT commands.

MIRROR   MI   <u>C</u>onstruct > <u>M</u>irror

R 1   Creates a mirror image of the selected objects, with the option to retain or discard the original objects. ***Notes:*** 1: Once the objects (to be mirrored) have been selected, you are prompted to enter two points which define the mirror line. (Any of the available input techniques may be used here including snap, ortho, typed input or object snap.) Finally you are given the option of retaining or discarding the original objects. 2: The MIRRTEXT setting controls the behaviour of Text during reflection. IF MIRRTEXT is set to 1, reflected text appears 'backwards', while a value of 0 causes text to be normally oriented. If it is important that reflected text should still be readable, then set MIRRTEXT to 1 before starting the MIRROR command. 3: You can also use the *grips* feature to mirror objects. ***See also:*** ARRAY, COPY and MOVE commands. MIRRTEXT setting.

MOVE   M   Modify > <u>M</u>ove

Moves the selected objects to a new location. The objects to be moved must first be selected, after which a 'Base point or displacement:' is given. Finally, the 'Second point of displacement:' is selected. (One method is to select a reference point using object snap and then type the displacement as a relative coordinate.)

R 1   ***Notes:*** 1: The COPY command leaves the original object(s) unaltered, while MOVE deletes the original selection set. 2: You can also use the *grips* feature to move objects. ***See also:*** ARRAY, COPY and MOVE commands.

MSLIDE	**ML**	<u>F</u>ile > <u>I</u>mport/Export > Make <u>S</u>lide

R 1   Creates a 'slide' of the information in the graphics area, which may later be viewed using the VSLIDE (view slide) command. ***Notes:*** 1: A common use of slides is with presentations, where a series of slides may be displayed in sequence. The SCRIPT command, together with a suitable script file, is commonly used to automate the process of displaying the slides. Suitable time delays may be introduced using the DELAY command, while the RSCRIPT command causes the script file to run in a continuous loop. A script file which has been halted (by pressing [Ctrl] + [C]) may be restarted using the RESUME command. 2: The second use of slides is in the creation of icons, which may be used in *icon menus*. Icon menus are used in conjunction with the pull-down menu system and allow options to be presented to the user in pictorial form (text fonts for example). It is normal practice to place all of the slides used by a pull-down menu into a single slide library file. The SLIDELIB (DOS) utility program is used for this purpose (see Chapter 8 for more details). ***See also:*** DELAY, RESUME, RSCRIPT and VSLIDE commands.

MSPACE	**MS**	(No menu pick sequence)

R 1   Switches from paper space to model space. ***Notes:*** 1: For the command to work, the TILEMODE setting must be zero. 2: With TILEMODE set to 1, viewports are controlled using the VPORTS command, and are not allowed to overlap. All drawing and plotting operations take place in model space and the paper space icon in the Toolbar cannot be accessed. 3: With TILEMODE set to 0, viewports are controlled using the MVIEW command and the paper space icon may be accessed to switch between model space and paper space. Model space is the space where the model is created – normally at life size. Paper space represents the paper on which the drawing is finally displayed. Viewports are created on the 'paper' using the MVIEW command, showing different views of the 'model'. 4: When a drawing is plotted from paper space, all model space viewports, together with any objects created in paper space (title Blocks etc.) are plotted. ***See also:*** MVIEW, PLOT, PSPACE and VPORTS commands. TILEMODE setting.

MULTIPLE	**MU**	(No menu pick sequence)

R 1   Causes the following command to repeat automatically, until it is cancelled (by pressing [Ctrl] + [C] or by clicking the Cancel icon in the Toolbar). ***Notes:*** 1: Use this option as an aid to productivity, if you will be using a particular command several times in succession. 2: Another way to repeat the last command is to enter a command separator ([↵], [Spacebar] or ⌐⌐) at the Command prompt.

MVIEW

MV   <u>V</u>iew > Viewp<u>o</u>rts

R 1   Creates and controls model space viewports. (For the command to work, the TILEMODE setting must be zero.) Available options are **ON**, **OFF**, **H** – Hideplot, **F** – Fit, **2**, **3**, **4**, **R** – Restore and ⌐ – indicate corners. ***Notes:*** 1: The ON and OFF options are used to enable or disable the display of model space information in a particular viewport. When a viewport is 'off', it does not display any model space information, and cannot be selected in model space. 2: The Hideplot option controls the removal of hidden lines in individual viewports, during plotting. 3: The Fit, 2, 3, 4, and Restore options are all used to create <u>new</u> viewport(s). The Fit option creates the largest possible viewport, while the 2, 3 and 4 options create the specified number of viewports within the indicated screen area. You are given considerable flexibility in the arrangement of these smaller viewports, with horizontal and vertical arrangements being possible, together with combinations of the two. 4: With TILEMODE set to 1, viewports are controlled using the VPORTS command, and are not allowed to overlap. All drawing and plotting operations take place in model space and the paper space icon in the Toolbar cannot be accessed. With TILEMODE set to 0, viewports are controlled using the MVIEW command and the paper space icon may be accessed to switch between model space and paper space. Model space is the space where the model is created – normally at life size. Paper space represents the paper on which the drawing is finally displayed. Viewports are created on the 'paper' using the MVIEW command, showing different views of the 'model'. 5: When a drawing is plotted from paper space, all model space viewports, together with any objects created in paper space (title Blocks etc.) are plotted. ***See also:*** MSPACE, PLOT, PSPACE, VPLAYER and VPORTS commands. TILEMODE setting.

NEW

N   <u>F</u>ile > <u>N</u>ew

R 1

Begins a new drawing. This command has been extended considerably in AutoCAD LT Release 2, and is now more powerful and flexible in use. The user has a choice of 3 different methods of starting a new drawing. These are **Quick**, **<u>C</u>ustom** and **<u>N</u>one** (with or without a prototype drawing). ***Notes:*** 1: Quick setup provides a dialogue box which allows the units of measurement, drawing limits and simple drawing aids (snap and grid) to be controlled. 2: The **<u>C</u>ustom** option provides slightly more detailed options than **<u>Q</u>uick** setup. For example, the drawing aids are now accessed by pressing a button, which activates the DDRMODES command. In addition to setting the model space drawing limits, it is also possible to load a range of different *Title blocks*, each of which is configured for a different paper size. The Title block information is displayed in paper space, together with a suitably sized model space viewport. When enabled, the **Date Stamp** checkbox causes a Block containing drawing revision information to be inserted into the drawing. (You can insert this Block manually using the REVDATE command.) The Attributes associated with this Block may be edited at any time using the DDATTE command. 3: The **<u>N</u>one** option allows a new drawing to be started, based on a prototype drawing, or on AutoCAD LT's internal default settings. If a prototype drawing is selected, then the new drawing is an identical copy of the prototype. ***See also:*** DDATTE, FILEOPEN, OPEN, QSAVE, QUIT, REVDATE, SAVE and SAVEAS commands.

OFFSET   OF   <u>C</u>onstruct > <u>O</u>ffset

R 1   Creates a second object, which is parallel to the first. ***Notes:*** 1: The created object is always of the same type as the original (Line, Arc, Polyline, or Circle). 2: There are two basic approaches, as indicated by the 'Offset distance or Through *<default>*:' prompt, with the default method being shown inside the angular brackets. If you enter an offset distance (5 drawing units for example), you are then asked to select the original object, and then to indicate on which side of the original object, the new object should be placed (use the mouse here). If you choose the Through option, then you are first asked to indicate the original object, and then to give a point which the new object should pass through. 3: Certain types of object cannot be offset (Solids for example). ***See also:*** DLINE command.

OOPS   OO   <u>M</u>odify > <u>O</u>ops

R 1   Recovers the most recently erased object(s). ***Notes:*** 1: Unlike the U command, OOPS does not undo the effect of the most recent command. It simply recovers any erased objects. Thus if a Block has just been created using the BLOCK command, the OOPS command will recover the objects used to create the Block without erasing the Block definition. (The BMAKE command, which is preferred to BLOCK, offers an option to 'retain entities' after creation of the Block.) ***See also:*** REDO, U and UNDO commands.

OPEN   OP   <u>F</u>ile > <u>O</u>pen

R 1

Opens an existing drawing using the Open Drawing dialogue box. ***Notes:*** 1: To change the Drive name, click in the **Dri<u>v</u>es:** area, which will display a drop-down list of available drives. In a typical system, 'A:' and 'B:' (if fitted) are used for removable diskettes, while 'C:' is normally the hard disk. (You might also have a CD-ROM drive referred to as drive 'D:'.) 2: The **Directories:** section shows the current drive and root directory ('\'), followed by each element of the pathname. Thus, if the pathname is 'C:\ACLTWIN\TEST', there will be entries of 'C:\', 'ACLTWIN' and 'TEST', with each being further indented. If there are any directories below the current one, then these are also displayed, with the current location highlighted. Thus to move up or down the directory structure, simply click on the required directory name. 3: Any files of the selected type are displayed in the Files list box. To open a file, click ⌐ to highlight the file and then press the **OK** button (or you can open the file in a single operation by double-clicking on the file name). 4: The **List Files of Type:** list box allows different types of files to be displayed, and in some cases opened. In Release 2, you can open drawing files ('.DWG') or drawing interchange format ('.DXF') files, while in Release 1, you can also open slide files ('.SLD'). Other types of files cannot be opened using this dialogue box. 5: When you open an existing drawing, AutoCAD LT creates a backup copy of the drawing, with a file extension of '.BAK'. In Release 1, you can open backup files directly using the OPEN command (set the file template to '*.BAK' and press ↵ to list backup files). In Release 2, you have to <u>rename</u> the drawing file before opening it. Similarly, with Release 1, you can load timed backups (having an extension of '.AC$' – as set by PREFERENCES) by using the OPEN command. In Release 2, the file must first be <u>renamed</u>.

'ORTHO   OR   (No menu pick sequence)

R 1

Constrains drawing operations to be aligned with the graphics crosshairs. By default, the crosshairs are horizontal and vertical but this can be modified. **Notes:** 1: To alter the angle of the crosshairs, use the **S̲nap Angle** option in the DDRMODES command's dialogue box. (This is 0° by default.) 2: To constrain drawing operations to be aligned with an isometric grid, use the DDRMODES command to enable the **I̲sometric Snap/grid** and **O̲rtho** checkboxes. 3: A new feature in AutoCAD LT Release 2, is *direct distance* entry. In normal use (drawing Lines for example), a start point is first given and Ortho is enabled. A direction and distance may then be specified by moving the cursor in one of the four possible directions and then typing the required distance. The combination of Ortho and direct distance entry both simplifies and accelerates the entry of typed coordinates. **See also:** DDRMODES, GRID and SNAP commands.

'OSNAP   O   (No menu pick sequence)

R 1

Allows running object snap modes to be controlled from the command line. Most users will prefer to use the DDOSNAP command, which uses a dialogue box. Available options are None, Off, ↵, Nearest, Endpoint, Midpoint, Node, Quadrant, Intersection, Insert, Perpendicular, Tangent and Quick. **Notes:** 1: The None, Off and ↵ (null response) options disable any previously selected object snap modes. 2: You can select more than one option by entering a list of object snap modes, separated by commas (no spaces). 3: Object snap options can be abbreviated to the first three letters, when typed. 4: You can also enter an object snap mode as a *single point override*. **See also:** DDOSNAP command.

'PAN   P   V̲iew > Pa̲n

R 1

Moves the displayed portion of the drawing area in the specified direction, without altering the 'magnification'. **Notes:** 1: You can also use the DSVIEWER command to perform dynamic zoom and pan operations. 2: The DVIEW command performs dynamic zoom and pan with 3-dimensional models. 3: The VPOINT command allows the viewpoint used with 3-dimensional drawings to be altered. **See also:** DSVIEWER, DVIEW and VPOINT commands.

PASTECLIP   PC   E̲dit > P̲aste

R 1

Pastes information from the Windows Clipboard into the drawing. **Notes:** 1: If the Clipboard contains graphical (vector-based) information then the command dialogue is similar to that used during Block insertion. 2: Textual information can also be pasted into the drawing. To do this, first start the DTEXT command and, at the 'Text:' prompt, select the **Paste C̲ommand** option from the **E̲dit** pull-down menu. Finally press ↵ twice to complete the DTEXT command. 3: You can also use 'drag and drop' techniques to paste an entire text file (having a '.TXT' file extension) into the drawing. At the above 'Text:' prompt, 'drag' the text file's icon over the AutoCAD LT window and then release the mouse button. **See also:** COPYCLIP, COPYEMBED, COPYIMAGE and COPYLINK commands.

PEDIT	**PE**	<u>M</u>odify > Edit Pol<u>y</u>line

R 1   Edits 2-dimensional (PLINE) and 3-dimensional (3DPOLY) Polylines. It may also be used to edit polygon meshes which have been created by another application, such as the full version of AutoCAD. The options available with 2-dimensional Polylines are **C** – Close, **O** – Open, **J** – Join, **W** – Width, **E** – Edit vertex, **F** – Fit, **S** – Spline, **D** – Decurve, **L** – Ltype gen, **U** – Undo and **X** – eXit. (A subset of these options are available with 3-dimensional Polylines.) ***Notes:*** 1: As their names suggest, the Open and Close options cause the Polyline to be opened or closed respectively. (A 'closed' Polyline has a segment drawn between the first and last points.) 2: The Join option allows other objects to be added to the currently selected Polyline. It may also be used to turn a series of (connected) Lines and Arcs into a single Polyline. 3: The Width option alters the thickness of the entire Polyline in a single operation. 4: The Spline and Fit options cause the Polyline to be replaced by a curve. The Spline option uses the original Polyline as the basis for a *B-spline curve*, in which the curve is 'guided' by the original points, but does not necessarily pass through them. A *quadratic* or *cubic* B-spline curve is drawn, depending on the value of the SPLINETYPE setting (5 = quadratic, 6 = cubic). The Fit option draws a smooth curve which actually passes through each Polyline vertex. 5: Use the Decurve option to recover the original Polyline, after using the Spline or Fit options. 6: The visibility of the original Polyline after a curve has been fitted is controlled by the SPLFRAME setting (0 = invisible, 1 = visible). 7: When a B-spline curve is drawn, the SPLINESEGS setting controls the number of individual segments which are drawn (higher values give more accurate curves). 8: The Edit vertex option allows Polyline vertices to be individually edited. Vertices may be moved, inserted or deleted and the width of individual Polyline segments may be altered. (These facilities are available from a subsection of the PEDIT command.)   9: The 'Ltype gen' option controls the appearance of linetype patterns at the vertices of the Polyline. When enabled, the linetype is drawn in a continuous sequence, possibly resulting in a gap at a vertex. When disabled, each segment is drawn separately, guaranteeing that there will be a solid line at each vertex. ***See also:*** 3DPOLY, DDMODIFY and PLINE commands. PLINEGEN, SPLFRAME, SPLINESEGS SPLINETYPE settings

PLAN	**PV**	<u>V</u>iew > <u>3</u>D Plan View

R 1   Returns to a plan view, in which the positive *Z* axis points 'out of the screen', and the *X* and *Y* axes are horizontal and vertical respectively. Available options are ⏎ – Current UCS, **U** – named UCS and **W** – World coordinate system (WCS). ***Notes:*** 1: Pressing ⏎ generates a plan view in the currently active user coordinate system (UCS). 2: The UCS option allows a plan view to be produced, based on a previously named UCS. 3: The World option returns to a plan view of the World coordinate system. (The World and user coordinate systems are the same, unless another UCS has been created and made current.) 4: Although the PLAN command alters the viewing direction, it does <u>not</u> alter the current UCS. Entered coordinates remain relative to this active UCS. 5: If the UCSFOLLOW setting is enabled (1 = enabled, 0 = disabled), then a plan view is automatically generated when the active UCS is changed. ***See also:*** DVIEW, VPOINT, UCS and UCSICON commands. UCSFOLLOW setting.

PLINE	**PL**	<u>D</u>raw > <u>P</u>olyline

R 1

Draws a 2-dimensional Polyline. The range of options changes, depending on whether you are drawing line or arc segments. Line drawing options are **A** – Arc, **C** – Close, **H** – Halfwidth, **L** – Length, **U** – Undo, **W** – Width, – Endpoint of line and ⏎ – exit command. Arc drawing options are **A** – Angle, **CE** – CEnter, **CL** – CLose, **D** – Direction, **H** – Halfwidth, **L** – Line, **R** – Radius, **S** – Second point, **U** – Undo, **W** – Width, – Endpoint of arc and ⏎ – exit command. *Notes:* 1: 2-dimensional Polylines use the default *Z* coordinate value, as set by the current drawing elevation, and by the active user coordinate system (UCS). You cannot explicitly enter a *Z* value during coordinate entry. (3-dimensional Polylines are drawn using the 3DPOLY command.) 2: The Line and Arc options switch between the two available drawing modes. 3: The Halfwidth and Width options allow the starting and ending width of the next segment to be defined. Subsequent segments inherit the ending width of the previous segment, by default. As its name suggests, the Halfwidth value gives the distance from the midpoint to one edge, which is half of the Polyline's Width. 4: When drawing line segments, the Length option causes a segment to be drawn having the specified length, using the default drawing direction. 5: The Close option causes the first and last points to be joined by the active segment type, and also exits the command. 6: When drawing Arc segments, the starting direction is inherited from the previous segment, by default. You can explicitly set this using the Direction option. 7: The Angle option allows the included angle of the next segment to be specified, while the Radius option defines its radius. The CEnter option allows the radius and starting direction to be given in a single operation. 8: You can also indicate a 3-point arc by choosing the Second point option. *See also:* 3DPOLY, DDMODIFY, DLINE, LINE and PEDIT commands. PLINEGEN, SPLINETYPE, SPLFRAME and SPLINESEGS settings.

PLOT	**PP**	<u>F</u>ile > <u>P</u>rint/Plot

R 1

☺

Plots the current drawing, either to the default Windows system printer, or to the specified file. A new feature in AutoCAD LT Release 2 is the ability to plot to a bitmap file (TIFF, PCX, GIF or BMP file formats are all supported). *Notes:* 1: The PLOT command allows the active drawing unit (inches or millimetres) to be selected and performs any scaling which may be necessary to fit the drawing onto the paper. 2: Use the **Size...** button to set the paper size, and the **Rotation and Origin...** button to arrange the drawing on the paper. The 'Plotted Units = Drawing Units' section then allows the printout scale to be specified. If the **Scaled <u>t</u>o Fit** checkbox is enabled, then this scale factor is calculated for you automatically. 3: Click the **Pr<u>e</u>view...** button to check that the drawing is arranged to your satisfaction, prior to producing an actual printout. The **Part<u>i</u>al** option shows the selected drawing area and the paper, without giving any drawing detail. The **F<u>u</u>ll** option is slower, but gives an accurate representation of the drawing on the paper, including any selected options (such as hidden line removal). 4: The Additional Parameters section is used to specify the area of the drawing which is to be plotted (the current display, drawing *extents*, drawing *limits*, a named *view*, or the specified *window*). 5: Hidden line removal (of 3-dimensional drawings plotted from model space) may also be controlled using the **Hide <u>L</u>ines** checkbox.

(The MVIEW command's Hideplot option is used when drawings are plotted from paper space.) 6: The **Adjust Area Fill** option, controls whether the width of the plotter pen is taken into account, when a solid area is filled. When enabled, the outer boundary is moved inwards by a distance equal to half of the pen width. 7: If the hard copy device is not currently available, then the printout may be written to a file. To do this, enable the **Plot to File** checkbox, and set the filename using the **File Name** edit box. This file may later be copied to the printer using a suitable DOS command. (A typical example would be **COPY TEST.PRN LPT1 /B**, where LPT1 is the printer port, and the /B option causes the information to be treated as a 'binary' (rather than ASCII) file.) 8: If your printer/plotter supports 'software' pen width control, then the pen width associated with individual screen colours may be controlled from the **Pen Assignments** dialogue box. (With pen plotters which support multiple pens, you can use a different plotter pen for each drawing colour. The line width is then controlled by the choice of physical pen – in 'hardware'.) 9: The **Print/Plot Setup & Default Selection...** dialogue box controls the type of output produced by the PLOT command, and its destination. You can use this option to print to the Windows System printer, or to produce a bitmap image. *See also:* MSLIDE, MVIEW and SAVEDIB commands.

POINT   PT   <u>D</u>raw > P<u>o</u>int

R 1

Draws a Point at the specified coordinate, using the currently active *point style*. *Notes:* 1: To alter the active point display format, use the DDPTYPE command. 2: Existing Points are automatically updated to the current point style when the drawing is regenerated. *See also:* DDPTYPE and REGEN commands. PDMODE and PDSIZE settings.

POLYGON   PG   <u>D</u>raw > **Polygon**

R 1

Creates a regular polygon. The polygon is defined by giving the number of sides (3–1024), followed by its position and size. The size and position can be entered in two different ways. You can either give the centre coordinate, followed by the distance to the midpoint of an edge, or you can give the two coordinates of one face of the polygon. (In this second method, it is assumed that the polygon is drawn in an anticlockwise direction.) *See also:* CIRCLE and RECTANG commands.

PREFERENCES   PF   <u>F</u>ile > Pre<u>f</u>erences

R 1

☺

Defines certain preferences which are retained between drawing sessions. Several new features have been added in AutoCAD Release 2. *Notes:* 1: The Settings area controls the drawing interface by enabling or disabling the Toolbox and Toolbar. You can also decide whether an audible beep should be produced following an error, and control the use of *file locking*. (File locking is used in networked environments and prevents two or more users from accessing the same file simultaneously.) 2: The active **Measurement** system determines whether metric or 'English' prototype drawings, hatch patterns or linetype definitions are used with the drawing project.

3: Automatic file saving may be enabled or disabled, and the time interval between save operations controlled using the options available in the Automatic Save region. The automatic save feature proves particularly useful in the event of a power supply failure, in which case the timed backup file may be first renamed and then opened in the normal way. 4: The Environment area controls the directory path where AutoCAD LT support files are located, and also allows the active pull-down menu system to be specified. (By default, the file ACLT.MNU is used, but you can create your own customized menu systems if you wish.) 5: The **User Name:** edit box contains the name which is inserted into the drawing (as an Attribute) when a Date Stamp Block is inserted into the drawing. 6: You can control the placement of temporary files, desktop colours and screen fonts using a series of subsidiary dialogue boxes. *See also:* NEW and REVDATE commands.

PSOUT	PU	<u>F</u>ile > <u>I</u>mport/Export > <u>P</u>ostScript Out

R 1 Creates an *encapsulated PostScript file* which may either be printed by a compatible printer, or imported into another application, such as a desktop publishing package. *Notes:* 1: Encapsulated PostScript files have a file extension of '.EPS'. 2: Once the filename has been specified, you must select the area of the drawing which will be used to form the EPS file. Available options are **D** – Display, **E** – Extents, **L** – Limits, **V** – View and **W** – Window. 3: A bitmap screen preview image may optionally be included in the EPS file, which may be either EPSI or TIFF format. The bitmap resolution may also be set to 128, 256 or 512 pixels per side. 4: The active drawing units (inches or millimetres), drawing scale and paper size must also be specified. 5: Some types of AutoCAD LT object are not directly supported by the PostScript language. Appropriate conversions are made when the EPS file is created. (See the *AutoCAD LT User's Guide* for more details.) *See also:* PSPROLOG and PSQUALITY settings.

PSPACE	PS	(No menu pick sequence)

R 1 Switches to *paper space* from *model space*. *Notes:* 1: For the command to work, the TILEMODE setting must be zero. 2: With TILEMODE set to 1, viewports are controlled using the VPORTS command, and are not allowed to overlap. All drawing and plotting operations take place in model space and the paper space icon in the Toolbar cannot be accessed. 3: With TILEMODE set to 0, viewports are controlled using the MVIEW command and the paper space icon may be accessed to switch between model space and paper space. Model space is the space where the model is created – normally at life size. Paper space represents the paper on which the drawing is finally displayed. Viewports are created on the 'paper' using the MVIEW command, showing different views of the 'model'. 4: When a drawing is plotted from paper space, all model space viewports, together with any objects created in paper space (title Blocks etc.) are plotted. *See also:* MVIEW, MSPACE, PLOT, and VPORTS commands. TILEMODE setting.

PURGE	**PR**	<u>M</u>odify > <u>P</u>urge

R 1   Removes named objects from a drawing, if those objects are not in current use. This may result in simplification of the drawing, and a reduction in the size of the drawing file. Available options are **B** – Blocks, **D** – Dimstyles, **LA** – LAyers, **LT** – LTypes, **S** – (text) Styles or **A** – All. ***Notes:*** 1: This option must be the <u>first</u> command to be issued after the drawing has been opened. 2: You cannot remove layer 0, the CONTINUOUS linetype, or the STANDARD text style. 3: To remove an unused user coordinate system (UCS), named view, or viewport configuration, use the UCS, VIEW or VPORTS options respectively. 4: You may need to issue the PURGE command several times to fully remove all unused objects from the drawing. This is because an object, such as a linetype, may only become unreferenced when an object that refers to it (such as an unused Block or an unused layer for example), is itself removed from the drawing. ***See also:*** OPEN, UCS, VIEW and VPORTS commands.

QSAVE	**(No abbreviation)**	<u>F</u>ile > <u>S</u>ave

R 1   Saves the current drawing to disk. If the drawing has been named, then this name is used automatically. If the drawing is unnamed, then the SAVEAS command's dialogue box is used. ***See also:*** END, QUIT and SAVEAS commands.

QTEXT	**QT**	**(No menu pick sequence)**

R 1   Draws Text as an outline box when it is displayed on screen, or plotted. This command is intended to speed up drawing regeneration and plotting operations for complex drawings, particularly when the drawing is at an intermediate stage. ***Note:*** After enabling or disabling the *quick text* feature, use the REGEN command to see the effect on screen. ***See also:*** FILL command.

QUIT	**ET / EXIT**	<u>F</u>ile > E<u>x</u>it

R 1   Abandons the current drawing session, without saving the current drawing. ***Note:*** If you make a bad mistake after opening an existing drawing, or simply want to start again, then this command may be useful. (Using the U or UNDO commands may be a better alternative in some circumstances.) ***See also:*** END, NEW, QSAVE, SAVEAS, U and UNDO commands.

RECTANG	**RC**	<u>D</u>raw > <u>R</u>ectan<u>g</u>le

 Draws a rectangle, based on the coordinates of two opposite corners. This command offers a small time saving, when compared with the use of the LINE or PLINE commands. ***See also:*** LINE, PLINE and POLYGON commands.

R 1

REDO   RE   <u>E</u>dit > <u>R</u>edo

R 1

Reverses the effect of the most recent U or UNDO command, provided that the REDO command is the <u>first</u> command to be issued after the undo operation. **Note:** When REDO follows U, then only <u>one</u> AutoCAD LT command is affected. You cannot 'step back' through a drawing. **See also:** OOPS, U and UNDO commands.

'REDRAW   R   <u>V</u>iew > <u>R</u>edraw

R 1

Redraws the graphics display. **Notes:** 1: One common reason for wanting to 'clean up' the display is the appearance of unwanted marker *blips*. You can disable the creation of blips using the DDRMODES command's dialogue box (or from the Command prompt by using the BLIPMODE command). 2: The REDRAW command simply causes the screen display to be refreshed, without recalculating display vectors from the drawing database. Some commands may update the drawing database or alter a setting (system variable). The REDRAW command may not take these changes into account, so the REGEN command should be used in these cases. **See also:** BLIPMODE and REGEN commands.

REGEN   RG   <u>V</u>iew > Re<u>g</u>en

R 1   Calculates all display vectors based on the drawing database and then redraws the graphics display. **Notes:** 1: Regenerating the drawing using the REGEN command is slower than redrawing with the REDRAW command. However some commands may alter the drawing database or update system variables, with the result that the graphics display does not reflect the true state of the drawing. In such cases, the REGEN command must be used, rather than REDRAW. 2: Most commands which alter the drawing database, also cause the drawing to be regenerated automatically. **See also:** REDRAW command.

RENAME   RN   (No menu pick sequence)

R 1   Allows certain types of (named) objects to be renamed from the Command line. Available options are **B** – Block, **D** – Dimstyle, **LA** – LAyer, **LT** – LType, **S** – Style, **U** – Ucs, **V** – View and **VP** – VPort. **Notes:** 1: Most users will prefer to use the DDRENAME command to rename objects, due to its use of a dialogue box. 2: The RENAME command may prove useful in some script files. **See also:** DDRENAME command.

'RESUME   (No abbreviation)   (No menu pick sequence)

R 1   Resumes execution of a script file which had been interrupted previously (by pressing Ctrl + C). **See also:** RSCRIPT and SCRIPT commands.

REVDATE   (No abbreviation)   Modify > Date and Time

R 1 Inserts a Title Block into the current drawing, or causes an existing Title Block to be updated. *Notes:* 1: At its simplest, a Title Block is a Block definition which contains three Attributes called USER, REVDATE and FNAME. The value of each Attribute is obtained automatically when the Title Block is inserted or updated. The **User Name:** edit box in the PREFERENCE command's dialogue box supplies the USER Attribute's value, while the current (system) date and time are used for the REVDATE Attribute. If the drawing has been named, then this value supplies the FNAME Attribute. 2: To create a basic Title Block (consisting of the above mentioned Attributes only), use the REVDATE command, or create a new drawing using the **Custom** option and then enable the **Date Stamp** checkbox. 3: More complex Title Blocks may be selected using the **Title Block...** button, which is available from the NEW command's dialogue box, during 'custom' drawing creation. *See also:* DDATTE and NEW commands.

ROTATE   RO   Modify > Rotate

R 1 Rotates the selected objects through a specified angle, about a given centre of rotation. *Notes:* 1: Once the selection set has been selected, you are prompted to enter the rotation angle (+ve angles are measured anticlockwise normally), or to enter **R** to select the Reference option. To use the Reference option, specify a base angle, followed by the new angle. (For example, if the base angle is 80° and the new angle is 90°, then the selected objects will be rotated through 10°.) 2: One use for the Reference option is where you want to alter the angle of inclination of an existing object (which may be unknown) to a new value. Use object snap to specify the base angle by giving two reference coordinates and then type the new angle. 3: Objects may also be rotated using the grips feature. *See also:* COPY, MOVE and SCALE commands.

RSCRIPT   (No abbreviation)   (No menu pick sequence)

R 1 Causes a script file to run in a continuous loop. *Note:* The RSCRIPT command should be the <u>last</u> command in a script file. *See also:* RESUME and SCRIPT commands.

SAVE   SA   (No menu pick sequence)

R 1 Saves the active drawing as either a '.DWG' (AutoCAD LT's native file format) or a '.DXF' (drawing interchange format) file. *Notes:* 1: If the file has not been named, then you are prompted to enter or select a filename using a dialogue box. With previously named drawings, the file is automatically written to the specified filename. (If you don't want to overwrite the existing file then use the SAVEAS command, which always asks for a filename.) 2: Save the drawing as a DXF file, if you want to transfer the file to another application which does not directly support the Autodesk's DWG file format. *See also:* DXFOUT, QSAVE, QUIT and SAVEAS commands.

SAVEAS (No abbreviation) File > Save As

R 1 Saves the current drawing with the specified filename. *Notes:* 1: Unlike the SAVE command, SAVEAS will always ask for the drawing filename, even if the drawing has already been named. 2: As with the SAVE command, you can save the loaded drawing in either 'DWG' or 'DXF' file format. *See also:* DXFOUT, QUIT and SAVE commands.

SAVEDIB (No abbreviation) File > Import/Export > BMP Out

R 1 Saves the loaded drawing as a bitmap image (having a file extension of '.BMP'. *Notes:* 1: The bitmap file format is supported by a wide range of word processing, desktop publishing and graphics editing software. 2: The PLOT command may also be used to create bitmap images, from where a range of commonly used image sizes and file formats are available. 3: Drawing information may also be transferred to other applications, via the Windows Clipboard. *See also:* COPYCLIP, COPYEMBED, COPIMAGE, COPYLINK, DXFOUT, PLOT, SAVE, SAVEAS and WMFOUT commands.

SCALE SC Modify > Scale

R 1 Makes the selected objects larger or smaller, based on a specified scale factor, and base point. *Notes:* 1: The scale factor acts as a 'multiplier', so values less than unity cause the selected objects to become smaller. Values greater than one increase the size of the selected objects. (Thus, for example, a scale factor of 2 will cause all sizes to be doubled.) 2: If you select the Reference option then you can give the scale factor as a reference length, followed by a new length. (So a reference length of 40 and a new length of 60 will cause all selected objects to increase in size by a factor of 1.5.) 3: One use of the reference option is to scale an object so that it becomes a particular length, even if the original length is unknown. To do this, use object snap to indicate two reference points on the original object (hence giving a distance), and then type the required new size. 4: You can also scale objects by using the grips feature. *See also:* COPY, MOVE and ROTATE commands.

'SCRIPT SR File > Run Script

R 1 Causes a series of commands to be executed automatically from a script file. *Notes:* 1: A script file is an ASCII text file, having a file extension of '.SCR'. 2: In principle, any series of AutoCAD LT commands may be placed into a script file, but in practice, only those which may be operated entirely from the keyboard are suitable. Bear in mind that many of the commands which use dialogue boxes, also have command line equivalents. 3: One common application of script files is to display a series of *slides* (created originally by the MSLIDE command), using the VSLIDE command. The DELAY command is used to provide a timed interval between on slide and the next. To cause the script file to run continuously, place the RSCRIPT command at the end of the script file. *See also:* DELAY, GRAPHSCR, RESUME, RSCRIPT, TEXTSCR and VSLIDE commands. CMDDIA setting.

SELECT   SE   <u>A</u>ssist > <u>S</u>elect

R 1   Places selected objects into a *selection set* – which may then be accessed by subsequent editing commands by using the Previous object selection option. ***Notes:*** Another approach is to enable **Noun/verb Selection** (using the DDSELECT command) which allows you to optionally select objects <u>before</u> selecting an editing command. ***See also:*** DDSELECT command.

'SETENV   (No abbreviation)   (No menu pick sequence)

R 1   Sets those system variables (or settings) which are stored in the AutoCAD LT initialization file, 'ACLT.INI'. ***Notes:*** 1: You can also display or alter a named system variable, simply by typing its name at the Command prompt. 2: The SETVAR command may also be used to display or alter AutoCAD LT's system variables, many of which are saved as part of the active drawing. 3: By preceding the command name by an apostrophe, you can alter the value of an AutoCAD LT setting *transparently*. However, the new value may not come into effect until the currently active command is completed. ***See also:*** GETENV and SETVAR commands.

'SETVAR   (No abbreviation)   (No menu pick sequence)

R 1   Displays or changes the values of AutoCAD LT's system variables or settings. ***Notes:*** 1: You can also display and alter a named system variable, simply by typing its name at the Command prompt. 2: The SETENV command may also be used to display or alter system variables which are stored in the file 'ACLT.INI'. 3: By preceding the command name by an apostrophe, you can alter the value of an AutoCAD LT setting *transparently*. However, the new value may not come into effect until the currently active command is completed. ***See also:*** GETENV and SETENV commands.

SHADE   SH   <u>V</u>iew > <u>S</u>hade

R 1   Displays a shaded image of the drawing in the active (or only) viewport. This proves particularly useful when visualizing 3-dimensional drawings. ***Notes:*** 1: The SHADEDGE and SHADEDIF settings control the detailed operation of the SHADE command. Values of 0 or 1 for the SHADEDGE setting give 256 colour rendering (display permitting). With a SHADEDGE value of 0, edges are not highlighted, while a value of 1, causes edges to be drawn in the background colour. In 256 colour rendering, the light source is assumed to be behind the 'observer', and the angle of each face to the light is used, together with the SHADEDIF setting, to determine the brightness of a particular face. The SHADEDIF setting gives the percentage of reflected light to ambient (background) light, thus controlling the depth of shading. 2: A SHADEDGE value of 2 causes edges to be drawn in the object colour, with faces drawn in the background colour (similar to the HIDE command). 3: Setting SHADEDGE to 3 causes faces to be drawn in the object colour, with edges drawn in the background colour. ***See also:*** DVIEW, HIDE and VPOINT commands. SHADEDGE and SHADEDIF settings.

'SNAP   SN   (No menu pick sequence)

R 1

When enabled, the snap feature causes the movement of the crosshairs to be restricted to a rectangular grid. Available options are **ON**, **OFF**, **A** – Aspect, **R** – Rotate, **S** – Style and **<>** – new snap spacing (numeric value). **Notes:** 1: An alternative to using the SNAP command is to use the DDRMODES command's dialogue box, which will be preferred by most users. 2: To turn snap on or off, click the appropriate button in the Toolbar, press function key F9, press Ctrl + B, or select the SNAP command's ON or OFF option. 3: The Aspect option allows different *X* and *Y* snap spacings to be selected. 4: The Rotate option allows the snap grid to be rotated by a specified angle, with respect to the active coordinate system. (Another way to rotate the snap grid is to define your own user coordinate system, with the UCS command.) 5: The Style option allows you to select between standard (orthogonal) and isometric snap grids. 6: With isometric snap enabled, the ELLIPSE command provides the facility to draw an isometric 'circle', in the active isometric plane (left, right or top). 7: A numeric input is taken as the new snap spacing. **See also:** DDRMODES, ELLIPSE, GRID and UCS commands.

SOLID   SO   <u>D</u>raw > <u>S</u>olid

R 1

Creates one or more (linked) polygons, which are filled in the current drawing colour. **Notes:** 1: To avoid creating 'bow ties', enter the third and fourth points in the same relation as the first and second points (left to right for example). 2: To create a three-sided Solid, enter a command separator at the 'Fourth point:' prompt. 3: When drawing linked Solids, the third and fourth point of the most recent Solid are taken to be the first and second points of the next. **See also:** FILL and PLINE commands.

STRETCH   S   <u>M</u>odify > <u>S</u>tretch

R 1

In normal operation, causes selected objects to be moved, while connections with other (unselected) objects are 'stretched' to maintain their relative positions. **Notes:** 1: The exact behaviour of the STRETCH command depends on whether a crossing or window selection is made during the object selection phase. With a window selection active, the command is similar to MOVE, with objects entirely within the selection window (only) being affected. If a crossing selection is made (which is the default) then objects entirely within the selection window are moved while objects partly within are 'stretched'. 2: A crossing selection is made automatically when STRETCH is selected from the Toolbox, or from the pull-down menu. You can force a crossing selection at other times by drawing the object selection window from right to left, or by typing **C** or **CP** at the Command prompt. 3: You can also stretch objects by using the grips feature. **See also:** MOVE command.

'STYLE	ST	(No menu pick sequence)

R 1 Creates a text style, which may then be associated with particular Text objects, thus defining their basic appearance. Each text style has a name (up to 31 characters long), together with a series of properties. Features controlled include whether the Text is drawn backwards, upside-down, vertically or horizontally. Other properties include the text height, width factor, obliquing angle and the name of the font file. **Notes:** 1: An enhanced version of the STYLE command is available by selecting the **Text Style...** option from the **Settings** pull-down menu. This uses an Icon menu to display the range of available fonts. 2: An existing text style can be renamed using the DDRENAME command. 3: To change the properties associated with a particular Text object – including its text style – use the DDMODIFY command. 4: To edit the text string associated with existing Text, use the DDEDIT command. 5: To create new Text, use either the DTEXT or TEXT commands. 6: To remove unwanted text styles, use the PURGE command. **See also:** DDEDIT, DDMODIFY, DDRENAME, DTEXT, PURGE and TEXT commands.

TEXT	TX	(No menu pick sequence)

R 1 Draws a single line of text in the currently active text style. Unlike the dynamic text command (DTEXT), the Text is not displayed in the drawing area until the ↵ key is pressed. Available options are **J** – Justification and **S** – Style. *Justification* refers to the arrangement of the Text, which may be *left*, *centre*, *right* or *middle* justified. The Text may also be *aligned* or *fitted* between two points. (See Figure 3–16 for details of these justification options.) The Style option allows a named *text style* to be selected, including such features as the *font*, *width factor* and *obliquing angle*. **Note:** See Table 3–5 for details of control sequences, which are used to produce effects such as underlining or special characters. **See also:** DDCHPROP, DDEDIT, DDMODIFY, DDRENAME, DTEXT and STYLE commands.

'TEXTSCR	(No abbreviation)	Edit > Text Window

R 1 Switches from the graphics window and the text screen. The same effect may be achieved by pressing function key F2. **Notes:** 1: This command may be useful during the operation of a script file, where function keys are unavailable. 2: The GRAPHSCR command switches from the text screen to the graphics window. 3: Typing an apostrophe before the command name causes the TEXTSCR command to be issued *transparently*. **See also:** GRAPHSCR command.

'TIME	TI	Assist > Time

R 1 Displays date and time information about the current drawing. **Notes:** 1: Information displayed includes the drawing's creation date and time, when the drawing file was last updated, and the total editing time. 2: A user timer may also be enabled, disabled or reset (using the ON, OFF and Reset options respectively). 3: The time to the next automatic save (if enabled), is also shown. 4: The TIME command may also be issued *transparently*. **See also:** PREFERENCES command.

TOOLBOX   TL   <u>S</u>ettings > Tool<u>b</u>ox Style

R 1

Controls the position and on/off status of the Toolbox by cycling through the range of available options. The sequence is left margin, off, right margin and floating (which then repeats again from the beginning). ***Notes:*** 1: Holding the cursor over a particular item causes a 'tool-tip' to appear, giving the name of that option. (This behaviour differs slightly from that of AutoCAD LT Release 1.) 2: The 'mobile' Toolbox may be moved to a more convenient screen location by first moving the mouse over the Toolbox's title bar and then *dragging* (moving the mouse with the left button depressed). ***See also:*** DSVIEWER command.

TRIM   TR   <u>M</u>odify > <u>T</u>rim

R 1

Causes the unwanted portion of a selected object to be erased. One or more *Cutting planes* (other objects) are used to define boundaries between the retained and discarded sections. ***Notes:*** 1: The command dialogue is in two distinct stages, which must be followed carefully. Firstly, one or more cutting planes is selected, after which you must press ⏎ to continue to the second stage. The object which is to be trimmed is then selected by using the mouse in the normal way. (The indicated point is on the section which is to be <u>discarded</u>.) 2: The BREAK, FILLET and CHAMFER commands may also be used to truncate objects. ***See also:*** BREAK, CHAMFER and FILLET commands.

U   (No abbreviation)   <u>E</u>dit > <u>U</u>ndo

R 1

Reverses the effect of the most recent (single) command. ***Notes:*** 1: The U command is functionally equivalent to using **UNDO 1**. 2: The effect of the most recent undo operation may be reversed by issuing the REDO command, but only if REDO is used immediately after U or UNDO. 3: Some operations – such as printing a drawing, or saving to a file – cannot be undone. ***See also:*** OOPS, REDO and UNDO commands.

UCS   (No abbreviation)   <u>A</u>ssist > Set <u>U</u>CS

R 1

Controls user coordinate systems. AutoCAD LT has a single World Coordinate System (WCS) and a potentially unlimited number of user coordinate systems (UCSs). The ability to create your own user-defined coordinate systems, and to switch between them, can greatly simplify the calculation of geometric data. For example, careful selection of UCS can allow 3-dimensional drawings to be produced by working in different 2-dimensional drawing planes, each of which corresponds to a named UCS. Available command options are **O** – Origin, **ZA** – ZAxis, **3** – 3point, **E** – Entity, **V** – View, **X** – *X* axis rotate, **Y** – *Y* axis rotate, **Z** – *Z* axis rotate, **P** – Previous UCS, **R** – Restore named UCS, **S** – Save as a named UCS, **D** – Delete named UCS, **?** – list named UCSs and ⏎ – return to WCS. ***Notes:*** 1: When working with UCSs, it is useful to have a visible UCS icon which moves to reflect the current UCS origin and orientation. To achieve this, use the UCSICON command (with the ON and OR options enabled). 2: The appearance of the UCS icon gives useful information regarding the current UCS status.

3: The UCSFOLLOW setting controls whether a plan view of the current UCS is automatically generated as the UCS is redefined. (0 = generate plan view, 1 = retain current viewpoint.) 4: The PLAN command may be used to generate a plan view in the current UCS or the WCS. 5: To move the UCS origin, select the Origin option and indicate the new origin coordinate (object snap is often useful here). 6: To rotate the UCS around the X, Y or Z axes, select the X, Y or Z options respectively. (You can use the *right hand corkscrew rule* to visualize positive rotation angles. Imagine a corkscrew which is aligned with the intended axis. A positive rotation will cause the corkscrew to move <u>away</u> from the origin.) 7: The View option produces a UCS which is aligned with the current viewpoint (without moving its origin). 8: There are several methods of simultaneously moving and orienting the UCS. The 3point option defines the UCS using an origin, a point on the positive X axis, and a point anywhere on the positive XY plane. The Entity option aligns the UCS to an indicated object, with the Z axis pointing along the object's direction of extrusion. The ZAxis option defines the new UCS by giving the origin, followed by a point on the positive Z axis. 9: There are several options which manipulate named user coordinate systems. The ? option lists named UCSs. The Save option saves the current UCS with the specified name. The Restore option makes the named UCS current. The Delete option removes the specified UCS from the drawing. 10: The DDUCS command allows named UCSs to be manipulated using a dialogue box, which will be preferred by most users. *See also:* DDUCS, PLAN and UCSICON commands. UCSFOLLOW, UCSNAME, UCSORG, UCSXDIR and UCSYDIR settings.

UCSICON   UI   <u>A</u>ssist > U<u>C</u>S icon

R 1   Controls the appearance and behaviour of the UCS icon. Available options are **ON** – UCS icon displayed, **OFF** – no UCS icon, **A** – All, **N** – Noorigin and **OR** – ORigin. *Notes:* 1: To cause the UCS origin to move as the current user coordinate system is redefined, the ON and OR options should both be selected. (The Noorigin option cancels this behaviour, leaving the UCS icon at the lower left corner of the screen always.) 2: The appearance of the UCS icon gives useful information regarding the current UCS status. A '+' indicates that the UCS icon is displayed at the UCS origin. A 'W' means that the current UCS and the WCS are identical. A 'broken pencil' icon indicates that the UCS is being viewed from the side (within 1°), so drawing operations are unlikely to produce the intended result. If the central area of the UCS icon is blank then the UCS is being viewed from below. 3: The UCS icon is <u>never</u> clipped, so if it cannot be displayed at the UCS origin, it is displayed at the lower left corner of the screen. 4: The All option causes the UCS icon to be updated in all open viewports, rather than in the current viewport only, which is the default. *See also:* DDUCS and UCS commands.

UNDO   **UN**   **(No menu pick sequence)**

R 1   Reverses the effect of the most recent command, or series of commands. (Most
users will find the U command to be simpler, and hence more useful in practice.)
Available options are **A** – Auto, **B** – Back, **C** – Control, **E** – End, **G** – Group, **M** –
Mark and **<number>** – undo the specified number of commands. ***Notes:*** 1: The
most common use of the command is to enter an integer which represents the
number of commands to be undone (which can be quicker than repeated use of
the U command). If you go too far back then use the REDO command (which must
be issued <u>immediately</u> after UNDO). 2: The Group and End options are used to
group together a series of commands so that they can later be undone in a single
operation. This is mainly intended for use with menu macros, as explained in the
next note. 3: The Auto option, when enabled, causes a series of commands
issued by a complex menu macro to be treated as a single command by UNDO.
This works because AutoCAD LT automatically places an UNDO GROUP at the
start of the command sequence, which is then followed by an UNDO END at the
end of the sequence. Thus the menu macro may be undone using a single
operation. 4: The Mark option is used to select a particular point in the command
sequence so that the UNDO command can quickly revert the drawing back to this
point (with the Back option). A typical application would be to place a mark, prior
to trying some drawing 'experiment'. If this proves to be unsuccessful, then the
UNDO BACK command may be used, before continuing from the point previously
reached. 5: The Control option determines whether undo information is stored in
memory for the entire drawing session (the All option, which is the default), for the
most recent command only (the One option), or not at all (the None option). If
memory is in short supply, then the One option may offer the best compromise
between speed and functionality. ***See also:*** OOPS, REDO and U commands.

'UNITS   **UT**   **(No menu pick sequence)**

R 1   Allows the measurement system used for coordinates, distances and angles to
be defined from the Command prompt. ***Notes:*** 1: Most users will prefer to use the
DDUNITS command, which allows these options to be set from a dialogue box.
2: Entering an apostrophe in front of the command name allows the UNITS
command to be entered *transparently*. ***See also:*** DDUNITS command.

'UNLOCK   **UL**   <u>F</u>ile > <u>U</u>nlock Files

R 1   Unlocks files which have been previously locked by AutoCAD LT. File locking is
a convention – mainly used on networked computer systems – which controls
who can open a file for reading or writing. The intention is to prevent multiple users
from simultaneously writing data to the same file (write locks), or from reading data
from a file which is being updated (read locks). ***Notes:*** 1: File locking may be
enabled or disabled using the PREFERENCES command. 2: On stand-alone
computers, the most likely reason for finding a locked file, is where an unexpected
power failure has prevented AutoCAD LT from removing the lock file at the
intended time. ***See also:*** PREFERENCES command.

'VIEW	V	<u>V</u>iew > <u>V</u>iew

R 1   Allows the current viewport's display settings to be saved and later restored. Available options are **?** – list currently defined views, **D** – Delete, **R** – Restore, **S** – Save and **W** – Window. Notes: 1: To save the current viewport's settings, use the Save option. (Valid view names may have up to 31 characters.) Parameters saved include the viewing direction, zoom factor and whether perspective mode is enabled (as set by the DVIEW command). 2: To restore a named view into the current viewport, use the Restore option. 3: To delete a previously saved view, use the Delete option. 4: To define a view, based on a window, use the Window option. (This is quicker than using the Zoom command, followed by VIEW.) 5: The VIEW command only affects the active viewport, unlike the related VPORTS command. *See also:* VPLAYER and VPORTS commands.

VPLAYER	VL	<u>V</u>iew > Viewport <u>L</u>ayer Visibility

R 1   Controls the visibility (or freeze/thaw status) of layers in individual viewports. Available options are **?** – list frozen layers, **F** – Freeze, **T** – Thaw, **R** – Reset, **N** – Newfrz and **V** – Vpvisdflt. *Notes:* 1: The TILEMODE setting must be set to 0 before using this command. 2: The DDLMODES command allows layers to be controlled on a global basis using a dialogue box. It also provides options to control the visibility of layers in the currently selected viewport, and default layer visibility in newly created viewports. 3: To list frozen layers in a particular viewport, select the ? option. 4: To freeze or thaw layers in one or more viewports, use the Freeze or Thaw options respectively. Once the layers to be frozen or thawed have been selected, use the All option to update all layers, the Select option to choose individual viewports, or the Current option to affect the current viewport only. 5: The Reset option resets the visibility of layers in selected viewport(s) to their default settings. To change the default visibility of individual layers, use the Vpvisdflt option. 6: To create a new layer which is automatically frozen on all layers, use the Newfrz option. (You can then manually enable the layer in particular viewports.) *See also:* DDLMODES command. TILEMODE setting.

VPOINT	VP	<u>V</u>iew > 3<u>D</u> Viewpoint

R 1   Alters the 3-dimensional viewing direction for the current viewport. Available options are **R** – Rotate and **↵** – View point. *Notes:* 1: As with the DVIEW command, the VIEWPOINT command is best understood using a 'camera' and 'target' analogy, with the observer positioned behind the camera, looking towards the target. By default, the target is the absolute coordinate (0,0,0), as held in the TARGET system variable, while the VPOINT command determines the camera coordinate. 2: The Rotate option allows the camera coordinate to be set in a manner which is similar to defining a spherical coordinate. The angle in the XY plane is given first (horizontal), followed by the angle of inclination (towards the Z axis). The View point option allows the camera position to be defined using a 'compass and tripod' display. The tripod shows the relative alignment of the X, Y and Z axes, while the compass shows a 'flattened sphere', having a 90° angle between each line and circle. *See also:* DVIEW command: TARGET setting.

VPORTS   VW   <u>V</u>iew > Viewp<u>o</u>rts

R 1   Controls viewport configurations, but only when the TILEMODE setting is enabled. (The MVIEW command performs a similar function when TILEMODE is set to 0.) Available options are **S** – Save, **R** – Restore, **D** – Delete, **J** – Join, **SI** – SIngle, **?** – list saved configurations, **2** – create 2 new viewports, **3** – create 3 new viewports and **4** – create 4 new viewports. **Notes:** 1: The Save option allows the current viewport configuration to be saved, while the Restore option makes a previously saved configuration current. 2: The Delete option removes a previously saved viewport configuration. 3: The ? option lists previously named viewport configurations. 4: The 2, 3 and 4 options allow the specified number of new viewports to be created. There is considerable flexibility in the arrangement of these new viewports, with horizontal, vertical or mixed arrangements being possible. 5: The Join option allows two existing viewports to be joined to create a single viewport. 6: The SIngle option returns the display to a single viewport. 7: Viewports created by the VPORTS command are 'tiled', meaning that they are joined edge to edge. The MVIEW command allows a more flexible arrangement of 'floating' (mobile) viewports. 8: When a drawing with tiled viewports is plotted, only the active viewport is displayed. To plot multiple viewports, create the viewports with the MVIEW command and plot with paper space active. **See also:** MVIEW command. TILEMODE setting.

VSLIDE   VS   <u>F</u>ile > <u>I</u>mport/Export > <u>V</u>iew Slide

R 1   Displays a slide which has been created previously by the MSLIDE command. Slides are used to produce 'snapshots' of drawings (perhaps as part of a presentation), and also in *Icon menus* (graphical pull-down menu selections, such as text styles). **Notes:** 1: Slide files have a file extension of '.SLD'. 2: The SLIDELIB utility program may be used to group slides together into a single slide library file, having a file extension of '.SLB'. 3: To clear the display after displaying a slide, use the REGEN or REDRAW commands. **See also:** REDRAW, REGEN and SCRIPT commands. SLIDELIB utility program.

WBLOCK   W   <u>F</u>ile > <u>I</u>mport/Export > <u>B</u>lock Out

R 1   Creates a Block definition as a separate drawing file, which may subsequently be inserted into other drawings. **Notes:** 1: Having specified the drawing file name which is to be created, you are then prompted for a 'Block name:'. You can either give the name of an existing Block definition (in the current drawing), or press ↵ and then select the required objects in the normal way. 2: A Block definition may also be created, simply by saving a drawing to disk in the normal way. In this case, the BASE command may be used to set the insertion point, if this is to be different from the drawing origin. (Where an entire drawing file is treated as a Block, only those objects which are in model space will be inserted into the new drawing.) 3: The related BLOCK and BMAKE commands allow a Block definition to be created as part of the current drawing. **See also:** BASE, BLOCK, BMAKE and XREF commands.

WMFIN **WI** <u>F</u>ile > <u>I</u>mport/Export > <u>W</u>MF In

R 1 Imports a *Windows Metafile* into the current drawing as a Block definition. ***Notes:*** 1: A WMF file is first selected using the Import WMF dialogue box. The selected WMF file may optionally be previewed, prior to actually opening the file. 2: The subsequent command dialogue is very similar to that used by the INSERT command. 3: The WMFOPTS command controls whether Solids and wide Polylines are filled in WMF files. 4: WMF files are best reserved for nontechnical applications, where absolute sizes are not important. To accurately scale a WMF file, you can use the SCALE command's Reference option. ***See also:*** INSERT, SCALE, WMFOPTS and WMFOUT commands.

WMFOPTS **(No abbreviation)** <u>F</u>ile > <u>I</u>mport/Export > WMF In <u>O</u>ptions

R 1 Controls whether Solids and wide Polylines are filled in imported WMF files (both options are enabled by default). ***See also:*** WMFIN and WMFOUT commands.

WMFOUT **WO** <u>F</u>ile > <u>I</u>mport/Export > W<u>M</u>F Out

R 1 Creates a *Windows Metafile*, which may be subsequently inserted into another drawing using the WMFIN command. You are first asked to specify the filename using the Export WMF dialogue box, after which the 'Select objects:' prompt appears. ***See also:*** WMFIN and WMFOPTS commands.

XBIND **XB** <u>D</u>raw > E<u>x</u>ternal Reference > Bind Sym<u>b</u>ols

R 1 Allows individual features of externally referenced drawings to be permanently attached to the current drawing. Available options are **B** – Block, **D** – Dimstyle, **LA** – LAyer, **LT** – LType and **S** – Style. ***Note:*** The XREF command's Bind option allows an entire externally referenced drawing to be attached to the current drawing, including any dependent features. The XBIND command allows dependent features to be attached (made permanent) in a more selective manner. ***See also:*** XREF command.

XREF **XR** <u>D</u>raw > E<u>x</u>ternal Reference > (6 options)

R 1 Attaches a drawing as an External Reference to the current drawing. Whenever the current drawing is opened, any External References are updated automatically by opening the associated drawing file(s). Available options are **?** – list External References, **B** – Bind, **D** – Detach, **P** – Path, **R** – Reload and **A** – Attach. ***Notes:*** 1: To link a drawing as an External Reference, use the Attach option (which is the default). 2: To make an External Reference a permanent part of the current drawing, use the Bind option. 3: To remove an External Reference, use the Detach option. 4: If an external referenced drawing has changed since the current drawing was opened, then use the Reload option to update the current drawing. 5: Use the Path option to modify the pathname of a currently loaded External Reference. 6: The ? option lists currently loaded External References. ***See also:*** XBIND command.

'ZOOM   Z   <u>Vi</u>ew > <u>Z</u>oom

R 1

Increases or decreases the apparent size of previously drawn objects. This affects the current viewport if model space is active, or the entire graphics area if paper space is selected. Available options are **A** – All, **C** – Center, **E** – Extents, **P** – Previous, **W** – Window and **S** – Scale (which is the default selection). **Notes:** 1: To zoom into a windowed area, select the Window option and then indicate two opposite corners. The indicated window will then be magnified so that it fills the available display area. 2: If the *implied windowing* feature has been enabled (see the DDSELECT command) then the ZOOM command automatically assumes that an indicated point is the first corner of a window. (There is no need to type **W** before picking the first coordinate) 3: AutoCAD LT remembers the 10 most recent zoom settings. These may be recalled in sequence by selecting the Previous option. 4: The Extents option zooms out so that the entire drawing just fits into the available display area. (If the drawing is empty, then the drawing limits are used.) 5: The behaviour of the All option varies depending on the current drawing. If the entire drawing is within the area defined by the drawing limits (see the LIMITS command), then the drawing limits are displayed. However, if part of the drawing is outside of the limits area, then the zoom magnification is altered so that the entire drawing is displayed. 6: The Center option allows the centre of the displayed area to be selected, as well as its magnification. Having selected the centre coordinate, you may give a scale factor (see note 7 for details), or specify the height of the display area in drawing units. (The current height is shown as the default, so pressing ⏎ here effectively pans the display.) 7: If a number is entered at the command prompt then this is taken to be a scale factor. This scale factor may be relative to the drawing limits, the current view, or to paper space drawing units. To scale the display relative to the drawing limits, enter a number such as **0.5**, **1** or **2**. A value of **1** causes the entire drawing limits to be displayed. Values less than unity reduce the apparent size of the display, while larger values increase it. (The centre of the display is inherited from the previous view.) To scale the display relative to the current zoom magnification, enter a scale factor such as **0.5x**, **1x** or **2x** (where the 'x' here indicates a multiplier). Thus entering a value of **2x**, for example, causes the apparent size of the displayed information to be doubled. The final option is to specify the zoom factor relative to paper space drawing units. In this case a scale factor such as **0.5xp**, **1xp** or **2xp** would be entered. To appreciate the usefulness of this feature, recall that paper space represents the paper on which the drawing is finally plotted. The normal plotting convention is that 1 paper space unit equals 1 measurement unit (1 mm or 1 inch for example). If the information in a model space viewport is to be accurately scaled on the final printout when a drawing is plotted from paper space, then it is necessary to scale the model space information relative to paper space. Entering a paper space scale factor which is less than unity causes model space objects to appear smaller than their actual size, while larger values cause their apparent size to increase. (Thus for example a line 100 units in length which is drawn in a model space viewport will appear 50 units long when plotted from paper space, if the viewport's scale factor is 0.5xp.) **See** *also:* DSVIEWER and PAN commands. PSLTSCALE setting.

Index

Numeric

3D
clipping planes. *See* DVIEW command
dynamic view. *See* DVIEW command
elevation and thickness 154–5
hidden line removal. *See* HIDE command
isometric style 3D viewpoints 153
perspective. *See* DVIEW command
printing/plotting drawings. *See* PLOT command
Polyline. *See* 3DPOLY command
shading images. *See* SHADE command
viewpoint. *See* VPOINT command
3DPOLY command 193

A

ABOUT command 193
absolute coordinates 43–5
ACLT.INI file 18, 184
ACLT.LIN file 19, 69, 71, 175
ACLT.MNU file 186
ACLT.MSG file 193
ACLT.PAT file 19
ACLT.PGP file 191
ACLTISO.LIN file 19, 69, 71, 175
ACLTISO.PAT file 19
Aerial View window. *See* DSVIEWER command
angular measurement. *See* DDUNITS command
APERTURE command 193
ARC command 16–17, 193
AREA command 158–9, 194
ARRAY command 104–6, 194
ATTDEF command 113, 194
ATTDIA setting 114, 117
ATTDISP command 114, 119, 194
ATTEDIT command 113, 119, 195
ATTEXT command 113, 195
ATTREQ setting 114, 117
Attribute
creating 118–20
editing 119–20, 195
extraction 180–2, 195

B

BASE command 114, 195
BHATCH command 125–8, 195–6

Bill of materials. *See* Attribute extraction
bitmap images
saving. *See* PLOT and SAVEDIB commands
BLIPMODE command 196
BLOCK command 113, 196
Blocks
Attributes 112–20
defining 111–6
External References 112–4, 124, 245
inserting 113–6
removing unused. *See* PURGE command
BMAKE command 113–5, 120, 197
BOUNDARY command 197
BREAK command 93–4, 197
buttons (mouse)
customizing 187–8
functions performed by 41
BYBLOCK object property 68–9, 124
BYLAYER object property 68–9, 89, 122

C

calculating
angles. *See* DISTANCE command
areas. *See* AREA command
coordinates. *See* ID command
distances. *See* DIST command
elapsed time (editing). *See* TIME command
cancelling active commands 15–6, 100
Cartesian coordinate 43–5
CHAMFER command 108–9, 197
CHANGE command 60, 90–1, 198
CHPROP command 198
CIRCLE command 109, 198
CLAYER setting 124
CMDDIA setting 178
COLOR command 198
Colour Display Button. *See* DDEMODES command
colours
changing existing 68
default 67–8
Dimensions 68, 140–1
Comma Delimited File (CDF) format. *See* DDATTEXT command
command
abbreviations 15, 39, 191
area and prompt 14